TAKE TEN:

NEW 10-MINUTE PLAYS

TAKE TEN:

NEW 10-MINUTE PLAYS

EDITED BY *Eric Lane*
AND *Nina Shengold*

VINTAGE BOOKS

A DIVISION OF RANDOM HOUSE, INC.   NEW YORK

CONTENTS

INTRODUCTION

A ten-minute play is a streak of theatrical lightning. It doesn't last long, but its power can stand your hair on end.

Not long ago, a ten-minute play might have seemed like a gimmick or novelty item, or even an alarming indication of our culture's diminished attention span: a kind of theatrical sound bite. With incredible speed, the ten-minute play has emerged as a recognized art form, practiced by such master craftsmen as Tony Kushner, Romulus Linney, John Patrick Shanley, Megan Terry, and August Wilson, as well as by newly emerging writers. The thirty-two plays in this collection are every bit as ambitious, as funny, and as dramatic as those you'll find anywhere. They're just a lot shorter.

The ten-minute play made its official debut at the Actors Theatre of Louisville's 1977 Humana Festival of New American Plays. Producing Director Jon Jory, the father of the genre, has said: "They are the American theatre's haiku. They must, by nature, imply rather than explain. They often depend on metaphor to extend their reach. They stick like glue in the mind because the viewer remembers the *whole* play."

The plays gathered here are extraordinary. From the quirky hilarity of David Ives's *The Philadelphia* to the breathtaking ferocity of Dana Yeaton's prize-winning *Helen at Risk*, these are gems of great writing. Cast sizes range from monologues (by John Augustine, Christopher Durang, David Mamet, and others) to John Guare's eight-character farce *New York Actor.* Many plays feature roles for minority actors, including Jane Martin's *Shasta Rue,* Chiori Miyagawa's *Yesterday's Window,* José Rivera's

Gas, Diana Son's *R.A.W.,* and August Wilson's *The Janitor;* still others, such as Shirley Lauro's *Railing It Uptown,* Nicole B. Quinn's *The Spirit is Willing,* and Megan Terry's *Breakfast Serial* encourage nontraditional casting. In fact, nearly any grouping of ten-minute plays allows flexible casting in multiple roles, freeing actors to leap across boundaries of age, race, gender—even species, in Sybil Rosen's *Duet for Bear and Dog.*

The plays in this collection—many in print for the first time—come from theatres all over the country. Some were commissioned for ten-minute play festivals at Actors Theatre of Louisville, Primary Stages, and Actors & Writers; others premiered in omnibus evenings of one-acts at Ensemble Studio Theatre, Circle Rep Lab, and New Dramatists; still others were part of anthology evenings of one playwright's work.

Ten-minute plays are eminently producible, most with a minimum of scenic requirements, in venues ranging from campus coffeehouses to Off-Broadway and regional theatres. They are beautifully suited to the classroom, providing student actors and directors with the full arc of character and story in ways that an excerpted scene from a longer play cannot. They're also exciting to read on the page, providing a crash course in what makes good drama. There is no room for slack in a ten-minute play. The sheer economy of the form demands both precision and boldness. You have to start strong and end stronger, like a sprinter completing a hundred-yard dash.

While editing this book, we read hundreds and hundreds of ten-minute plays. Many of them seemed to blur together (the generic ten-minute play might be Boy Meets Girl in a Restaurant) but the good ones, to quote Raymond Chandler, "stood out like a tarantula on a slice of angel food cake." We were amazed by the diversity and distinctiveness of the playwrights' voices, and the rich, complete worlds conjured up in a few daring strokes.

Whether you read, produce, or act in these ten-minute plays, here are thirty-two stunning examples of "less is more."

—Eric Lane and Nina Shengold,
May 1996

TAKE TEN:

NEW 10-MINUTE PLAYS

SIOBHAN

John Augustine

———————————————————————

SIOBHAN is originally from a longer play, *Temporary People*. It was added to Augustine's evening of short plays, *GENERATION X. HOME* for Contemporary Theatre, at HERE, New York City, 1993. Bill Russell directed.

SIOBHAN   Sherry Anderson

ACTOR NOTE

The original actress, Sherry Anderson, was blond and, roughly speaking, looked like Linda Evans. If you are not blond and do not remotely resemble Linda Evans, change the line "People say I look like Linda Evans although her shoulders are about seven times wider than mine are" to "People say that I look like Linda Evans . . . just kidding. But people always think I'm somebody else." Then change the references to Bo Derek and Olivia Newton-John that follow to references that suit you; you don't actually have to look like the people, just roughly in the same ballpark.

Lights up. SIOBHAN *is sitting at a table in an automat. There is a Hostess Twinkie and a diet Shasta Cola on a small table beside her. She is reading Louise Hay's* You Can Heal Your Life. *Perhaps a heavy sigh.*

SIOBHAN: Well THIS is no help at all. For eight ninety-five plus tax, I expect to feel better in a hurry. I've tried everything else. And boy oh boy am I tired of being IN recovery. I am tired of being spiritual. I am tired of rocks that supposedly change our moods. I don't want to see another crystal unless it's on Dynasty reruns in the form of Linda Evans. People say that I look like Linda Evans although her shoulders are about seven times wider than mine are.

People always think that I'm somebody else. Bo Derek . . . Olivia Newton-John . . . in a certain light . . . if I wash my hair and wear clean clothes. They think that they know me. They think they saw me on the TV. I tell them, "NO! YOU DON'T KNOW ME. BUT I USED TO WORK AT A NURSING HOME AND MAYBE YOU SAW ME CLEANING YOUR GRANDMOTHER'S TOILET!!"

I hated that job. Cleaning all these toilets.

Sometimes people's number two would stick to the inside of the toilet bowl and I would have to scrub to get it off. I would ask . . . "HEY! What are you feeding these people?? I can't get their NUMBER TWO off of the toilet!!"

Sometimes I would use my own money and buy one of those things that make the water blue 'cause then you can't see the number two.

(*realizes what she said and how it must sound*)

I'm sorry. I honestly had no intention of talking about number two. But you see I'm just so tired of everything so I was reading this book and I am tired of trying to be spiritual. I'm just not getting it. It's EXHAUSTING to say "I Love You" to people when what you really want to do is to run them over with your car. I don't have a car and I can't even rent one cause you need a driver's license AND a credit card. And not just Macy's or one like that. It has to be a MAJOR credit card. God. They act like you're going to steal the damn thing.

(*takes a sip of soda—or just looks off in thought for a beat*)

What else.

I am sick and tired of self-help seminars . . . self-help books . . . I'm tired of my A.A. meetings. I go to A.A., A.C.O.A., C.A., S.A., D.A., B.A., M.A., Blae, Blae. And quite frankly, I don't have a fuckin' clue as to what I am doing in these meetings.

I should go to the "I DON'T HAVE A FUCKIN' CLUE" meeting. I don't have a clue . . . . Well I don't.

I hope that I am not too negative for you people. Some of you look scared. Some of you look negative. I like you guys better. I wanted to tell you about my job, but if you'd like we could have an A.A. meeting instead.

OK. I'll start. Hello. My name is Siobhan, and I am an alcoholic. I am also the adult child of five transsexual parents and two bisexual grandparents. And I'm addicted to love and giving to charities and following the Commandments and work . . . . . . work is just so hard!

I quit the nursing home a while ago. I decided that I needed sort of a break from cleaning the toilets until I could figure out if I was going to (*referring to book*) HEAL myself or not.

So, I figured I'd get a job as a temporary worker. Something without responsibility, till I got my head together. So anyway, somebody gave me this newspaper intended for people in show business and there were all these ads advertising jobs. Lots of jobs. And they said things like . . . "BE THE *STAR* OF YOUR NEXT JOB. Call *STAR* TEMPORARIES!" Or things like . . ."Actors and Actresses wanted! Open call! AA Temporaries!"

Now THAT one caught my eye originally because of the AA. But the AA stood for Actors and Actresses. So I thought, well, I'm not an actress, but if they can get jobs, I should be able to.

So I go to this temp place called Madame Flora's Tempting Temps or something like that. I felt like I was going to apply to work in a brothel.

So I get there and I say . . ."Hello. My name is Siobhan, and I would like to register with your firm for possible employment." I thought that this sounded like a person who can work.

And the girl behind the desk said: "Do you know WORD-STAR? WORDPERFECT? MACROWORD? MICRO-WORD? MULTIMATE? MINIMATE? BLAE, BLAE, BLATE?"

I mean, GOD! Whatever happened to . . ."Can you answer a phone?" So I said . . . I'm terrified of computers, but I type thirty-five w.p.m. Words per minute. Then I had to take all these tests that show if I could file the word BOOK after BIRD and stuff like that. Then I needed to type endless forms and meet endless lines of people all to determine if I can be the STAR of my next temp job.

I listed twenty-three previous jobs, seventeen previous addresses . . .

. . . ONE personal reference.

And by now, I'm beginning to regret the fact that I didn't just stick to cleaning other people's shit. I was considering answering one of those ads you see on the subways advertising the Wilfred Academy of Beauty. "Hello? Mom? I made it! I'm a hairdresser!"

(She smiles wildly. Maybe takes a bite of the Twinkie.)

I wondered if there were temp agencies for people with more skills than I had. Like I wonder if a doctor is out of work if he can go to a temp agency to be the star of his next job. "What is your area of expertise? Heart Surgeon? Ohh . . . We have a two-day engagement at Cabrini Medical Center for six hundred dollars an hour." "What? You're a movie producer? We have a stint in Hollywood for two weeks producing a movie for Eight Thousand Dollars an hour because you have really great typing skills . . . and you can file the word book after bird . . . !"

(beat)

Maybe we should begin the meeting again. "Hi. My name is Siobhan and I am the adult child of two graduates of the Wilfred Academy of Beauty."

This is not really the point . . . but where is being a temp going to get me?

Was I really the star of this job or not? And if I was the STAR of this job, then couldn't I fire everybody there? I tried. It didn't work. They just looked at me. Wow! I really tired myself out! I wonder if I can get a job as someone who talks on the street. "Special Skills?" Well, I can talk on and on and on and on and on . . . *(sigh)* I think I better go now. I need a pill or a nap or something. I'm actually on my break from my current temp job. I'm filling in for Jane Pauley on the *Today* show. She's pregnant again. Okay, I'm not actually filling IN for her, but I do work in the OFFICE there. Well, not IN the office but I do work down the hall from the office . . . All right! I work in the building. At night. Cleaning. I don't know why I lied about filling in for Jane Pauley just now. It's not even a very good lie. You know she's not on the show.

Do you ever lie for no reason at all? . . . Just no reason at all?

The people I clean with think I look like Jane Pauley. People always think I'm someone else . . .

I'm not someone else . . .

I don't know WHO I am, but I'm not someone else.

(*start fade out*)

I'm not someone else . . .

Dark.

END

ANYTHING FOR YOU

Cathy Celesia

ANYTHING FOR YOU was originally produced at the Circle Repertory Lab in New York City, June 1993. Scott Segall directed the following cast:

LYNETTE   Johanna Day
GAIL   Jo Twiss

CHARACTERS

LYNETTE: thirtyish, stylish
GAIL: same age, a bit more conservative

TIME: the present

PLACE: an urban café

At Rise: LYNETTE *sits alone at a table for two, staring into her drink.* GAIL *approaches the table, a bit harried. She kisses the preoccupied* LYNETTE *on the cheek, sits.*

GAIL: Sorry I'm late. I was just about to walk out when this rap artist of ours plops himself in the outer office, announces he's not leaving until somebody acknowledges his artistic crisis. This is a kid, nineteen years old mind you, who has a house in the Hamptons and a hot tub for every day of the week, and he's having an artistic crisis. That needs acknowledgment. (*She picks up a menu.*) Have you ordered yet? (*perusing the menu*) So I have to sit there for twenty minutes trying to sound sincere when I tell him "It's not so bad, Roger. Money doesn't compromise your art. It just makes it more affordable." When what I really wanted to say was, This is the legal department. We work here. You're feeling screwed up or dysfunctional, go to artistic, bother them. So anyway . . . the squab looks good. What do you think?

(GAIL *continues to study the menu.* LYNETTE *leans forward in her chair.*)

LYNETTE: I need to have an affair.

GAIL: Hmm? Did you say something?

LYNETTE: I said, Gail, that I need to have an affair.

GAIL: (*looking up*) You don't mean that.

LYNETTE: Yes I do.

GAIL: An affair?

LYNETTE: Yes.

GAIL: You?

LYNETTE: Uh-huh.

GAIL: But you and Richard—

LYNETTE: I know.

GAIL: Then I don't understand.

LYNETTE: Neither do I.

GAIL: So basically you're sitting here telling me for no good reason that you want to—

LYNETTE: Not want. Need. Capital N. The big guns.

GAIL: Why?

LYNETTE: I don't know. An overwhelming biological necessity for alternate body types. I don't know.

GAIL: I don't think this is the place we should be discussing this.

LYNETTE: This is exactly the place. You are exactly the person. Gail. If I don't sleep with someone other than my husband very soon, I won't be responsible for myself.

GAIL: Lynette.

LYNETTE: Time bomb. Tick tick tick.

GAIL: Don't you think you're being a little overdramatic?

LYNETTE: No. Tick.

GAIL: Have you met someone?

LYNETTE: No. Although when you get right down to it, everybody's a candidate.

GAIL: You're kidding, right? All right, joke's over, very funny, ha ha, you're kidding.

LYNETTE: Gail, you don't know what it's like. I can't work. I can't sleep. All I know is I want a hot roll in the hay. That's the extent of my cognizant abilities.

GAIL: I think you should try to show a little control.

LYNETTE: Yesterday I looked at a clock. I forgot how to tell time.

GAIL: What are you drinking?

LYNETTE: I'm losing my mind.

GAIL: You certainly are. Richard—

LYNETTE: Is sweet and kind and good, I know. He adapts, no matter how crazy I am. "You're right honey, I'll be more careful, I'll try not to let my heels touch the floor in that irritating manner anymore." I could tell him I want to chuck it all for a sugar cane farm in Borneo and he'd be researching farming techniques and plane fares within the hour.

GAIL: So it seems to me you have nothing to complain about.

LYNETTE: I'm not complaining. But God, if I don't find someone to sear me to the bones I am going to explode. Little pieces of me flying out my office window and over New York, settling on some old ladies in the park. Explode.

GAIL: I don't know what to say. You've put me in a difficult position. I love Richard.

LYNETTE: I do too.

GAIL: He and George are best friends.

LYNETTE: Like brothers.

GAIL: And you're my best friend—

LYNETTE: (*expectantly*) Yes?

GAIL: Yes what?

LYNETTE: I'm your best friend.

GAIL: Yes.

LYNETTE: You'd do anything for me.

GAIL: Of course I would, you know that. What are you driving at?

LYNETTE: Sleep with me.

GAIL: What?!

LYNETTE: Sleep with me, Gail. Make love to me until I beg you to stop.

GAIL: You can't be serious.

LYNETTE: I couldn't live with myself if I did it with another man, not to mention what it would do to Richard if he found out. But you—

GAIL: Are astonished.

LYNETTE: You're a woman, Gail. It wouldn't be cheating. It would be experimenting.

GAIL: You're out of your mind.

LYNETTE: Will you do it?

GAIL: Of course not.

LYNETTE: Why not?

GAIL: In the first place, no offense, but I'm not physically attracted to you.

LYNETTE: Liar.

GAIL: What did you call me?

LYNETTE: You're lying. You've wanted me from the day we met.

GAIL: Oh, now I agree with you, Lynette, you have gone over the deep end.

LYNETTE: You stare at me. You watch my mouth when I speak. When we kiss hello you let your nose linger in my hair a little bit longer than necessary and you breathe in.

GAIL: I can't really have this conversation anymore, okay? Can we order? (*pause*) I think you should see a doctor.

LYNETTE: You're angry.

GAIL: I'm not, I'm flabbergasted. To think that after all these years of what I thought was a close friendship you would suddenly come up with this insane notion that I—that we— I'm married, Lynette.

LYNETTE: I know.

GAIL: And I love George. Not to mention I'm one hundred percent heterosexual.

LYNETTE: I'm going out of my mind.

GAIL: I wish I could help you. I really do.

LYNETTE: You love me.

GAIL: Of course I do. But that doesn't mean I desire you in a sexual manner.

LYNETTE: What about New Year's Eve?

GAIL: (*after a pause*) What about it?

LYNETTE: New Year's Eve, 1991. The four of us spent it together. I drank too many peach margaritas.

GAIL: I remember.

LYNETTE: I got sick. Richard ended up carrying me into the bathroom and you stayed to help.

GAIL: You were so sick. Richard was so angry.

LYNETTE: I thought I'd never stop throwing up. When I finally did, I laid down on the bathroom floor, closed my eyes, and you kissed me. On the mouth.

GAIL: I didn't.

LYNETTE: You did. For a good long time.

GAIL: You must have dreamt it, Lynette, I think I would remember—

LYNETTE: I remember thinking, "how soft her mouth is." You held my lower lip for an extra second. Then you let go and the air hissed out of me like a balloon.

GAIL: I did not kiss you, Lynette. I mean, I may have given you a peck on the cheek because I felt sorry for you, but beyond that, you are mistaken.

LYNETTE: I felt your tongue.

GAIL: Lynette! (*She looks around, lowers her voice.*) This is really inappropriate.

LYNETTE: Why are you so against this? You have me, I have my fling—everybody wins.

GAIL: Except Richard, and George.

LYNETTE: We don't tell them. This is a secret between friends. Inviolable.

GAIL: It's not that simple.

LYNETTE: Why not?

GAIL: Lynette, look—do you want me to fix you up with someone? There are a lot of lesbians in the music business.

LYNETTE: I want you.

GAIL: No you don't.

LYNETTE: I do. You're my friend, I can trust you, there's no danger of falling in love. I was going to say you're honest but you can't even admit to kissing me when we both know—

GAIL: All right, all right, I kissed you, I kissed you! I'd had a little to drink myself that night— (*to an unseen patron*) Can I help you?

LYNETTE: You were stone cold sober. The antibiotics, remember?

GAIL: (*helplessly*) You looked so pretty. Lying there with your hair spread out over the mat. So vulnerable and so . . . beautiful, actually.

LYNETTE: Sleep with me, Gail.

GAIL: I can't.

LYNETTE: Why not?

GAIL: Because I'm in love with you.

LYNETTE: What?

GAIL: I'm in love with you, Lynette. You think I go around kissing drunken smelly women on the mouth because it's a thing of mine?

LYNETTE: But I thought—

GAIL: That my heart couldn't possibly leap every time I see you? That I don't feel profound jealousy when you and Richard reach for each other like any other happily married couple? That my feelings can't be real?

LYNETTE: No, I mean . . .

GAIL: What, Lynette? What did you think?

LYNETTE: I don't know. A harmless crush. Like schoolgirls.

GAIL: Not exactly.

LYNETTE: No. (*pause*) So where does this leave us?

GAIL: I don't know.

LYNETTE: (*after a pause*) Maybe I do drink too much.

GAIL: Maybe.

LYNETTE: I have a problem.

GAIL: Yes.

LYNETTE: And you have a problem.

GAIL: Yes.

LYNETTE: What do you think we should do?

GAIL: I think we should order.

(*They return to looking at their menus.*)

END

FLOP COP

Laura Cunningham

FLOP COP premiered in New Dramatists' "Sanctuary" Festival in New York City, March 1992. It was directed by Lisa Petersen; the stage manager was Troy Michael Rowland; Director of Artistic Programs was Elena Greenfield. The cast was as follows:

PLAYWRIGHT Chris McCann

MIKE MURPHY (OFFICER) Damian

CAST

OFFICER MIKE MURPHY: a trooper with the (name the state) Police Department, Arts Division. Young, fit, but must be impassive. Flat delivery. (Actor should familiarize himself with cop show monotone narration.)

PLAYWRIGHT: Any physical description, but must emote highest anxiety. Speaks in high, choked tones. Range—inchoate agony to unbearable pain. Sweating, near tears: a febrile look.

SCENE: (Name of the presenting theatre)

TIME: Any dreary night.

NOTES FOR *Flop Cop*

References should be timely and local, for impact.

For example, when performed at New Dramatists, the theatre named is "New Dramatists," a former church, and the P.D. is NYTD (New York Theatre Department), Arts Division. The coffee shop and other theatre references should also be made familiar to the audience.

The date, so often repeated by the cop, should be the night of the performance.

The interior of the (Name of theatre). It is night. The stark hall appears empty save for some scarred folding chairs, an empty pizza box, and a gallon jug of Chilean wine. In the darkness, we hear the ragged breathing, near sobs of THE PLAYWRIGHT, *at first unseen, cowering near the wings. Sound of police sirens. The red-white-and-blue swivel alarm plays as if projected from the roof of a squad car outside the building.* OFFICER MIKE MURPHY *walks stolidly into center stage and stares into the audience.*

OFFICER MIKE MURPHY: (*flattest monotone*) I am not a professional actor. What you are about to see is a reenactment of an actual crime, in which I, Officer Mike Murphy, third generation in law enforcement, was the arresting officer.

(*continuing, even flatter*)

As a rookie with the (*State*) State Police Arts Division, I had very little experience in the field on that night of (*tonight's date*). Most of my knowledge was strictly textbook or from the classroom. But on this night in question, (*date*), I would be faced with the real thing. And I confess, if I had had time to think, I would have been frightened. I had never before seen an out-of-control playwright, although I knew that this area, especially around the vicinity of (*give locale*), was full of them. But this was the night of (*date*), and TD was launching a new policy on how to deal with these so-called "actors and writers" and their alleged "works-in-progress." When I set forth on that damp, chill night, I was—truthfully—only thinking of getting some coffee from the (*local coffee shop*). I had no idea that the new policy would almost cost me my life, and lead me to take the most drastic action an officer can take. I responded at exactly 7:03 P.M. to a radio call that a deranged playwright, male or possibly masculinate female, Caucasian or possibly light-skinned Afro-American, Asian, or Native American, weighing approximately 145 to 230 lbs., was holed up in a former (*building*) now known as (*name theatre*), a hangout for known offenders. The suspect had already been spotted in (*nearby locale*) abusing a Xerox machine, and there had been . . .

(*Sounds of recorded typing, mixed with the* PLAYWRIGHT's *sobbing, moans.*)

OFFICER MIKE MURPHY: (*continued*) . . . several rounds of staccato typing. As the building was filled with people who had entered to attend a so-called "Fest," it was deemed necessary to subdue the subject, before he could subject unarmed civilians to his misdirected anger. He was rumored to be armed with a pretty heavy invective. He had been holed up in the building all day, subsisting on cold, take-out pizza, and flat-canned Coke. He claimed to have a new monologue, and was wild enough to deliver . . . no matter how unprovoked. It was my duty to stop him. I hoped to do so without using undue force. I drew on my training in Abnormal Psych.

(PLAYWRIGHT, *wild-eyed, holding manuscript in one hand, pizza in the other, leaps into center stage. He circles, completely crazed. He takes occasional swigs of the jug wine, and then fires off a word or two on an open typewriter.*)

PLAYWRIGHT: (*in full yowl*) Ooooooooowwwwweeeeeeeee! Awwwwwwwwwggggggh! Nada! Rien! Merde!

(OFFICER MIKE MURPHY *moves tentatively to the* PLAYWRIGHT's *side.* MURPHY *barely conceals his gun and walkie-talkie. He crouches beside the distraught* PLAYWRIGHT.)

OFFICER MURPHY: (*to audience*) I knew from my course in "Subduing Hostile Individuals" that I must establish rapport and trust.

(*to* PLAYWRIGHT)

Hey, I know you. I caught one of your plays at the (*another theatre*). I thought it showed "promise."

PLAYWRIGHT: The fuckin' promise they said I didn't keep. That's why they say you have promise, so later they can say—you haven't lived up to it.

OFFICER MURPHY: (*with false, flat warmth*) Hey, what do they know? Huh? A Bad review in the (*local paper*). "Nada. Rien. Merde."

(PLAYWRIGHT *snuggles up to the* OFFICER, *eager for his sympathy.*)

OFFICER MURPHY: (*flat to audience*) My only goal was to get him to turn his back, so that I could cuff him and get him out of the theatre.

(*warm, to* PLAYWRIGHT)

Hey, man, tonight looks dark, but it can only get better, right, Man. Sometimes, you got to touch bottom, to feel solid ground.

PLAYWRIGHT: *Terra firma.* Terror, firmer. I don't just touch bottom, Man, I live here. I am scraping the remains of my NEA, Man . . . My life is merde, that translates to shit. Make that "undiluted." *Shit.*

OFFICER MURPHY: I feel the same way, Man.

(*He fingers his gun.*)

. . . but I hang it up after my shift, and go home to the family. The family can be your oasis, your shelter from the cold.

PLAYWRIGHT: I want to weep.

OFFICER MURPHY: Let it out . . .

(*aside to the audience*)

Even if it is . . . *unmanly.*

(*warm, to* PLAYWRIGHT)

Call for your mother, if it helps.

PLAYWRIGHT: (*flaring, wild anger*) My *mother!* That demented pathetic woman. She loved me, I guess . . . but her love was sick, sicker than my Dad's and he used the stick. Their love was sick; it was a sick, sick thing. They passed the blows rained upon them onto me. I could feel their pain, but it added to my own!

OFFICER MURPHY: Surely there's someone in your life to whom you turn for comfort? Your wife?

PLAYWRIGHT: (*jumping out of his skin*) My wife! My wife . . . is from . . . Mythology! Medea is mellow, the Medusa laidback . . . compared to *her.* People are frightened of her at parties. She's frigid and unfaithful . . . a bad combination!

(OFFICER MURPHY *steps in front of the* PLAYWRIGHT, *who is pacing and venting his rage.*)

OFFICER MURPHY: The playwright fit the psychiatric profile— hostile to his parents. Seductive mother, brutal Dad. Psychosexual love/hate for his romantic partners. Probably suffering from psychosomatic physical complaints . . .

PLAYWRIGHT: (*wailing*) Now, I can't even pee! I'm prostrate with prostate! Unspilled seed turned toxic, love, unshed, backed up . . . is bile, vile. I can't come, I can't go!

OFFICER MURPHY: (*to audience*) See.

(*into walkie/talkie*)

Suspect is beginning a monologue, the one about his deadly dick. Can I have some reinforcements? The situation's going

to explode. I don't know how long I can hold him although . . .

(*He checks the fevered face of the* PLAYWRIGHT.)

He is warming to me. I think I have his trust.

(*Ratlike, the* PLAYWRIGHT *nibbles his pizza, swills the Chilean wine.
He storms the* OFFICER, *grapples with him, grabs his walkie-talkie.*)

OFFICER MURPHY: (*still condescending*) Would you like to make a
call? You're allowed one call. To a Buddy?

PLAYWRIGHT: I had a friend. He went to the O'Neill. Without
me. But I didn't resent him, he resented me.

OFFICER MURPHY: Maybe if you picked up a check once in a
while.

PLAYWRIGHT: With what? I was turned down for a McKnight! I
was living in Minneapolis . . . in *winter,* and they turned me
down. Do you know what I had to do? I considered *teach-
ing.* But then I moved in with a woman with money.

OFFICER MURPHY: You found love.

PLAYWRIGHT: She had a laptop and a printer.

(*He buries his head in his lap, cries.*)

I wanted love. Love is the cure . . . so they say!

OFFICER MURPHY: (*into walkie-talkie*) Suspect is becoming maudlin
and trite.

(PLAYWRIGHT *staggers, begging for understanding.*)

PLAYWRIGHT: (*sad whisper*) As soon as I get close to anyone, I
take . . . an extreme dislike.

(*He kneels toward a* WOMAN *in the front row of the audience.*)

PLAYWRIGHT: The second a woman offers me anything, I pull
away. I fall into hate as I want to fall into love. The feeling

deepening on each new-discovered detail. (*groveling on his knees*) I can't bear to see them naked from the back. Their asses depress me. (*crying*) I hate my hatred.

(OFFICER MURPHY *sneaks toward the wings, kneels, radioing for help.*)

OFFICER MURPHY: He's firing off indiscriminately at everyone in his life! He's warming to a theme which is rife with self-pity, and which, with my training, I can assess as having psycho-sexual homophobic and homophilic tendencies . . .

(PLAYWRIGHT *stiffens, overhearing.*)

PLAYWRIGHT: Oh, why don't you get it over with, and fire your big hot gun!

OFFICER MURPHY: (*false, soothing*) Nothing has really happened here, that would get you in really deep. You might not even have to do time. You might get off with "suspended.". . . It's not too late. We can just go outside . . . Go to (*local bar*), have a beer . . . talk things over . . .

(*He tries to escort the* PLAYWRIGHT *from the room.*)

OFFICER MURPHY: (*flat, to audience*) I wanted to get him out, and lock him in the squad car. (*kind but even flatter to* PLAY-WRIGHT) I said you had "promise."

PLAYWRIGHT: That I didn't keep. That cut!

OFFICER MURPHY: There wasn't much I could say after seeing your one-act in Louisville.

PLAYWRIGHT: That was entirely the Production! The Director was crazy, the set designer was his lover!

OFFICER MURPHY: Sure he was. (*fast, firing tone*) The original voice I thought I heard downtown was gone, replaced by a derivative tone, the pathos turned to bathos.

PLAYWRIGHT: You should have seen it in Buffalo! When I directed it myself! My wife played my mother! It still wasn't right, but there was something there.

(PLAYWRIGHT *starts banging his head against the wall.*)

PLAYWRIGHT: (*continued*) I got to let it out! It scares even me. I'm on fire! I can't pee. I can't screw! I can't sleep!

OFFICER MURPHY: But I bet you can still work through the night.

PLAYWRIGHT: (*sweet, sinking to his knees*) Oh, thank the Lord, for so often I am taken by surprise, by the sunrise.

OFFICER MURPHY: Suspect slipping into cheap rhyme and may fall back on his false but facile habit of alliteration.

(*into walkie-talkie again, the alert*)

Calling 10-11! 10-11! 10-11! All cars! (*to audience*) 10-11 is police shorthand for performance. This guy's going to go. This guy's going to go!

(PLAYWRIGHT, *wildest, rushes him, screaming.*)

PLAYWRIGHT: You totalitarian turd! Night-crawling nerd!

(OFFICER MURPHY *draws his gun.*)

OFFICER MURPHY: While the suspect's work was often perceived as antisocial, there was no way of knowing, until the night of (*date*) that he would finally snap . . . (*to audience*) Please stand back. We don't want you to be hurt. Drop it! Drop that script!

PLAYWRIGHT: (*ultimate yowl*) I have nothing left but this! Life is *merde,* but it can still be beautiful to say so! I'll go to . . . Ontario and give a staged reading!

(OFFICER MURPHY *fires, and the* PLAYWRIGHT *staggers.*)

OFFICER MURPHY: (*deadest pan*) I knew then that I could not avoid the use of force. He had pulled the trigger when he said "staged reading." The (*State*)TD policy had been given strict instruction: "Don't wait till it's a play. Bust it at the beginning. Catch it in nonperformance, don't let it go into even a cold reading." It can hit people then, kill them with inchoate feeling and unoriginal ideas.

(PLAYWRIGHT *falls dead at his feet.* OFFICER *steps over him.*)

> I had never wanted to draw my weapon, but I had no choice. I consulted with my fellow officers, and even went to counseling . . . Everyone said I was completely justified. If I hadn't fired, he would have done at least a monologue . . . He would never have made it into a full production, but he would have continued to be included in these "Fests." It was obviously necessary to take him out. . . . He is still in print, in a few seldom-read, never-performed anthologies . . . but he never had a real opening night. He was dead on arrival. . . .

(PLAYWRIGHT *has a spasm, and bites the* OFFICER *on the ankle.* OFFICER *drops the gun.* PLAYWRIGHT *seizes the weapon, and fires, killing* MIKE MURPHY.)

PLAYWRIGHT: *(manic and gleeful, rising to his feet)* Heh, heh . . . I'm counting on being a posthumous success! Everybody loves a dead playwright!

Thank you! I'm flyin'!

With a delirious spin, he dances past the body of the slain officer. Jumps from stage, runs through audience to EXIT.

BLACKOUT

MRS. SORKEN

Christopher Durang

MRS. SORKEN was the opening play of the six-play evening, *Durang, Durang,* which premiered on November 14, 1995, at Manhattan Theatre Club, Stage II, New York City. Lynne Meadow, artistic director. Barry Grove, managing director. Scenery by Derek McLane. Costumes by David C. Woolard. Lighting by Brian Nason. Sound by Tony Meola. Production stage manager was Perry Kline; stage manager was Gregg Fletcher. Directed by Walter Bobbie.

The six plays had a company of seven actors: Becky Ann Baker, David Aaron Baker, Patricia Elliott, Marcus Giamatti, Lizbeth Mackay, Patricia Randell, Keith Reddin. Understudies were John Augustine, Judith Hawking, Margo Skinner.

MRS. SORKEN   Patricia Elliott

Note: The playwright offers the alternative ending published here for when the piece is performed separately from the rest of *Durang, Durang.*

(*Enter* MRS. SORKEN *to address the audience. She is a charming woman, well-dressed and gracious, though a little scattered. She is happy to be there.*)

MRS. SORKEN: Dear theatregoers, welcome, and how lovely to see you. I've come here to talk to you about theatre, and why we all leave our homes to come see it, assuming we have. But you have left your homes, and you're here. So, welcome!

Now I have written down some comments about theatre for you, if I can just find them.

(*searches through her purse*)

Isn't it refreshing to see someone with a purse?

(*looks some more through the purse*)

Well, I can't find my notes, so I'll have to make my comments from memory.

(*From here on, she is genuinely winging it—some of it may be thoughts she prepared, much of it is thoughts that pop into her head as she is speaking. She is not nervous, though. She loves talking to the audience.*)

Drama. Let's begin with etymology, shall we? . . . etymology, which is the history of the word.

The word "drama" comes from the Greek word "dran," which means to do, and which connects with the English word "drain," meaning to exhaust one totally, and with the modern pharmaceutical sedating tablet, Dramamine, which is the tradename of a drug used to relieve airsickness and seasickness and a general sense of nausea, or "nausée" as Jean-Paul Sartre might say, perhaps over a cup of espresso at a Paris bistro. How I love Paris in the spring, or would, if I had ever been there; but Mr. Sorken and I haven't done much traveling. Maybe after he dies I'll go somewhere.

We go to the drama seeking the metaphorical Dramamine that will cure us of our nausea of life.

Of course, sometimes we become nauseated by the drama itself, and then we are sorry we went, especially if it uses the F-word and lasts over four hours. I don't mind a leisurely play, but by 10:30 I want to leave the theatre and go to sleep. Frequently, I prefer Dramamine to drama, and only wish someone would renew my prescription for Seconal.

Secondly . . . we have the word "theatre," which is derived from the Greek word "theasthai," which means to view.

And nowadays we have the word, "reastat," a device by which we can dim the lights in one's house slowly, rather than just snapping them off with a simple switch.

And thirdly, we have the Greek god "Dionysus," the last syllable of which is spelled "s-u-s" in English, but "s-o-s" in Greek, the letters which in Morse code spell *help*— "Dionysos" is the god of wine and revelry, but also the father of modern drama as we know it.

The Greeks went to the theatre in the open air, just like the late and wonderful Joseph Papp used to make us see Shakespeare. Shakespeare's language is terribly difficult to understand for us of the modern age, but how much easier it is when there's a cool breeze and it's for free. If it's hot and I have to pay, well, then I don't much like Shakespeare. I'm sorry, I shouldn't say that. He's a brilliant writer, and I look forward to seeing all 750 of his plays. Although perhaps not in this lifetime.

But back to the Greeks. They went to the open-air theatre expecting the drama they saw to evoke terror and pity.

Nowadays we have enough terror and pity in our own lives, and so rather than going to the theatre looking for terror, we go looking for slight irritation. And rather than looking for the theatre to evoke pity, we look merely for a generalized sense of identification as in "Evita was a woman, I am a woman." Or "Sweeney Todd was a barber, I go to the hairdresser." Or "Fosca in *Passion* should have her moles removed, I know a good dermatologist." That sort of thing.

But did the Greeks really experience terror and pity? And if so, what was it in all that matricide-patricide that so affected them?

I know that seeing Greek drama nowadays, even with Diana Rigg in it, really rather baffles me, it is so very different from my own life. My life with Mr. Sorken is not something that Diana Rigg would wish to star in, even on PBS. My life, I'm sorry to say, is not all that interesting.

Indeed, addressing you at this very moment, I'm sorry to say, is the highpoint of my life to date.

Could I have lived my life differently? Women of my generation were encouraged to marry and to play the piano, and I have done both those things. Is there a piano here? I don't see one. I might have played a sonata for you, or a polonaise.

But back to my theme—Drama, from the Greek word "dran."

When we leave the drama, we return to our homes feeling "drained." And if it's been a good night in the theatre, we leave feeling slightly irritated; and feeling identification with Evita or Fosca or that poor Mormon woman in *Angels in America*.

And so, drained, we get into our nightgowns, we adjust our reastats from light to darkness, we climb into bed next to

Mr. Sorken, we fall into a deep REM sleep, dreaming God knows what mysterious messages from our teeming unconscious; and then in the morning we open our eyes to the light of the new day, of the burgeoning possibilities.

Light from the Greek word "leukos," meaning white, and the Latin word "lumen" meaning illumination. In German, *der licht;* in French, *la lumière.* All art leads to light.

Light. Plants need light to grow. Might people need art to grow? It's possible. Are people less important than plants? Some of them are certainly less interesting.

But there is some connection between theatre and light, and people and plants, that I am striving to articulate. It's about photosynthesis, I think, which is the ingestion of light that plants go through in order to achieve growth.

And you see, it's "light" again—"photo" comes from the Greek word, "phos," which means light and which relates to phosphoresence, or the "light given off." And "synthesis" comes from the Greek prefix, "syn-" meaning together, and the Greek word "tithenai," meaning to place, to put.

Photosynthesis—to put it together with light.

We go to the theatre, desperate for help in photosynthesis.

The text of the play is the light, the actors help put it together, and we are the plants in the audience.

Plants, lights, theatre, art. I feel this sense of sudden interconnection with everything that's making me feel dizzy. And Dramamine, of course, is good for dizziness.

Now to wrap up.

Dear theatregoers. I hope you enjoy your evening this evening. I'm not quite sure what you're seeing, but whatever it is, I'm sure it will be splendid.

And, by the way, if you are ever in Connecticut, I hope you will drop in and say hello to me and Mr. Sorken. He prefers that you call first, but I love to be surprised. So just ring the bell, and we'll have cocktails.

And I hope you have enjoyed my humbly offered comments on the drama. I have definitely enjoyed speaking with you, and have a sneaking suspicion that in the future, it is going to be harder and harder to shut me up.

(*Either end with that, or possibly add and end with: "And so, the high-point of my life to date being over, I leave you with the play."*)

BROTHER

Mary Gallagher

BROTHER was originally produced at HOME for Contemporary Theatre and Art, in New York City, December 1988. It was directed by Melia Bensussen; set designer was Geoffrey Makstutis; lighting designer was Danianne Mizzy; and stage manager was Randy Rollison. The cast was as follows:

JANET   Janet Zarish
PHIL   Phil Soltanoff

It's five o'clock in the morning. KITTY's *entering in her bathrobe and heading for the refrigerator as* CHARLIE *enters from outside, wearing a worn-looking winter jacket.*

CHARLIE: Oh great—   KITTY: Oh God,
   I was afraid Mom was   you scared me—
   up—How the hell are ya?   Hi! How *are* you . . . ?

(*They kiss and hug awkwardly, he whirls her around as:*)

CHARLIE: Jeez, whenja get so skinny?

KITTY: God, I don't know . . . has it been that long since we—?

CHARLIE: Yeah, gotta be   KITTY: Well, yeah, I guess
   a couple years   we didn't make it last
   or something . . .   Christmas, so—

KITTY: You look big! I always forget, I expect you to look weedy, like when you were sixteen or something . . .

CHARLIE: That was many moons ago.

KITTY: I know, but I forget. Listen, I still picture you in that dalmatian outfit you had to wear in the kindergarten play.

CHARLIE: Oh, yeah? You wanta wrestle? Now that you're a flyweight. Give you two falls out of three. How was the trip down?

KITTY: Average. There was a wreck on 90 so everything was backed up—and poor Matt got carsick, twice—your average turnpike nightmare. . . . Are you just getting home?

CHARLIE: Yup. Had too good a time tonight, couldn't tear myself away. What is it, five o'clock or something? What're you doing up?

KITTY: I just *got* up, I've gotta make this damn potato salad for the reception and I want to get it done before the kids get up. I must've been crazy to say I'd do this . . .

(*She takes a bowl of hard-boiled eggs from the fridge and starts peeling them.*)

KITTY: So what's the story, you seeing somebody?

CHARLIE: Nah. I was just up at Dink's.

KITTY: That biker bar? I mean, it *was* . . . now is it . . . like, fun, or—?

CHARLIE: That's my club. There're some good guys hang out there. They call me the King. I walk in, they say, "The King is here." Plus they got a pool table—

KITTY: You didn't walk home, did you? God. I mean, it's none of my business, but you don't want to get mugged again—

CHARLIE: I was a kid when I got mugged, I don't even remember it. *You* remember—

KITTY: Well, but it's cold out, too—

CHARLIE: Haddaya *think* I get around? It's not like I can use Mom's car. Hey, I'm the champeen walker.

KITTY: Right . . . don't you have gloves, at least?

CHARLIE: I had some great gloves. Did you give me those? Blue wool with leather pads?

KITTY: Yeah, probably . . .

CHARLIE: They were great. But I lost 'em. That red shirt you gave me was great too, I lost that too. They're great while

they last, though. Man, I am starving. Mom made that
chicken stuff for dinner, right?

KITTY: We killed it.

CHARLIE: Thanks, guys.

KITTY: There's salad left, though.

CHARLIE: Salad! Hey, this is me you're talking to—Oh shit, I better close this door or Mom'll be out here bitching, make me
do the Breathalyzer . . .

(*He closes the door to the hall, goes to cupboards, takes out a can of Chef
Boy-ar-Dee Ravioli and a loaf of Wonder Bread, opens the can and
makes cold ravioli sandwiches.*

CHARLIE: Couple months ago I was a bad boy, really let myself
go . . . she tell you about this?

KITTY: (*nods yes, but blankly*) What.

CHARLIE: It was pretty funny, or it woulda been if somebody'd
been there to see it besides us . . . I came in real late, and I
mean I was loaded, and coming through the living room, I
tripped over her fucking sewing box and I fell flat, like, with
this huge crash! And I couldn't get back up. It was wild, the
whole room was going nuts around me . . . and then, Jesus,
here comes Mom, with the electric carving knife!—she
thought someone was breaking in—

KITTY: (*appalled but has to laugh*) What was she gonna do with the
electric knife, she would've had to go get the extension cord
so she could plug it in—

CHARLIE: (*laughs*) Yeah, right . . . yeah . . . but she doesn't sleep
through stuff like she used to. That was great, how when she
was sleeping, we'd go in and ask her stuff, like if we could
do stuff or buy stuff, like donuts or something, and she'd
always say—

BOTH: "Sure, honey . . ."

KITTY: She'd still be asleep . . .

CHARLIE: We got away with fucking everything. Forget it, *now*. The slightest thing, she wakes up screaming . . .

KITTY: Listen though, Mom says you're doing great at your new job, she says they really like you.

CHARLIE: Well, my boss keeps telling me I'm the best worker they got . . .

KITTY: Well, good for you . . . just keep it up. I mean I always knew if you got on a good roll . . .

CHARLIE: I figure she'd be telling you to shape me up—

KITTY: No, listen . . . I mean sure, she . . . she *cares*, that's all . . . but I don't want to . . . be telling you . . . we oughta be past that . . .

CHARLIE: Jesus, *I* think so, but Mom . . . she's really getting crotchety. Like ever since that night, she won't give me a ride anywhere except to work, and that's just if I oversleep. It's like, in her mind, the only life I should have is work. You know? I go, "Hey, Ma, I'm not gonna just work and come straight home and sit around watching the boob tube all night long, like the living dead . . ."

(*starts eating ravioli sandwiches, sees her watching*)

What.

KITTY: You really do still eat like that.

CHARLIE: Hey, the Chef's my man. Mom, once in a while she'll try to palm off some gourmet brand, what they call "pasta" now. I tell her, "Ma, I got my loyalties."

KITTY: So you psyched for the wedding?

CHARLIE: . . . Oh, right! Right . . . great!

KITTY: All the cousins are coming in—

CHARLIE: Oh yeah? Old Eddie's coming, too?

KITTY: Yeah, didn't Mom tell you?

CHARLIE: Hey. You're the one she talks to.

KITTY: Well . . . that's because I'm gone. But listen, Jen has hot plans to dance with you. Uncle Charlie. Like, rad.

CHARLIE: Oh, yeah?

KITTY: Oh, please. Don't tell her I said so, but she never stops playing that Jackson Browne tape you gave her.

CHARLIE: She's a babe, that kid, she's gonna break some hearts. Yeah, I wanted to make it home to see her tonight, but . . .

KITTY: And Matt's dying to see you too. You'll have to show him your MAD collection one more time.

CHARLIE: He remembers that?

KITTY: Are you serious? That's on the list now, that's required.

CHARLIE: Oh, shit.

KITTY: What.

CHARLIE: I think I have to work today.

KITTY: Oh, no, Charlie, you can't miss this—

CHARLIE: Shit. Get me up at eight, I'll call in sick.

KITTY: Well . . . wait . . .

CHARLIE: Nah, fuck it. If he doesn't like it, he can fire me.

KITTY: No, wait, Charlie, I shouldn't've . . . that wouldn't be too cool with Mom, or . . . you know, just . . . for *you*, I mean . . . this is a decent job . . .

CHARLIE: Pearl-diving, it's a privilege—

KITTY: Well, but if you stick it out there, maybe you can move up—

CHARLIE: Move up, how? To waiter? I'd rather wash dishes my whole life than be a fucking waiter. You know how much shit they have to take from these assholes? Come in ordering "Chivas and Coke," like that's a sign of class!

KITTY: Well, but you'd make a lot more money—

CHARLIE: Hey, I go in, I do my job, and I don't have to take any shit from anybody—including my "superior." The crew chief? What a dickhead! Keeps telling me about "technique"—which he doesn't know zilch what he's talking about—and when I tell him "Back off," he goes, "I am your superior!" Dickhead's never read a book, can't even speak English hardly, here he is telling me . . .

KITTY: Well, sure, but on any job—

CHARLIE: Then yesterday, I had a couple beers in the bar on my lunch hour—then my boss comes in and tells me the staff isn't *allowed* to drink on the "premises"—how's that for life in a democracy?

KITTY: That stinks. But, you know, why give them your money anyway—

CHARLIE: Man, I was seeing red, I went back in the kitchen, my "superior" starts in on me about "technique," I told him, "Yeah, you spent your whole life washing other people's dirty dishes, and you think that makes you my *superior?* I find that sad."

KITTY: Well, but Charlie, don't . . . this looks like a job you can keep for a while, right?

CHARLIE: Listen, there are a million—a zillion jobs like this. Pearl-diving, busing tables, washing floors—nobody wants these fucking jobs. Every kitchen is a zoo, they got no-shows, they got walkouts, guys right off the boat who can't even speak English, you gotta do a pantomime to show 'em what they're sposeta do. . . . This is one thing I know more about than you, okay? With my experience, I can walk into any restaurant and any bar in this city, and I can get hired, and I am not exaggerating, any day I ask—

KITTY: Okay, but asking is the hard part, and—Jesus, I swore I wasn't getting into this—Mom wants you to be working—

CHARLIE: No matter what scutwork it is—

KITTY: Now that's not fair—or true—God, Charlie—you're so bright—

CHARLIE: Oh shit, what, did you guys spend the whole night talking about getting me motivated—?

KITTY: (overlapping) No, I told her, I told everyone, I don't want to get into this! But when I hear you talking about—

CHARLIE: (overlapping) You come home every two years—

KITTY: (overlapping) It's not just me who's saying it—

CHARLIE: You wouldn't last one day washing dishes in a restaurant.

KITTY: Okay, fine . . . let's not do this, huh? I'm really . . . want to see you, I want to spend some time with you—

CHARLIE: You know, she keeps ragging me about "if you'd just get your equivalency"—like a high school diploma's gonna open the golden doors—McDonald's, that's the golden doors it'll open—and I'd rather haul shit! Listen, I couldn't make Mom happy unless I wore a suit to work—Shit.

KITTY: What.

CHARLIE: I forgot to get my good pants cleaned.

KITTY: I'll just iron 'em, they'll be fine—

CHARLIE: No, they're gross, got puke on 'em or something . . .

KITTY: Well, maybe Joe brought extra pants—

CHARLIE: Well, I was gonna ask him if he brought extra shoes. All I've got is tennis shoes.

KITTY: God, I sort of doubt it. Joe's not exactly Mr. Style, you know. I mean you don't have to worry about family standards here. Last week his boss took us out to dinner, and they wouldn't even let Joe in the restaurant because no tie, right?

CHARLIE: (*half-listening*) Assholes . . .

KITTY: So Joey takes off down the street and zips into some discount store and zips out with this plastic tie—God, did it feel sleazy, like it was made out of a shower curtain, or—well, most likely he'll wear it tomorrow at the wedding—

CHARLIE: I've got ties to lend him, God, they're still in the boxes—but I better find that white shirt, throw it in the washer. Can you wake me? Like at nine. And I'll call in. What time's the wedding?

KITTY: Noon. I'll prob'ly still be making this goddamn potato salad as they're marching down the aisle . . .

CHARLIE: Joe's gonna wear a suit, right?

KITTY: No, just a sportscoat, you don't have to—

CHARLIE: Would he have an extra one?

KITTY: . . . I don't think . . . but you don't have to . . . or we can go buy one, in a couple hours here. We can put it on the card and you can pay us back.

CHARLIE: Yeah? When?

KITTY: Oh, who cares? Shoes, too. Charlie. You should have a decent pair of shoes, you know? A decent jacket . . . for your life. Okay?

CHARLIE: (*beat; then:*) I can get away with a shirt and tie, huh?

KITTY: . . . Sure, this is very casual . . . home-catering, the whole trip . . .

CHARLIE: Okay, I'm gonna hit the rack. Wake me up, okay? Wake me at ten, ten's good enough.

KITTY: I'll send the kids in—

CHARLIE: Better not, you ain't seen my room.

(*as he exits*)

And listen, at the wedding? Just keep Uncle Bill away from me. I can get through anything if he just doesn't ask me what I'm "up to these days."

(*He exits, with remains of sandwiches. She keeps peeling eggs.*)

BLACKOUT

NEW YORK ACTOR

John Guare

NEW YORK ACTOR was first performed at a benefit at the American Repertory Theater in Cambridge, Massachusetts, in April 1992. It was also presented at the New York Public Library for the Performing Arts Reading Room Series on February 1, 1993, under the direction of Neel Keller, with the following cast:

CRAIG	John Vickery
NAT	Stephen Pearlman
EILEEN	Marion Seldes
BARRY	Jerry Stiller
CRITIC	Andre Gregory
CRITIC'S WIFE	Harriet Harris
SAMMY	Barry Sherman
PATRON	Sharon Washington

A theater bar in the west 40s of Manhattan, Joe Allen's to be precise. One wall is lined with brightly colored theater posters of shows with one thing in common.

CRAIG, NAT, BARRY, *and* EILEEN *sit at a table.*

CRAIG: To see these posters. I know I'm back in New York. (CRAIG *raises his glass to the wall in question.*) To you, "Rachel Lily Rosenbloom."

NAT: Cheers, "Mata Hari."

BARRY: Hail, "Fig Leaves Are Falling."

EILEEN: Hey, "Dude!"

CRAIG: "Here's Where I Belong!"

NAT: "Come Summer!"

BARRY: "Hot September!"

EILEEN: I still remember you, "Carrie!"

CRAIG: "Breakfast at Tiffany's."

NAT: Arriverderci "Via Galactica!"

CRAIG: "I'm Solomon!"

EILEEN: The disaster wall. Hail to you shows that ran only one performance.

CRAIG: Yes! Flaunt your failure so it can't hurt you! Oh Christ it's good to be back in New York!

(BARRY *looks up at the TV screen.*)

BARRY: Here it is! Here it is!

EILEEN: Yes! Quiet! Omigod!

(*They all look up.* EILEEN *and* BARRY *recite along with their TV voices.*)

EILEEN'S VOICE: Why would our old cereal want us to get cancer?

BARRY AND EILEEN (*together*): NU-TRIX Bran wants us to live a long long time.

(*They watch in silence for five seconds and then the commercial is over. Everyone applauds.*)

CRAIG: You were great!

NAT: You'll save lives!

EILEEN: You looked like a bank president.

BARRY: Very Katharine Hepburn you.

EILEEN: I hope we work together again.

NAT: This is going to go national.

CRAIG: You'll make a lot of money.

EILEEN: Don't you have a commercial coming up?

NAT: Athlete's foot. The third toe. But it can't all be *The Oresteia.*

EILEEN: Did you see the Peter Brook?

NAT: Out in Brooklyn? So so. (*To* CRAIG) But here's to you. To be on Broadway!

BARRY: Your series finally over!

NAT: I liked "Lawyer from Another Planet."

CRAIG: Indentured slavery. Five years of torture.

EILEEN: I've never been to California.

NAT: But it gave you recognizability.

BARRY: Plus cash. And those residuals.

CRAIG: We *were* like a family. Our own repertory company. For a while. But still—

EILEEN: But "The Locksmith." To be in the play of the year. Everyone on tenterhooks!

BARRY: You open in a month?

NAT: I've got *my* tickets. I'm a Tony voter.

BARRY: No disaster wall for you.

EILEEN: Not after two years in London.

NAT: They'll give you respect.

BARRY: But no residuals.

CRAIG: Katinka and I let our place go in L.A. Half an acre in Studio City. Took an apartment here. Talk about "Little Shop of Horrors." The kids didn't want to move east but I said, Look! your father is back being the greatest thing anyone can be—a New York actor. The British director's crazy about us. Says the American cast has an energy the English lack. Although I'm not crazy about some of the cast.

BARRY: Who are you? I saw it in London.

CRAIG: The Locksmith.

BARRY: The Locksmith! The guy in London won a prize.

NAT: The Oliver!

BARRY: You got the Locksmith!

CRAIG: They called me. I read. I got it. Simple.

NAT: You went to London?

CRAIG: They came to L.A.

NAT: They skipped New York? Fuck 'em. Although I'm glad for you.

EILEEN: I've never been to London. Always afraid to leave New York. Always afraid the big call would come and I'd miss it.

BARRY: Well, this bran flakes will give you financial freedom.

EILEEN: And residuals.

CRAIG: It's like what Laurence Olivier said: "If acting decides to embrace you and take you to its heart, it will hurl you up there among the gods. It will change your wooden clogs overnight and replace them with glass slippers." I'm not saying I'm Sir Larry—

EILEEN and BARRY: No no no—

CRAIG: but I'm thrilled to be back in New York. Out there I was ready to kill myself.

NAT: Kill yourself?

CRAIG: Terminal likability. Any time you read a freeway fatality, know it's an L.A. actor who crashed his Volvo into an overpass, sick of being likable. That's . . . that's what happened to me.

EILEEN: No!

CRAIG: I tried to crash my new Volvo into a rail guard. I pulled over to the side of the road. Asthmatic. Sweating. Freezing. My series was cancelled. I took it as a sign. I knew I had to get out.

EILEEN: I'm so glad you're back.

NAT: Bravo.

BARRY: I was up for a Volvo commercial. Voice-over.

CRAIG: The difference between being an L.A. actor and a New York actor is in L.A. you don't ever dare be tuned out of

somebody's living room. Never be unpleasant or compli-
cated. But a New York actor is fearsome. A New York actor
changes his soul. A New York actor has a soul to change.
Christ, listen to me. I'm alive! Being what God meant me
to be!

NAT: That's why I could never make it out there. I'm not likable.
I like that about me.

CRAIG: An L.A. actor has to make Jack the Ripper likable.

BARRY: Charlie Manson a sweetheart—

NAT: Richard Nixon a heartbreaker—

CRAIG: Although I got offered an interesting part wouldn't you
know the day before I left. Richard Nixon's hairdresser.
True story. Haircuts he gave during crises.

BARRY: Vietnam?

NAT: Watergate?

CRAIG: Snip snip snip. Very moving.

BARRY: You don't think of Richard Nixon having haircuts.

NAT: I suppose he must have.

BARRY: Richard Nixon with his hair down to his shoulders.

NAT: Richard Nixon with a ponytail.

EILEEN: Nixon in a beehive. I like it. But you turned it down.

CRAIG: because I'm the greatest thing there can be

NAT: New York actor!

CRAIG: A killer! A giant! A teller of truths! Brando! Monty Clift.

EILEEN: George Scott.

BARRY: Jimmy Dean.

NAT: Jason.

BARRY: Eli.

EILEEN: Rip.

CRAIG: New York actors. They played Broadway. I'll tell you a secret. It's driven me crazy all these years. (*Draws chair closer.*) I never played Broadway.

NAT and BARRY and EILEEN: What? No? Really?

CRAIG: I'd wake up in the middle of the night and say my life is worthless because I never played Broadway. And then along came the Locksmith. Another round? My treat.

BARRY: There's life beyond Broadway. You ever played Seattle Rep? You ever played Yale Rep? Hartford? The Arena?

CRAIG: Readings at the Taper. I kept my hand in.

EILEEN: Seattle Rep. The Goodman. Trinity Square.

BARRY: Williamstown. New Jersey Shakespeare. ART.

NAT: That's our national theater. Broadway's a dream for you but it's not for me. Shakespeare in the Park. I won an Obie.

BARRY: An ensemble Obie. The whole cast got the Obie.

NAT: You ever even been suggested for anything resembling an Obie?

(CRITIC *and* CRITIC'S WIFE *sit at the next table and pick up menus.*)

EILEEN (*sotto voce*): See who's at next table? The new guy at the *Times.*

NAT: The new guy?

EILEEN: They're going to have a Tuesday lynching party. A reviewer reviews the reviews. That's him. That's Tuesday. Don't look.

BARRY: What the world needs now. More reviews. Don't look.

NAT: Well, this guy loves me. You read my reviews on *Tomorrow's Meadow*? A love letter from him.

EILEEN: That's six years ago in a small weekly magazine.

CRAIG: So what! Today he's the *Times.* Tell him—

NAT: Tell him what?

CRAIG: Thank him for your review. Someone who appreciates your craft. God, we're all in this together! The Theater! This endangered medium! A precious craft like lace weaving! Essential to our souls like water. He wrote about you? Thank him for what he wrote. Appreciate appreciation. Stick up for yourself! You're a New York Actor.

(NAT *pauses and then gets up and stands over the table until the* CRITIC *looks up.*)

CRITIC: I'll have the black bean soup.

CRITIC'S WIFE: No, dear. You have an opening tonight. Try the consommé.

NAT: I'm Nat Boyle.

CRITIC: Yes—and the La Scala salad.

NAT: "Tomorrow's Meadow"?

CRITIC: Is that a horse?

NAT: A play. (CRITIC *and* CRITIC'S WIFE *laugh.*) I was in it.

CRITIC'S WIFE: We have a curtain—

CRITIC: Can we order?

NAT: Sir, you wrote this review of me—

CRITIC'S WIFE: You cannot hold him responsible—

(NAT *takes out a clipping from his wallet.*)

NAT: You said I was "almost perfect." I had you laminated.

CRITIC: *Tomorrow's Meadow?*

NAT: I just heard your good news and wanted to tell you it's great news for the theater community having more reviews and how everyone admires you and what an addition and privilege you are. Your judgments are synonyms for perspicacity and insight into the craft of where we theater artists are striving and it's a great day for the New York theater and I speak for all of us personally looking forward to reading you and if you some Tuesday find yourself writing a column about "Down Memory Lane," about performances you've admired over the recent years—Nat Boyle! Meeting you. It's a privilege. And let me order you a waiter! Waiter! Pronto!

(NAT *returns to his table.*)

NAT: Oh Christ, was I an ass kisser?

BARRY: Oh no! A blow job doesn't make you an ass kisser.

CRAIG: Bravo! Bravo!

(SAMMY *enters, sits down.*)

SAMMY: Congratulate me! I just came from a great audition! I think I got the part! This new English play! They're replacing the guy who's doing the Locksmith. Some L.A. actor. Where's a waiter! I am thirsty! I auditioned my heart out! I sang! I swear to you I sang! Waiter! A bottle of champagne! No, the Krug—

(CRITIC'S WIFE *looks for something.*)

CRITIC'S WIFE: It was right here. It was right here.

CRAIG: One moment. One fucking moment.

(*The* CRITIC *taps* CRAIG *on the shoulder.*)

CRITIC: Did either of you gentlemen see my wife's purse?

CRITIC'S WIFE: It was right here. It was right here.

CRAIG: Shut up, asshole, I'm talking!

BARRY: Shut up! That's *The New York Times* Tuesday.

CRITIC'S WIFE: I hung my purse over the chair.

CRAIG (*to* SAMMY): What is this? April fools?

(BARRY *whispers to* SAMMY.)

SAMMY: What did you say?

(BARRY *whispers to* SAMMY, *now audibly.*)

BARRY: Locksmith. Him.

SAMMY: What did you say?

(CRAIG *stares at* SAMMY.)

CRITIC'S WIFE: It was right here. It was right here.

SAMMY (*to* CRAIG): Oh fuck. I'm really sorry.

CRITIC (*to* NAT): Could we have it back?

NAT (*to* CRITIC): What are you looking at me for?

CRITIC'S WIFE: I had it. And then you leaned over. *Tomorrow's Meadow.*

BARRY: Cover your face.

EILEEN: Move to another table!

(EILEEN *and* BARRY *move away, napkins over their faces.*)

CRITIC: You leaned over my wife.

NAT: To talk to you. To talk you got to lean.

CRITIC'S WIFE: I hung my purse over the chair.

CRAIG: What are you saying you got a part?

SAMMY: It was only sort of definite. Look—don't take it personal.

CRAIG: Who's got a quarter?

SAMMY: Here's a quarter.

CRAIG: I don't want a quarter from you.

(CRAIG *runs off.*)

SAMMY: Be happy for me.

(SAMMY *runs off after* CRAIG. *The* CRITIC'S WIFE *is down on all fours looking under the table.*)

CRITIC'S WIFE: It had everything in it. Keys. Money.

(NAT *gets down on the floor.*)

NAT: Why would I take anything from you?

CRITIC: Because you're sick! Now I'm in a foul mood and I have to view a play I don't want to see anyway. Wait! I remember you! Nat Boyle! That's your name!

NAT: No! Not Nat Boyle. Pat Doyle. Doyle! That's my name. You need money? Here—take mine? You want eyeglasses? A wallet?

(NAT *empties his pockets.* CRAIG *returns,* SAMMY *following.*)

CRAIG: There's a message on my machine to call the producers.

SAMMY: Maybe they want me for understudy. Maybe it's for the tour.

CRAIG: I can't go back to L.A. But how will I stay here in New York? Out there I tried to kill myself. Maybe that's the answer. Why not! Why not!

(CRAIG *runs out of the theater bar.*)

SAMMY: Come back!

(SAMMY *follows. The* CRITIC'S WIFE *holds* NAT *by the leg.*)

CRITIC'S WIFE: Thief! Thief!

(*The* CRITIC *pulls his* WIFE *away.*)

CRITIC: Sweetheart! Quiet! I don't want my name in the paper!

NAT: Oh but you can put my name in the paper! "Almost perfect" yesterday. Thief today!

(NAT *punches the* CRITIC. *The* CRITIC'S WIFE *punches* NAT.)

CRITIC'S WIFE: Thief! Thief!

(*They fall off, fighting.* EILEEN *and* BARRY *reappear, very excited.*)

BARRY: Here it is again!

EILEEN: Everyone! Quiet!

(EILEEN *and* BARRY *look up as before. They recite along with their voices.*)

EILEEN/WIFE: Why would our old cereal want us to get cancer?

BARRY/HUSBAND: Let's be grateful NU-TRIX wants us to live a long long time.

(*The commercial is over.*)

BARRY: You gave me so much.

EILEEN: You gave *me* so much.

(*Two* OUT OF TOWNERS *sit at the vacated table and look around, thrilled.*)

OUT OF TOWNERS: *Rachel Lily Rosenbloom!*
Mata Hari!
La Strada!
Fig Leaves Are Falling!
Dude!
Home Sweet Homer!
Pretty Belle!
Come Summer!
Breakfast at Tiffany's!
Carrie!
This place is adorable!

BLACKOUT.

END

THE PHILADELPHIA

David Ives

THE PHILADELPHIA was presented as part of *All in the Timing* at Primary Stages (Casey Childs, Artistic Director), in New York City, in December 1993. It was directed by Jason McConnell Buzas; the set design was by Bruce Goodrich; the costume design was by Sharon Lynch; the lighting design was by Deborah Constantine and the production stage manager was Christine Catti. The cast was as follows:

AL	Ted Neustadt
WAITRESS	Wendy Lawless
MARK	Robert Stanton

CHARACTERS

AL: California cool; 20s or 30s
MARK: frazzled; 20s or 30s
WAITRESS: weary; as you will

SETTING

A bar/restaurant. A table, red-checkered cloth, two chairs, and a specials board.

This play is for Greg Pliska, who knows what a Philadelphia can be.

AL *is at the restaurant table, with the* WAITRESS.

WAITRESS: Can I help you?

AL: Do you know you would look fantastic on a wide screen?

WAITRESS: Uh-huh.

AL: Seventy millimeters.

WAITRESS: Look. Do you want to see a menu, or what?

AL: Let's negotiate, here. What's the soup du jour today?

WAITRESS: Soup of the day you got a choice of Polish duck blood or cream of kidney.

AL: Beautiful. Beautiful! Kick me in a kidney.

WAITRESS: (*Writes it down.*) You got it.

AL: Any oyster crackers on your seabed?

WAITRESS: Nope. All out.

AL: How about the specials today, spread out your options.

WAITRESS: You got your deep fried gizzards.

AL: Fabulous.

WAITRESS: Calves' brains with okra.

AL: You are a *temptress.*

WAITRESS: And pickled pigs' feet.

AL: Pigs' feet. *I love it.* Put me down for a quadruped.

WAITRESS: If you say so.

AL: Any sprouts to go on those feet?

WAITRESS: Iceberg.

AL: So be it. (*Waitress exits, as* MARK *enters, looking shaken and bedraggled.*)

MARK: Al!

AL: Hey there, Marcus. What's up?

MARK: Jesus!

AL: What's going on, buddy?

MARK: Oh man . . . !

AL: What's the matter? Sit down.

MARK: I don't get it, Al. I don't understand it.

AL: You want something? Want a drink? I'll call the waitress—

MARK: (*Desperate.*) *No!* No! Don't even try. (*Gets a breath.*) I don't know what's going on today, Al. It's really weird.

AL: What, like . . . ?

MARK: Right from the time I got up.

AL: What is it? What's the story?

MARK: Well—just for an example. This morning I stopped off at a drugstore to buy some aspirin. This is at a big drugstore, right?

AL: Yeah . . .

MARK: I go up to the counter, the guy says what can I do for you, I say, Give me a bottle of aspirin. The guy gives me this funny look and he says, "Oh we don't have *that,* sir." I said to him, You're a drugstore and you don't have any aspirin?

AL: Did they have Bufferin?

MARK: Yeah!

AL: Advil?

MARK: Yeah!

AL: Extra-strength Tylenol?

MARK: Yeah!

AL: But no aspirin.

MARK: No!

AL: Wow . . .

MARK: And that's the kind of weird thing that's been happening all day. It's like, I go to a newsstand to buy the *Daily News,* the guy never even *heard* of it.

AL: Could've been a misunderstanding.

MARK: I asked everyplace—*nobody* had the *News!* I had to read the Toronto Hairdresser. Or this. I go into a deli at lunch time to buy a sandwich, the guy tells me they don't have any *pastrami.* How can they be a deli if they don't have pastrami?

AL: Was this a Korean deli?

MARK: This was a kosher from *Jerusalem* deli. "Oh we don't carry *that,* sir," he says to me. "Have some tongue."

AL: Mmm.

MARK: I just got into a cab, the guy says he doesn't go to 56th Street! He offers to take me to Newark instead!

AL: Mm-hm.

MARK: Looking at me like I'm an alien or something!

AL: Mark. Settle down.

MARK: "Oh I don't go *there,* sir."

AL: Settle down. Take a breath.

MARK: Do you know what this is?

AL: Sure.

MARK: What is it? What's happening to me?

AL: Don't panic. You're in a Philadelphia.

MARK: I'm in a what?

AL: You're in a Philadelphia. That's all.

MARK: But I'm in—

AL: Yes, physically you are in New York. But *meta*physically you are in a Philadelphia.

MARK: I've never heard of this!

AL: You see, inside of what we know as reality there are these pockets, these black holes called Philadelphias. If you fall into one, you run up against exactly the kinda shit that's been happening to you all day.

MARK: Why?

AL: Because in a Philadelphia, no matter what you ask for, you can't get it. You ask for something, they're not gonna have it. You want to do something, it ain't gonna get done. You want to go somewhere, you can't get there from here.

MARK: Good God. So this is very serious.

AL: Just remember, Marcus. This is a condition named for the town that invented the *cheese steak.* Something that nobody in his right mind would willingly ask for.

MARK: And I thought I was just having a very bad day . . .

AL: Sure. Millions of people have spent entire lifetimes inside a Philadelphia and never even knew it. Look at the city of Philadelphia itself. Hopelessly trapped forever inside a Philadelphia. And do they know it?

MARK: Well what can I do? Should I just kill myself now and get it over with?

AL: You try to kill yourself in a Philadelphia, you're only gonna get hurt, babe.

MARK: So what do I do?

AL: Best thing you can do is wait it out. Someday the great cosmic train will whisk you outa the City of Brotherly Love and off to someplace happier.

MARK: *You're* pretty goddamn mellow today.

AL: Yeah well. Everybody has to be someplace. (WAITRESS *enters.*)

WAITRESS: Is your name Allen Chase?

AL: It is indeed.

WAITRESS: There was a phone call for you. Your boss?

AL: Okay.

WAITRESS: He says you're fired.

AL: Cool! Thanks. (WAITRESS *exits.*) So anyway, you have this problem . . .

MARK: Did she just say you got *fired?*

AL: Yeah. I wonder what happened to my pigs' feet . . .

MARK: Al—!? You *loved* your job!

AL: Hey. No sweat.

MARK: How can you be so calm?

AL: Easy. You're in a Philadelphia? *I* woke up in a Los Angeles. And life is beautiful! You know Susie packed up and left me this morning.

MARK: Susie left you?

AL: And frankly, Scarlett, I don't give a shit. I say, go and God bless and may your dating pool be Olympic-sized.

MARK: But your job? The garment district is your life!

AL: So I'll turn it into a movie script and sell it to Paramount. Toss in some sex, add a little emotional blah-blah-*blah,* pitch it to Jack and Dusty, you got a buddy movie with a garment background. Not relevant enough? We'll throw in the hole in the ozone, make it E.C.

MARK: E.C.?

AL: Environmentally correct. Have you heard about this hole in the ozone?

MARK: Sure.

AL: Marcus, I *love* this concept. I *embrace* this ozone. Sure, some people are gonna get hurt in the process, meantime everybody else'll tan a little faster.

MARK: (*Quiet horror.*) So this is a Los Angeles . . .

AL: Well. Everybody has to be someplace.

MARK: Wow.

AL: You want my advice? *Enjoy your Philadelphia.* Sit back and order yourself a beer and a burger and chill out for a while.

MARK: But I can't order anything. Life is great for you out there on your cosmic beach, but whatever *I* ask for, I'll get a cheese steak or something.

AL: No. There's a very simple rule of thumb in a Philadelphia. *Ask for the opposite.*

MARK: What?

AL: If you can't get what you ask for, ask for the opposite and you'll get what you want. You want the *Daily News,* ask for the *Times.* You want pastrami, ask for tongue.

MARK: Oh.

AL: Works great with women. What is more opposite than the opposite sex?

MARK: Uh-huh.

AL: So. Would you like a Bud?

MARK: I sure could use a—

AL: No. Stop. (*Very deliberately.*) *Do you want . . . a Bud?*

MARK: (*Also deliberately.*) No. I *don't* want a Bud. (WAITRESS *enters and goes to the specials board.*)

AL: Good. Now there's the waitress. Order yourself a Bud and a burger. But do not *ask* for a Bud and a burger.

MARK: Waitress!

AL: Don't call her. She won't come.

MARK: Oh.

AL: You're in a Philadelphia, so just figure, fuck her.

MARK: Fuck *her.*

AL: You don't need that waitress.

MARK: *Fuck* that waitress.

AL: And everything to do with her.

MARK: *Hey, waitress! FUCK YOU!* (WAITRESS *turns to him.*)

WAITRESS: Can I help you, sir?

AL: *That's* how you get service in a Philadelphia.

WAITRESS: Can I help you?

MARK: Uh—no thanks.

WAITRESS: Okay, what'll you have? (*Takes out her pad.*)

AL: Excellent.

MARK: Well—how about some O.J.

WAITRESS: Sorry. Squeezer's broken.

MARK: A glass of milk?

WAITRESS: Cow's dry.

MARK: Egg nog?

WAITRESS: Just ran out.

MARK: Cuppa coffee?

WAITRESS: Oh we don't have *that*, sir. (MARK *and* AL *exchange a look, and nod. The* WAITRESS *has spoken the magic words.*)

MARK: Got any ale?

WAITRESS: Nope.

MARK: Stout?

WAITRESS: Nope.

MARK: Porter?

WAITRESS: Just beer.

MARK: That's too bad. How about a Heineken?

WAITRESS: Heineken? Try again.

MARK: Rolling Rock?

WAITRESS: Outa stock.

MARK: Schlitz?

WAITRESS: Nix.

MARK: Beck's?

WAITRESS: Next.

MARK: Sapporo?

WAITRESS: Tomorrow.

MARK: Lone Star?

WAITRESS: Hardy-har.

MARK: Bud Lite?

WAITRESS: Just plain Bud is all we got.

MARK: No thanks.

WAITRESS: (*Calls.*) *Gimme a Bud!* (*To* MARK.) Anything to eat?

MARK: Nope.

WAITRESS: Name it.

MARK: Pork chops.

WAITRESS: (*Writes down.*) Hamburger . . .

MARK: Medium.

WAITRESS: Well done . . .

MARK: Baked potato.

WAITRESS: Fries . . .

MARK: And some zucchini.

WAITRESS: Slice of raw. (*Exits, calling.*) Burn one!

AL: Marcus, that was excellent.

MARK: Thank you.

AL: *Excellent.* You sure you've never done this before?

MARK: I've spent so much of my life asking for the wrong thing
    without knowing it, doing it on purpose comes easy.

AL: I hear you.

MARK: I could've saved myself a lot of trouble if I'd screwed up on purpose all those years. Maybe I was in a Philadelphia all along and never knew it!

AL: You might've been in a Baltimore. They're practically the same. (WAITRESS *enters, with a glass of beer and a plate.*)

WAITRESS: Okay. Here's your Bud. (*Sets that in front of* MARK.) And one cheese steak. (*She sets that in front of* AL, *and starts to go.*)

AL: Excuse me. Hey. Wait a minute. What is that?

WAITRESS: It's a cheese steak.

AL: No. I ordered cream of kidney and two pairs of feet.

WAITRESS: Oh we don't have *that,* sir.

AL: I beg your pardon?

WAITRESS: We don't have that, sir. (*Small pause.*)

AL: (*To* MARK.) You son of a bitch! *I'm in your Philadelphia!*

MARK: I'm sorry, Al.

AL: You brought me into your fucking Philadelphia!

MARK: I didn't know it was contagious.

AL: Oh God, please don't let me be in a Philadelphia! Don't let me be in a—

MARK: Shouldn't you ask for the opposite? I mean, since you're in a Philad—

AL: Don't you tell *me* about life in a Philadelphia.

MARK: Maybe you're not really—

AL: I taught you everything you know about Philly, asshole. Don't tell *me* how to act in a Philadelphia!

MARK: But maybe you're not really in a Philadelphia!

AL: Do you see the cheese on that steak? What do I need for proof? The fucking *Liberty Bell?* Waitress, bring me a glass of water.

WAITRESS: Water? Don't have that, sir.

AL: (*To* MARK.) "We don't have *water*"—? What, you think we're in a sudden drought or something? (*Suddenly realizes.*) Holy shit, I just lost my job . . . ! Susie left me! I gotta make some phone calls! (*To* WAITRESS.) 'Scuse me, where's the pay phone?

WAITRESS: Sorry, we don't have a pay ph—

AL: Of *course* you don't have a pay phone, of *course* you don't! Oh shit, let me outa here! (*Exits.*)

MARK: I don't know. It's not that bad in a Philadelphia.

WAITRESS: Could be worse. I've been in a Cleveland all week.

MARK: A Cleveland. What's that like?

WAITRESS: It's like death, without the advantages.

MARK: Really. Care to stand?

WAITRESS: Don't mind if I do. (*She sits.*)

MARK: I hope you won't reveal your name.

WAITRESS: Sharon.

MARK: (*Holds out his hand.*) Good-bye.

WAITRESS: Hello. (*They shake.*)

MARK: (*Indicating the cheese steak.*) Want to starve?

WAITRESS: Thanks! (*She picks up the cheese steak and starts eating.*)

MARK: Yeah, everybody has to be someplace . . . (*Leans across the table with a smile.*) So.

BLACKOUT

THE MAN
WHO COULDN'T DANCE

Jason Katims

The attic of Gail's house in Connecticut. ELIZABETH *sleeps in her crib.*
ERIC *and* GAIL *enter.*

GAIL: Not too loud.

(They walk to crib. Look in.)

GAIL: Eric, this is Elizabeth.

ERIC: Oh my God. She's really . . . ugly.

GAIL: What?

ERIC: The kid is like a raisin or something.

GAIL: (*To* ELIZABETH, *whispering.*) Don't listen to him Elizabeth.
He's jealous. (*To* ERIC.) I've been wanting so much for you
to meet her. It's like it would make the whole thing real or
something.

ERIC: God. She's a beautiful little raisin, isn't she? It's what was
behind door number two.

GAIL: What?

ERIC: I don't know. All night I haven't been able to shake this
feeling. It's like I'm visiting the life I could have had. A
baby. A house in Connecticut. A subscription to *House and
Garden.*

GAIL: You won't let me outlive that one will you?

ERIC: Come on Gail. *House and Garden.*

GAIL: I put it in the basket in the bathroom for *you*, you know. I remember how frightened you used to be of bathrooms without reading material.

ERIC: Don't make me into some sort of like neurotic old boyfriend Gail.

GAIL: Are you going to deny your severe fear of bathrooms?

ERIC: Bathrooms are frightening, horrible places. Cold. Lonely. Sterile. But you should not use that to make me into some kind of little anecdote. Like a chapter of your life that was some little situation comedy. Do not mistake neurotic fears and obsessions for light comedy. Very dangerous, Gail.

GAIL: I don't want to get into a discussion like this now, Eric.

ERIC: What kind of discussion is it, and when *would* you like to get into it?

GAIL: A discussion about us. And never. They're waiting.

ERIC: They're fine on their own.

GAIL: What is that supposed to mean?

ERIC: What?

GAIL: They're *fine* on their own. *Fine?*

ERIC: It doesn't mean anything.

GAIL: Are you saying that my husband is attracted to your girlfriend. Is that it?

ERIC: Wooo. Hold on Gail. All I said was they're fine on their own.

GAIL: Fred and I happen to be very, very happy. Together. He's not interested in some twenty-three-year-old music student and her stupid thesis on Todd Rundgren.

ERIC: You seemed very interested over dinner.

GAIL: Who the hell would write a thesis on Todd Rundgren? Is she going to hand out T-shirts and loose joints at her orals?

ERIC: She's just a date, Gail. A date.

GAIL: It didn't sound like that on the phone. "She's beautiful. She's intelligent. She's not hung up by society's rules." These are your words. I think you should grow up.

ERIC: Why?

GAIL: Why should you grow up? Are you asking me why you should grow up?

ERIC: Yes. I'm interested in hearing about it from someone who thinks she has.

GAIL: That is what people do. They get married. They have kids. They remember their ideals fondly. They try to stick to them in their own way. They donate to public television. They get by.

ERIC: Don't cry, Gail. Please do not cry.

GAIL: Oooh that gets me. What makes you think I'm going to cry?

ERIC: Because you regret your choices. And now you're going to cry.

GAIL: I regret my choices? Fuck you.

ERIC: I'm sorry. I said what I thought. I broke the unwritten rule between us since we broke up. I'm supposed to smile, and talk to you like I'm really interested in just the right amount of sugar to put into the pecan pie recipe.

GAIL: I can't believe you said that thing about *my* pie.

ERIC: I liked the pie. I thought it had a little too much sugar. I just don't understand why everyone who makes pecan pie is obligated to put too much sugar in it because every other pecan pie has too much sugar in it. It's like a world doomed to repeat its horrors. I eat that pecan pie and I think we're just marking time until the next goddamn Holocaust.

GAIL: Are you saying I baked a Nazi pie?

ERIC: Not intentionally.

GAIL: You shouldn't have criticized my pie in front of company.

ERIC: Gail, I am the company.

(*A beat.*)

GAIL: Oh am I glad that you are not the father of my daughter. I am so happy to not have to worry for her about your inconsistency, your stubbornness, your uncanny ability to make the most politically and philosophically interesting choices leaving yourself and your loved ones in the shit heap. Let's just spend the rest of the night playing Pictionary. All right?

ERIC: This is the fourth time tonight you brought up Pictionary. Are you forcing me to play fucking Pictionary?

GAIL: It's just a game, Eric. Or am I wrong. Is it actually going to join forces with pecan pie to cause the next Holocaust?

ERIC: It's a waste of time. People sit around and solve meaning-less little puzzles and form arbitrary alliances for no other reason than to pass time. Well, time is passing well enough for me without games, Gail. Fred wastes enough of my time talking about his fucking boat. Does he really think I care about his fucking boat? All right, great. He bought a motor-ized flotation device. Does he really think I want to go on for hour after hour about it?

GAIL: So good. It's good to know how you feel about Fred.

ERIC: How do I feel about Fred?

GAIL: I always knew you didn't like him.

ERIC: How can I like him or not like him? I don't know him. I know his boat. I could draw the blueprints for his fucking boat. I don't know *him*.

GAIL: It's so goddamn easy for you.

ERIC: What?

GAIL: It's so easy for you *not* to play Pictionary. You're funny, verbal, provocative. Do you know how intimidated my husband is by you?

ERIC: Play fucking Pictionary, Gail. Play your heart out. I'll stay here with Elizabeth.

GAIL: You belong with Elizabeth.

ERIC: Purity-wise?

GAIL: Maturity-wise.

ERIC: (*Change of tone.*) You don't love Fred.

GAIL: What?

ERIC: You don't love Fred.

GAIL: That's it. I demand that you play Pictionary, Eric. I god-damn insist.

ERIC: Why did you marry a man you didn't love?

GAIL: I never said I don't love him.

ERIC: Christ, Gail. Tell me you love him. Please.

GAIL: YOU GOT ON THAT FUCKING BOAT. The crucial point. The pinnacle time. The absolute quintessential turn-ing point of our relationship and you're on a fucking boat to fucking Saint John.

ERIC: That has nothing to do with it.

GAIL: It's got everything to do with it.

ERIC: You make it sound like you made some kind of choice between two men. Like it was me or him.

GAIL: It was.

ERIC: It was? Come on Gail. It's a huge world. If it were a choice between me or Fred most women would just fucking shoot themselves.

GAIL: You threw it away.

ERIC: I never threw you away.

GAIL: Not *me*. It. Everything. Eric you're such an asshole. Everyone's goddamn guru. Living by your values. True to yourself. The ascetic. The Twentieth Century Philosopher. Eric, I have a question for you. A real question. Why are you working on a farm? Why? It's like I'm supposed to admire you or something. I'm so sick of your untraditional paths. The Farm Boy from Bensonhurst. You're wasting your intelligence. You're wasting your intelligence to pick vegetables. There is nothing to admire about that. It's stupid.

ERIC: You're right. Why work with my hands to produce a reasonably priced source of nourishment for my fellow human beings while I could be getting fat and playing Pictionary.

GAIL: I gained four pounds. *Four.* Don't you dare say I'm getting fat. And there is nothing wrong with playing Pictionary, you goddamn all-knowing fool. You lost me.

ERIC: I know.

GAIL: It pisses me off. It really pisses me off. That thing you said about me regretting my choices. At least I made a choice.

ERIC: But you do regret it.

GAIL: I love Fred, Eric. I do love him. Not like I loved you. But we have these things together. This family. This feeling. This sureness.

ERIC: I don't consider your need for structure your strongest trait.

GAIL: Look, Eric, I don't think I can have this conversation with you. I'm sorry things had to happen the way they happened. Let's go downstairs.

ERIC: Right. I'm sorry.

GAIL: You're just being yourself.

ERIC: That's what I'm sorry for. I should say good-bye to Elizabeth. Who knows when I'll see her again.

(ERIC *walks to the crib. He looks down. In a moment he bends over to her.*)

GAIL: Eric! She'll wake up.

(*But* ERIC *lifts her into his arms. When he turns back his face is flush with tears.*)

GAIL: Eric. What is it?

(ERIC *cuddles* ELIZABETH. *He puts his lips to her forehead. He places her gently back in the crib.*)

GAIL: What?

ERIC: It's um. It's this thing I need to tell you. I can't dance, Gail.

GAIL: You can't dance. This is why you're crying? Eric, a lot of people can't dance.

ERIC: I don't know why I can't dance. But it's—I can't. I can't make my body move in these ways that the music is demanding that I move. It's just so goddamn embarrassing. The situation. I mean, standing in public around hundreds of people who are displaying their purest, truest selves. I mean, it takes them no more than two drinks and their souls are out there on the dance floor. Their goodness. Their sensuality. They're sharing and loving. I watch that, look at

that. But my body fights it. I start to analyze the music.
The rhythm. The time signature. I understand the theory of
dancing. The *idea* of spontaneously sharing in this moment
that exists now and only now. The give and take with your
partner. Two mirrors on a land where gravity holds you to
this point and then leaves you free. And that the universe
happens right there and then. Like, truth. I understand this
intellectually. But Gail, I never have experienced it. I can't
dance.

GAIL: How did Elizabeth make you think of that?

ERIC: When we were together. There were all these times when
you would arrange for us to be in these places. These parties.
And invariably there would be a band, or music playing and
invariably people would start dancing.

GAIL: I would arrange this? Like I did this to you?

ERIC: Invariably you would want to dance. And I wouldn't
dance with you. I wouldn't dance with you, Gail. And I
could see the hurt register on your face. I could see the
anger build within you. I could see that this just wouldn't
do for you.

GAIL: Why didn't you just say I can't dance. Why didn't you just
tell me?

ERIC: Because it was the dam holding the water. If I let that out.
That one thing, everything would follow. I couldn't dance. I
couldn't have a normal talk about the weather with a neigh-
bor without getting into a conversation about God, love
and eternity. I mean, after all, the weather has these huge
connotations. I couldn't act correctly in social situations. I
couldn't sacrifice truth for a relationship. I couldn't hold you
when you needed to be held because I wanted you to be
stronger. Because I wanted to be stronger. I couldn't ask you
for the warmth of your touch out of need. I couldn't let myself. I would only ask for your touch out of strength. Out of

something that wouldn't become sick and interdependent and symbiotic. I wasn't able to do these things. I don't know, Gail. I mean, you marrying Fred didn't really say anything to me. It was like something in this continuum. This cycle. I mean, it was this thing that happened in my life. The love of my life got married to another man. It didn't seem permanent. But the fact that Elizabeth . . . The fact that this angel . . . this unbelievable gift isn't mine. And will never be mine. This is killing me.

GAIL: Oh my God, Eric. You're human.

ERIC: I'll never have a daughter, Gail.

GAIL: Yes, you will.

ERIC: I'm thirty-seven. I have done nothing but make myself more isolated, unavailable, and unappealing. Believe it or not, it's difficult picking up women with this type of conversation. I work for four dollars an hour, Gail. I never earned a college degree. I can't bring myself to work for someone who is not producing something with some kind of goodness. That rules out ninety-eight percent of job openings. And the other two percent pay approximately four dollars an hour. I am not really going to change. I don't know why this is. People think I make these choices. But you've got to believe me, Gail, I have no control. I can't dance.

GAIL: I never knew you *couldn't* dance. I always thought it was that you *wouldn't* dance.

ERIC: Could you hold me?

GAIL: I don't think so, Eric. I mean, I don't think I would be able to let go.

ERIC: Yeah. You're right. (*Pause.* ERIC *wipes his eyes.*) Gail, there were these things that you needed. Just to breathe you needed them. And it was so clear that there was no way I was going to provide you with them. And it was this thing that I did. This thing that I did. It wasn't that horrible. You needed to find someone. I felt that you needed me off the continent. Please believe me, Gail. When I got on that boat, I was thinking of you. Not of me.

GAIL: I believe you.

ERIC: Well, this is a sign of times to come. The first time we had a conversation where your eyes stayed dry and mine didn't.

GAIL: I cried.

ERIC: We better get downstairs before Marie tells Fred about her orgy with the British invasion.

GAIL: There was one time you danced with me.

ERIC: I don't remember.

GAIL: On my wedding day.

ERIC: I couldn't have.

GAIL: You did. I remember it clearly. I remember thinking how strange it was to be in this wedding gown. On my wedding day. Dancing with you. And you weren't my groom.

ERIC: Oh yeah. That. I wasn't dancing, Gail. I was walking. I convinced myself that I was walking very slowly and sideways. It was the only way I could do it.

GAIL: Eric, maybe one day . . .

ERIC: Please don't say it.

GAIL: Right.

ERIC: Gail, I cannot stand Marie. I can't stand her. Please, find something to say to her about me so she won't expect me to sleep with her tonight.

GAIL: I'm sure you'll do just fine on your own.

ERIC: She was just an excuse to see you. I figured, I'd call with this woman in my life. I'd be less of a threat to the home. It was really stupid of me.

GAIL: No. It was human.

ERIC: Thank you for showing me your daughter. She is absolutely the single, greatest thing I've ever looked at in my entire life.

(*They are about to leave.*)

GAIL: Eric.

(ERIC *turns.* GAIL *walks up to him slowly. She puts her head into his chest. His arms fold around her.*)

GAIL: Eric, you are Fred Astaire. You are Fred Astaire.

ERIC: No, no. Sweetheart. I'm Eric.

GAIL: You are Fred Astaire. Just move the slightest bit. You have nothing to prove to anyone. Just move a little slowly. The slightest bit. Don't worry.

ERIC: We should go down there.

GAIL: In a minute. Just one minute.

(GAIL *rocks back and forth musically.* ERIC *makes a slight movement trying to follow her. In a moment, he relaxes. He is dancing.* GAIL *reaches over, still holding him, and pulls the light cord.*)

BLACKOUT

HOLD FOR THREE

Sherry Kramer

CHARACTERS

SCOTTIE: A young woman, very early 20s, maybe late teens
BARTEY: A young woman, very early 20s, maybe late teens
ED: A young man, very early 20s, maybe late teens

Scottie, Bartey, and Ed are at the beach, at the water's edge. The horizon exists on a line parallel with the top of the audience.

SCOTTIE: (*Points at the horizon, excited.*) There——(*She is pointing at the moon, which has just started to rise.* ED *takes in a huge breath of air.*) She's up——she's up——

BARTEY: This is ridiculous——he's not going to be able to hold his breath while the moon comes up——

SCOTTIE: Come on, come on, look at your watch——

BARTEY: Okay, okay. It is exactly——

(*She looks at her watch, and reports whatever time it actually is.*)

_____ and seventeen seconds.

SCOTTIE: Let's subtract five seconds to adjust for operator error, shall we?

BARTEY: What do I care, Scottie? Really . . .

SCOTTIE: Okay, now, Ed, the first thirty seconds or so are easy. Just relax and save yourself.

BARTEY: (*Looking at* ED, *shaking her head.*) You're weird.

SCOTTIE: Adjusted time from start?

BARTEY: Uh——twenty-three seconds.

SCOTTIE: Okay. Allllllllllright.

(*Coaching sequences are down directly to* ED, *as excited as possible.*)

Now. I want you to imagine that you are in a Movie of the
Week disaster film with Evette Minaux. You are underwater
in—in a nuclear submarine. Evette is trapped in the com-
partment where Polaris missiles are armed and ready to fly.
You got to hold your breath long enough to get in, rescue
her, disarm six missiles, and save the world from nuclear
holocaust. Got that?

(ED *nods, and mimes spinning open bulkheads, disarming missiles, etc.*)

Well. That ought to take him a while. Time?

BARTEY: He's never going to make it.

SCOTTIE: Give me a break. It's almost a third of the way up.

BARTEY: A third? A third? His eyebrows just popped up—

SCOTTIE: The man in the moon does not have—

BARTEY: Well, if he did, that's what we'd—oooh—here come the
eyes—

SCOTTIE: Time, damn it, time—I got a man here trying to do a
job—

BARTEY: Fifty-three seconds.

SCOTTIE: Okay. Here we go. (*To* ED.) You're Anne Frank. Three
storm troopers with boots polished to a shine hard enough
to bounce laser beams enter the room. You're hiding in a
pile of dirty laundry. One breath out of you—you'll feel the
cold steel of their bayonets.

(ED *crouches on the floor, his hands covering his head, keeping very, very
still.*)

Not bad, huh?

(ED *makes a mezzo, mezzo gesture with one hand.*)

BARTEY: (*Looking closely at* ED.) He's turning blue.

SCOTTIE: (*Looks carefully, too.*) He just didn't shave this morning, that's all.

BARTEY: And he's shaking, I think—

SCOTTIE: (*Looking at the moon.*) It's close to halfway, wouldn't you say?

BARTEY: Why is he shaking like that—

SCOTTIE: Oh, differences in temperature in the atmospheric layers, something like that I guess. Distorts the air waves.

BARTEY: No, not the moon. Ed.

SCOTTIE: So he's shaking a little. Look—the bridge is up!

BARTEY: What?

SCOTTIE: Of his nose. Bridge is up, get it?

BARTEY: I hope he doesn't pass out or anything—I mean what if he hyperventilates in reverse or something—what if he forgets how to breathe—

SCOTTIE: (*As Carl Sagan.*) It took the genetic ancestors of Ed Carmichael billions and billions of years to learn to use their lungs. (*As herself.*) Even Ed can't screw all that up in three minutes. Time!

BARTEY: One minute, thirty-eight seconds.

SCOTTIE: And the boy is sweating bullets. I know you're gonna love this one, Ed. It's 1969. You're president of your university's SDS. The anti-war protest seems to be coming along fine when—TEAR GAS!!!! The pigs have just lobbed in the tear gas—one whiff and you're reduced to a slobbering flower child—you've got to hold your breath long enough to take over the dean's office—GO FOR IT!!!!!

(ED *mimes running, choking on tear gas, fighting with policemen, etc.*)

Time?

BARTEY: One minute, fifty-eight.

SCOTTIE: (*Looking at the moon.*) Looks like we're getting into the mouth now. Ed—Ed, hang on, just a couple lips to go.

(ED *indicates that he just can't go on.*)

> Ed—Ed—don't give up now—come on, come on, you can do it—all you have to do is pretend you're—pretend you're—GOD!!! Yes, you're God, and it's Day One of Creation. You've got a whole world of things to make before you get around to breathing the breath of life into Adam, so you hold it—you hold your breath for five days of creatures and firmament and shrubs—only you can do it, Ed, because you're GOD!

(ED *is past making a rude response to this one. He struggles on.* SCOTTIE *is near hysteria.*)

> TIME!!!

BARTEY: Two minutes, twenty-three.

SCOTTIE: THE HOME STRETCH!!! We're getting into the chin, now. You'll never *guess* what I've saved for the home stretch. (ED *struggles to his feet and stands, ready.*) You've been unjustly convicted of murder, and sentenced to the gas chamber. You're strapped in—when NEW EVIDENCE PROMPTS A PARDON FROM THE GOVERNOR—but—THE GAS PELLETS HAVE ALREADY BEEN RELEASED!!!!!! The guards are rushing to the door to save you—if only you can hold your breath till—

(ED *pretends sitting in the chair, ripping off the restraining straps, going wild trying to hold his breath in the gas chamber.*)

> TIME!!!

BARTEY: Two minutes, forty-four—

SCOTTIE: They're rushing to save you—

BARTEY: Clearing the chin now—

(BARTEY *is now caught up in the excitement.*)

SCOTTIE: They're almost to the door now—

BARTEY: Just this much more to go—

(*Makes an eighth of an inch with thumb and first finger, after measuring on the horizon.*)

SCOTTIE: They're at the door—

BARTEY: Two minutes and—you can do it, come on—

SCOTTIE: They're opening the door—

BARTEY: TEN—

SCOTTIE: No, it's stuck—

BARTEY: NINE—

SCOTTIE: They're using brute force—

BARTEY: EIGHT—

SCOTTIE: The guards have asked for help from—

BARTEY: SEVEN—

SCOTTIE: —the people from the press—

BARTEY: SIX—

SCOTTIE: The reporters are throwing their weight around—

BARTEY: FIVE—

SCOTTIE: The door starts to give—

BARTEY: FOUR—

SCOTTIE: It starts to give—

BARTEY: THREE—

SCOTTIE: (*Looking at the moon rather than* ED.) Come on, come on, it's starting to give now—

BARTEY: TWO—

SCOTTIE: It's—it's—it's UP!!!!

(ED *collapses on the floor.*)

BARTEY: ONE!!!! HE DID IT!!!! THREE MINUTES FLAT!!!

(BARTEY *and* SCOTTIE *gaze at the moon for several seconds.*)

SCOTTIE: Beautiful, isn't it, Ed.

ED: (*Raises his head, looks at the moon for the first time.*) Yeah.

(*Beat.*)

BLACKOUT

REVERSE TRANSCRIPTION

SIX PLAYWRIGHTS BURY A SEVENTH

A Ten-Minute Play that's nearly Twenty Minutes Long

Tony Kushner

REVERSE TRANSCRIPTION premiered at Actors Theatre of
Louisville's 1996 Humana Festival.

CAST

HAUTFLOTE: a playwright in his late thirties. He writes beautiful plays
everyone admires; he has a following and little financial success.
He was Ding's best friend, the executor of his will and his wishes.

ASPERA: a playwright in her early thirties. She writes fierce, splendidly intelligent, challenging plays, frequently with lesbian characters, and cannot get an American theater to produce her for love
or money. So she lives in London, where she is acclaimed. She is
cool and is beginning to sound British.

BIFF: a playwright in his late thirties. Scruffy, bisexual, one success,
several subsequent failures, cannot stay away from political themes
though his analysis is not rigorous. He is overdue; he should be
home, writing; he should not be here.

HAPPY: a playwright in his late thirties. His early plays were widely
admired, then one big success and he's become a Hollywood
writer, TV mostly, rich now, a little bored, but very happy. He
plans to go back to writing for the theater someday.

OTTOLINE: a playwright in her fifties. African-American, genuinely
great, hugely influential experimentalist whom everyone adores
but who is now languishing in relative obscurity and neglect,
though she continues to write prolifically. She is the best writer of
the bunch and the least well remunerated. Hers is a deep bitterness; the surface is immensely gracious. She teaches playwrights
and has a zoological fascination, watching them. Ding was her
protégé, sort of. She is an old friend of Flatty's.

FLATTY: a playwright in his late forties. Colossally rich. An easy target for negativity of all kinds though he is in fact a good writer,
hugely prolific, very hard-working and generous to his fellow
'wrights.

DING: a dead playwright wrapped in a winding sheet. A very talented
writer, whom everyone admired for wildly different reasons.

The play takes place in Abel's Hill cemetery on Abel's Hill, Martha's Vineyard, in December near midnight. Abel's Hill is a real place, a spectacularly beautiful, mostly nineteenth-century Yankee graveyard; it's way too expensive for any mortal to get a plot in it now. Lillian Hellman and Dashiell Hammett are buried there. So is John Belushi, whose tombstone kept getting stolen by fans till Dan Aykroyd put a gigantic boulder on Belushi's grave, too huge for anyone to lift. From the crest of the hill you can see the ocean.

Everyone has shovels, and several have bottles of various liquors. The night is beautiful and very cold.

They are writers, so they love words. Their speech is precise, easy, articulate; they are showing off a little. They are at that stage of drunk, right before sloppy, where you are eloquent, impressing yourself. They are making pronouncements, aware of their wit; this mustn't be pinched, crabbed, dour, effortful. They are having fun on this mad adventure; they relish its drama. Underneath is a very deep grief.

They all really loved Ding.

(*High atop Abel's Hill, a cemetery on Martha's Vineyard. Just athwart the crest. Tombstones all around. As the voice of the playwright is heard on tape, with an accompanying obbligato of a typewriter's clattering,* BIFF, HAPPY, ASPERA, OTTOLINE, *and* FLATTY *gather, facing downhill.* HAUT-FLOTE *appears, carrying the body of* DING, *wrapped in a winding sheet.* HAUTFLOTE *places the body before them, then runs off, then returns with six shovels. The other playwrights look about uneasily, and then sit. They have come to bury him illegally. It's nearly midnight.*)

THE VOICE OF THE PLAYWRIGHT: *Dramatis Personae:* Seven characters, all playwrights. BIFF, scruffy, bisexual, one success, several subsequent failures, cannot stay away from political themes though his analysis is not rigorous. He is overdue; he should be home, writing; he should not be here. HAPPY, his early plays were widely admired, then one big success and he's become a Hollywood writer, TV mostly, rich now, a little bored, but very . . . um, well, happy. He plans to go back to writing for the theater someday. ASPERA writes fierce, splendidly intelligent, challenging plays, frequently with lesbian characters, and she cannot get an American theater to produce her for love or money. So she lives in London where she is acclaimed. OTTOLINE, African-American, genuinely great, hugely influential experimentalist whom everyone adores but who is now languishing in relative obscurity and neglect, the best writer of the bunch and the least well remunerated. She is an old friend of FLATTY, colossally successful, colossally rich. An easy target for negativity of all kinds

though he is in fact a good writer, hugely prolific. HAUT-
FLOTE, writes beautiful experimental plays, has a small loyal
following and little financial success; the best friend and executor of the estate of DING, a dead playwright wrapped in a
winding sheet, very talented, whom everyone admired for
wildly different reasons. Seven characters are too many for
a ten-minute play. It'll be twenty minutes long! Fuck it.
One of them is dead and the others can all talk fast. The play
takes place in Abel's Hill cemetery, a spectacularly beautiful
mostly nineteenth-century Yankee graveyard, way too expensive for any mortal to get a plot in it now. On Abel's Hill,
Martha's Vineyard, in December near midnight.

(*When the voice is finished,* HAUTFLOTE *goes to a nearby headstone, on
the side of which is a light switch. He flicks it on; a full moon appears
in the sky.*)

HAUTFLOTE: Ah!

(*The play begins.*)

HAUTFLOTE: Here. We should start digging.

ASPERA: Athwart the crest. Facing the sea. As Ding demanded.

OTTOLINE: Isn't this massively illegal?

FLATTY: Trespass, destruction of private property, destruction of
a historical landmark I shouldn't wonder, conveyance of tissue, i.e. poor Ding, in an advanced state of morbidity, on
public transportation . . .

HAUTFLOTE: He's been *preserved*. He's hazardous to no one's
health. He traveled here in a steamer trunk. The porters
helped.

BIFF: (*apostrophizing*) O please come to me short sweet simple
perfect *idea*. A seed, a plot.

HAUTFLOTE: He's under a deadline.

BIFF: I'm doomed.

HAUTFLOTE: Now shoulder your shovels . . .

BIFF: There's no dignity, have you noticed? In being *this*. An American playwright. What is that?

OTTOLINE: Well, we drink.

HAPPY: No one really drinks now. None of us, at least not publicly.

FLATTY: I can't remember something.

HAPPY: We're . . . (*looking for the word*)

FLATTY: A name.

HAPPY: Healthier!

HAUTFLOTE: What name?

FLATTY: The name of the country that makes me despair.

HAPPY: But tonight we are drunk.

BIFF: In honor of Ding.

HAUTFLOTE: What letter does it begin with?

BIFF: Poor Ding.

(*They all look at* DING. *Little pause.*)

ASPERA: "And Poor Ding Who Is Dead."

(*Little pause. They all look at* DING.)

FLATTY: R.

HAUTFLOTE: Rwanda.

FLATTY: *That's* it.

OTTOLINE: How could you *forget*, Flatty? Rwanda?

FLATTY: I've never had a head for names. Not in the news much anymore, Rwanda.

OTTOLINE: We are afraid to stick the shovel in.

HAUTFLOTE: Yes.

OTTOLINE: Believing it to be a desecration.

HAUTFLOTE: Of this holy earth.

OTTOLINE: Not *holy:* Pure. Authentic.

HAPPY: Yankee.

OTTOLINE: Pilgrim.

HAPPY: Puritan.

OTTOLINE: Forefatherly. Originary.

ASPERA: Oh fuck me, "originary"; John Belushi's buried here!

FLATTY: And he had enough drugs in him when he died to poison all the waters from here to Nantucket.

OTTOLINE: And the people steal his tombstone.

FLATTY: No!

OTTOLINE: Or the hill keeps swallowing it up. It doesn't rest in peace. A pretender, you see.

ASPERA: Lillian Hellman's buried here. She's a playwright.

HAUTFLOTE: Appropriate or no, it's what Ding wanted.

OTTOLINE: And that's another thing. It cost two hundred thirty-seven dollars and fifty cents for a round trip ticket. From New York. This is an *island*. Martha's Vineyard is an *island!* Did Ding *realize* that? One has to *ferry* across. Fucking Ding. Maybe *you all* have money. For ferry passage. I don't have money. I've got no money.

FLATTY: I told you I'd pay for you.

OTTOLINE: Well we all know *you've* got money.

BIFF: O come to me short sweet simple idea!

FLATTY: I want something magical to happen.

BIFF: A plot. The Horseleech hath two daughters. It's a start. And these daughters . . . Do . . . What?

HAPPY: They cry!

OTTOLINE: Give, give!

BIFF: Brecht in exile circumnavigated the globe. Berlin. Skovsbostrand. Stockholm. Helsinki. Leningrad. Moscow. Vladivostok. Manila. L.A. Quick stop in D.C. to visit the HUAC. New York. Paris. Zurich. Salzburg. Prague. Berlin. An American playwright, what is that? Never in exile, always in extremis. The list of cities: AIDS, loss, fear of infection, unsafe sex he says gazing upon the corpse of a fallen comrade, I fuck men and women. I dream my favorite actor has been shot by the police, I dream I shoot Jesse Helms in the head and it doesn't kill him . . .

FLATTY: Eeewww, *politics.*

BIFF: I dream we are intervening in Bosnia merely to give Germany hegemony over Eastern Europe. Why, I dream myself in my dream asking myself, do you dream that? You do not dream a play, you *write* a play. And this play is due, and there's (*pointing to* DING's *corpse*) the deadline. I write in my notebook that I am glad we are sending troops to former Yugoslavia but I (*he makes the "in quotes" gesture with his fingers*) "inadvertently" spell troops "T-R-O-U-P-E-S" as in troupes as in theatrical troupes, traveling players, we are sending *troupes* to former Yugoslavia.

HAUTFLOTE: I don't think we can avoid it any longer. The digging.

FLATTY: I imagine it's worth serious jail time for us all.

HAPPY: Incarcerated playwrights. Now *that* has dignity. Until it's learned what for.

BIFF: I repulse myself, I am not of this earth; if I were more serious I would be an essayist if I were more observant a novelist more articulate more intelligent a poet more . . . succinct more *ballsy* a screenwriter and then I could buy an apartment.

HAUTFLOTE: Fuck the public. It's all Ding asked for. He never got his own, alive.

ASPERA: Poor poor Ding.

HAUTFLOTE: He grew obsessed with this cemetery, in his final months. We visited it years ago. On a day trip, we could never afford . . . to *stay* here. Or anywhere. Or anything. Health insurance. "Bury me on Abel's Hill." His final words. I think he thought this place would give him a retroactive pedigree.

OTTOLINE: That's it, *pedigree,* not *holiness.* Blood, genes. Of which we playwrights are envious. We're mutts. Amphibians.

ASPERA: Not of the land not of the sea. Not of the page nor of the moment.

HAPPY: Perdurable page. Fleeting moment.

FLATTY: Something magical should happen now.

HAUTFLOTE: Ding wanted to belong. Or rather, he never wanted not to. Or rather he never didn't want to, he *wanted* to not want to, but did. In his final months he grew finical.

ASPERA: When I saw him he wasn't finical, he was horrible. He looked horrible and he screamed at everyone all day and all night and there was no way he could get warm, ever. It was quite a change. I hadn't seen him in months, I was visiting from London, WHERE I LIVE, *IN EXILE,* PRODUCED, APPLAUDED, *LAUDED* EVEN and NO ONE IN AMERICA WILL **TOUCH** MY WORK, but anyway he was somehow very very angry but not bitter. One felt envied, but not blamed. At Ding's deathbed.

HAUTFLOTE: Ding Bat. Der Dingle. Ding-an-Sich.

HAPPY: I remember being impressed when I learned that the HIV virus, which has robbed us of our Ding, reads and writes its genetic alphabets backwards, RNA transcribing DNA transcribing RNA, hence *retro*virus, reverse transcription. I'm not gay but I am a Jew and so of course I, too, "read backwards, write backwards"; I think of Hebrew.

FLATTY: You're not gay?

HAPPY: No.

FLATTY: You're *not?*

HAPPY: No.

FLATTY: Everyone thinks you are. Everyone wants to sleep with you. Everyone. *Everyone.*

Oops.

You were saying?

HAPPY: I was saying that in my grief I thought . . . Well here I attempt a metaphor doomed to fail . . . I mean here we are, playwrights in a graveyard, here to dig, right? So, digging, I think: HIV, reverse transcribing, dust to dust, writing backwards, Hebrew and the Great and Terrible magic of that backwards alphabet, which runs against the grain, counter to the current of European tradition, heritage, thought: a language of fiery, consuming revelation, of refusal, the proper way, so I was taught, to address oneself to God . . . (*He puts his hands on* DING's *body.*) Perhaps, maybe, this backwards-writing viral nightmare is keeping some secret, subterraneanly affianced to a principle of . . . Reversals: good reversals and also very bad, where good meets bad, perhaps, the place of mystery where back meets forth, where our sorrow's not the point, where the forward flow of life brutally throws itself into reverse, to reveal . . . (*He lies alongside the body, curls up to it, head on* DING's *shoulder, listening.*) What? Hebrew always looked to me like zipper teeth unzipped. What awesome thing is it we're zipping open? To what do we return when we write in reverse? What's relinquished, what's released?

What does it sound like I'm doing here?

ASPERA: It sounds like you're equating Hebrew and AIDS.

HAPPY: I'm . . .

ASPERA: I'm not Jewish but I am a dyke and I think, either way, AIDS equals Hebrew or the reverse, you're in BIG trouble. I'm going to beat you up.

HAPPY: Not *equals,* I . . . I'm lonely. I'm among playwrights. Back East for the first time in months. So I get to talk. And none of you listen anyway. In Culver City everyone listens, they listen listen listen. They take notes. They take you at your word. You are playwrights. So be inattentive. If you paid attention you'd be novelists.

FLATTY: Aspera has spent five years in London. She's acquired the listening disease.

OTTOLINE: Soon, unless she watches herself, she will be an American playwright no longer but British, her plays will be all nuance, inference.

FLATTY: Yes, nuance, unless she's careful, or a socialist feminist.

BIFF: Everyone hates you Flatty.

OTTOLINE: Oops.

FLATTY: (*unphased, not missing a beat*) And then there will be no nuance at all.

ASPERA: *Does* everyone hate you?

FLATTY: No, they don't.

ASPERA: I live in London now, I'm out of the loop.

FLATTY: They don't hate me, they envy me my money.

ASPERA: (*To* HAPPY) I wouldn't *really* beat you up.

FLATTY: I could buy and sell the lot of you. Even *you* Happy and *you write sitcoms*. There. I've said it. I am wealthy. My plays have made me wealthy. I am richer than essayists, novelists, at least the respectable ones, and all poets ever. Envy is rather *like* hatred but as it's more debilitating to its votaries and votaresses (because it's so inherently undignified) it's of less danger ultimately to its targets.

BIFF: I don't envy your money. I envy your reviews.

HAUTFLOTE: I think we should dig now and bury Ding. This ground is patrolled. The night doesn't last forever. Ding's waiting.

OTTOLINE: (*Softly, firmly*) Ding's dead.

I love this place. It was worth two hundred and thirty-seven dollars and fifty cents to get here. Yes Flatty you can pay my way. Send me a check. Biff's got a point. It's the reviews, isn't it. I've worked tirelessly for decades. Three at least. What I have done no one has ever done and no one does it nearly so well. But what I do is break the vessels because they never fit me right and I despise their elegance and I like the sound the breaking makes, it's a new music. What I do is make mess apparent or make apparent messes, I cannot tell which myself. I signal disenfranchisement, dysfunction, disinheritance well I *am* a black woman what do they expect it's hard stuff but it's life but I am *perverse* I do not want my stories straight up the narrative the narrative the miserable fucking narrative the universe is post-Cartesian post-Einsteinian it's not at any rate what it's post-to-be let's throw some curve balls already who cares if they never cross the plate it's hard too hard for folks to apprehend easy so I get no big money reviews and no box office and I'm broke, I'm fifty or sixty or maybe I've turned eighty, I collected the box at the Cafe Cinno yes I am THAT old, and poor but no matter, I have a great talent for poverty. Oblivion, on the other hand, scares me. Death. And this may shock you but (*To* FLATTY) I ENVY you . . . your RENOWN. (*Roaring*) *I DON'T WANT ANOTHER OBIE! I want a hit!* **I want to hit a home run! I WANT A MAR-QUEE!** I'm too old to be ashamed of my hunger.

BIFF: O come to me short sweet. (*He blows a raspberry.*) There's just no dignity. I am oppressed by theater critics.

FLATTY: I gave up on dignity *years* ago. I am prolific. That's my revenge. If you want dignity you should marry a lighting designer.

OTTOLINE: Perhaps now we have worn out our terror, or at least winded it.

HAUTFLOTE: At darkest midnight December in the bleak midwinter athwart the crest of Abel's Hill on Martha's Vineyard six moderately inebriated playwrights stood shovels poised to inter . . .

FLATTY: Illegally.

HAUTFLOTE: . . . the earthly remains of a seventh.

HAPPY: Who might at least have agreed to the convenience of a cremation.

HAUTFLOTE: Being a creature of paper as well as of the fleeting moment Ding naturally had a horror of fire. *I knew him best.* For a long time now. I loved him.

OTTOLINE: We all did.

HAUTFLOTE: Yet not one of us dares break ground.

HAPPY: Wind perhaps, but never ground.

ASPERA: Wind for sure but not the Law. But is it the law or what's underground which immobilizes us? Incarceration or an excess of freedom? Enchainment or liberation? For who knows what dreams may come? Who knows what's underneath? Who knows if anything is, if the shovel will strike stone, or pay dirt, or nothing whatsoever?

BIFF: It's the Nothing stopping me. I can speak only for myself.

FLATTY: Bad thing in a playwright.

BIFF: The horseleech hath two daughters. There's a play in there, somewhere, of course. I used to say: it won't come out. Fecal or something, expulsive metaphor. I was stuffed, full and withholding. In more generous times. Before the fear . . . of the Deficit, before the Balanced Budget became the final face of the Angel of the Apocalypse. Now instead I say: I'm not going to go there. A geographical metaphor. Why? *I'm nearly forty* is one explanation. *"There"* meaning . . . That bleachy bone land. Into that pit. That plot. To meet that deadline.

OTTOLINE: The play is due?

BIFF: Day after yesterday.

HAPPY: Rehearsals starting . . . ?

BIFF: Start*ed*.

ASPERA: What, without a script?

BIFF: They're *improvising*.

(*Everyone shudders.*)

FLATTY: You shouldn't be here! You should be home writing!

BIFF: Did I mention how much I hate you, Flatty.

FLATTY: Marry a lighting designer. It worked for me. Sobered me right up.

HAPPY: I never meant . . . This reverse transcription thing. I'll work on it.

ASPERA: You do that.

HAPPY: I never meant to equate Hebrew and . . . It's just the words: reverse transcription. *Thinking* about it. Something I can't help doing. Writing began with the effort to record speech. All writing is an attempt to fix intangibles—thought, speech, what the eye observes—fixed on clay tablets, in stone, on paper. Writers *capture*. We playwrights on the other hand write or rather "wright" to set these free again. Not inscribing, not *de*-scribing but . . . *ex*-scribing (?) . . . "W-R-I-G-H-T," that archaism, because it's something earlier we do, cruder, something one does with one's mitts, one's paws. To claw words up . . . !

(HAPPY *falls to his knees beside* DING *and starts to dig with his hands.*)

HAPPY: To startle words back into the air again, to . . . evanesce. It is . . . unwriting, to do it is to die, yes, but. A lively form of doom.

ASPERA: Ah, so now you are equating . . .

HAPPY: It's not about *equation*. It's about the transmutation of horror into meaning.

ASPERA: Doomed to fail.

HAPPY: Dirty work . . . (*He shows his hands.*)

ASPERA: A mongrel business. This Un-earthing.

HAUTFLOTE: For which we Un-earthly are singularly fit. Now or never.

BIFF: I'm nearly forty. My back hurts.

FLATTY: Whose doesn't? No dignity but in our labors.

(*They hoist their shovels.*)

ASPERA: Goodnight old Ding. Rest easy baby. And flights of self-dramatizing hypochondriacal hypersensitive self-pitying paroxysmical angels saddlebag you off to sleep.

BIFF: (*apostrophizing* DING's *corpse.*) Oh Dog Weary.

HAUTFLOTE: Many of these graves are cenotaphs, you know, empty tombs, honorifics. Sailors lost on whalers, lost at sea, no body ever found, air and memory interred instead. All other headstones in the graveyard peristalithic to these few empty tombs, whose ghostly drama utterly overwhelms The Real.

(HAUTFLOTE *waves his hand in the air, a downbeat. Ella sings "When They Begin The Beguine."*)

OTTOLINE: Dig. Shovel tips to earth.

(*They are.*)

OTTOLINE: The smell of earth will rise to meet us. Our nostrils fill with dark brown, roots ends, decomposing warmth and manufactory, earthworm action. The loam.

FLATTY: I don't want to go to jail. Doesn't David Mamet live around here somewhere?

OTTOLINE: Push in.

(*They do.*)

THE END

A BOWL OF SOUP

Eric Lane

A BOWL OF SOUP was originally performed as part of *The Gary & Rob Show,* a longer play consisting of ten ten-minute pieces. It was presented by Orange Thoughts Theater & Film at the LaMama LaGalleria New Voices/New Plays Series (Lawry Smith, Curator) in New York City, October 1994. Martha Banta directed the following cast:

EDDIE   Frank Deal
ROB   Mark Bateman

The Gary & Rob Show was developed with the additional help of Thomas Keith, James Georgiades, Oliver Wadsworth, and New York Theatre Workshop.

CHARACTERS

ROB: mid-twenties to thirties. Sweet, gentle, physically and emotionally exhausted.
EDDIE: Rob's older brother. In the tile business.

SETTING: Rob's studio apartment with a makeshift kitchenette.

NOTE

While Rob doesn't speak until the end of the piece, his presence is equally important as that of Eddie. He hears what Eddie is saying although he doesn't overtly respond.

(EDDIE *opens a can of soup with a can opener.* ROB *sits, stares.*)

EDDIE: I got you the chicken. The onion I can't eat. I eat the onion I'm tasting it for days. Ma's the same way. You like that? . . . I didn't know if you was like that so I got the chicken. The chicken's good. What? Something's wrong with the chicken. Nothing's wrong with it, it's good. Improved. New and improved. You'll like it. I promise. You'll try it, you'll see. Just wait. Improved.

(*He puts the open can in a pot of water without emptying soup. Puts pot on hotplate, which he turns on. Soup heats in can without dirtying pot. Stirs occasionally.*)

You know, you shouldn't just buzz somebody in, you know. You should ask. I know you knew it was me but what if it wasn't. What if it was somebody else. Like somebody not your brother but I don't know—deranged-like. You know, mental. You don't know. There are a lot of crazy people out there. You gotta be careful. Not that I'm telling you what to do. You do what you want. That's up to you. Just be careful, you know. Safe.

You O.K., Robbie? . . . You O.K.? . . . Of course you're O.K. What'm I even asking. Forget I even said, just forget it, O.K. O.K.

'Cause that's the way it is now, the world. We're talking about the world here—outside. It's—what—it's scary, that's

what. Terrifying. You think—you think a lot of stuff but you
know what I'm saying. It's like walking a highwire act—like
you need your net just in case. God forbid,

(*Knocks wood*)

anything should, you know, happen you want your net in
place. That's all I'm saying. You want your net.

(*Stirs*)

You remember that mayonnaise jar we buried in the backyard behind the fireplace. You remember that. What? That's
over what? Twenty years ago. I was trying to remember what
we put in there. Like a time capsule. That's what we called
it. Stuck some stuff in there from around the house so
that when they dug it up sometime—like some time in
the future there'd be this stuff to remember us. That was
what? Like twenty, maybe more years ago. Behind the
fireplace—not, you know, bar-be-que. (*Realizes it wasn't
behind the fireplace, but behind the bar-be-que.*) That's it, behind
the bar-be-que. You remember that? . . . Anyway, Ma
says the other night some dog was digging back there and
I thought of it. Some stray probably roaming the neighborhood digging and I was wondering maybe he knew—
like all these years something inside there, in that jar he
wanted to get at. You think? I mean, after all these years
could he be remem—I mean, like smelling that jar. Something inside he wants to get at. Maybe, I don't know. You
think? . . . And like what? What'd we put in there. To
remember us, I try to remember but—Some pennies maybe.
And a note. Some kinda note like a letter but—You remember. I don't know. Something. Like . . . What? Maybe
some change and a letter and who remembers, I don't.
You remember that? Some marbles maybe. String. I don't
know. Just forget about it. Forget I even brought it up.
O.K. We'll just act like I never even said it. You know. Just
forget it . . .

You cook much? . . . How you gonna cook much, you don't even got a kitchen. A kitchenette. That's what it is. A little kitchenette. So what's wrong with a kitchenette. What you need anything bigger. You cook your soup. You toast your bread. You got a meal. There. There's a meal. And you didn't even dirty a pot. No dishes to wash. Just a spoon. And that's if you don't use plastic. You use plastic, you don't even got a spoon. It's done. You cook. You eat. You're done. Not a trace. Not a friggin' clue you was even here. You know. You could write a mystery. A detective story. If you could write, you could write a story. "The Case of the Disappearing Soup." You could sell that. You think people don't sell stories. I could sell it. Forget you, I'll sell it myself. Move to L.A. Give up the tile business and set myself up round some pool. I'll dictate, that's it. Won't even touch the pad, just dictate to some secretary in a two piece, her name's Gloria. Gloria Towers. Takes shorthand. She'll write it out. All you gotta have's an idea. A story to tell. You know some story, Robbie? . . .

You O.K. on money? 'Cause you need money, I got. Not that it means anything to me. I mean, like it's only money. But you need, I got so all you gotta do's say and it's here. Don't even say, it's here.

(*Takes out money, slips it in* ROB's *hand.*)

Here. You take it. What do I need. You take yourself out for dinner. Someplace nice, on me. Someplace you wouldn't usually go. Like special. You know.

(*Slips him another bill.*)

And take yourself a cab home. You don't wanna be taking the train late at night. I heard about the train. I watch the news. You take a cab, 'cause I say so, O.K.

(*Money drops from* ROB's *hand. Eddie picks it up. Lays it out on counter, flattening it out.*)

I'm putting it here. I'm putting it down here. It's for you. You put it away. But it's for you, O.K.? O.K. . . . How's the soup?

(*He checks.*)

Almost there.

You hear that dog? Digging. In the backyard. That was looking for that jar. It was the night you slept over. At Ma and Dad's. You hear it? . . . What're you gonna hear? It's just a dog. Just digging. Forget I even said it. Just forget it.

(*Zips his lips shut. Throws away key.*)

Gone. Look.

(*Tries to talk, can't. His lips are sealed.*)

My seals are lips. Get it. Ah, you got it. Smart kid like you, of course you got it. How're you not gonna get it.

(*Checks soup.*)

All I'm saying is, you want to go to Orlando, you go. You see where he's buried, you go. I'm offering you the money. I just got a raise two weeks ago. A lot. I won't say how much but a lot of money. It means nothing to me. You want it, it's yours. Don't even think about it, O.K. If that's the question—the problem. It's not a problem so O.K.—it's up to you.

Look, I understand they're in pain. His parents. Their son dies of AIDS. They haven't spoken to him for two years. Two years they haven't spoken and now he's gone. They grab. At whatever they can.

His body. What's his body. Like some empty jar, you know. Like that mayonnaise—

(*He stops himself.*)

I just—

(*A beat*)

I understand they're in pain and just wish they could see somebody else might be, too. You know. That's all.

You love him? David. I think so. I think you're lucky, you know. You probably don't want to hear this so I'll shut up, but you really loved him. And like, what? I never had that. Like who's gonna love me, right? Like . . . You know, you had that with him, like with David and half of that was you. You was like half and you'll find that again. Maybe not right away. Maybe like what, in time, you know. Some period of time. But like if you could have that with him then maybe with, not maybe. But like with somebody else. You know. That's all I'm saying. That's all.

ROB: It wasn't a dog. It was me.

EDDIE: What?

ROB: In the backyard. I kept thinking he was in that jar. David. I kept seeing him. I mean, I knew he wasn't. Part of me. Knew. But I just had to see.

(ROB *starts to cry.* EDDIE *holds him. He starts to weep.* EDDIE *rocks him.* ROB *stops crying.*)

EDDIE: You want some soup?

ROB: Put it in a bowl. I want to know we were here.

(*A moment. Lights fade.*)

RAILING IT UPTOWN

A SHORT PLAY

Shirley Lauro

RAILING IT UPTOWN was originally produced by Primary Stages in THE NEW YORK PROJECT, October 1995. Andrew Leynse directed the following cast:

THE WOMAN IN BLACK   Marilyn Rockafellow
THE WOMAN IN WHITE   Nicole Quinn

CHARACTERS

THE WOMAN IN BLACK: White. Middle-aged. WASP. Something aristocratic about her, an educated woman, although she is slightly unkempt, something ajar. Faded black taffeta, frayed dressy raincoat with ruffle around collar and down the front. Gray straggly hair. Hat with feather or flower. Torn suede pumps. Carries some kind of small dress bag. A slight limp.

THE WOMAN IN WHITE: Black. Thirty-fiveish. Well-dressed. Attractive. New York sophisticated woman. Extremely kempt. Hair, nails perfect. White designer trenchcoat. White Dior-type scarf with print around her neck.

The women bear a strange resemblance to each other in some way.

(*Playwright's Note:* I've designated one black and one white actress for the two roles. However, I feel the play would work equally well with other racial combinations: two white actresses, two black actresses, two Asian actresses, one white, one Asian, etc. etc.)

(In black. Lights up. Glaring, harsh fluorescent. Black velours. Center stage, raked a little left, a two-seat subway unit with window on one side and pole flanking outside seat. A subway double-door unit, open, stage right. A single-door unit to next car, closed, stage left. WOMAN IN BLACK discovered in outside seat. WOMAN IN WHITE enters through double-door unit. She carries several Macy's shopping bags. She sees empty seat, slides past WOMAN IN BLACK and sits in inside seat, putting bags at her feet. Double doors shut. Sound (slightly abstracted, surreal) of subway starting, roaring down track.

(A pause)

WOMAN IN BLACK: I get off at 42nd St.

(WOMAN IN WHITE startled, looks at WOMAN IN BLACK.)

You jumped! Like I was assaulting you!

WOMAN IN WHITE: No!

(She laughs a little.)

WOMAN IN BLACK: Yes you did!

WOMAN IN WHITE: Well—I—

WOMAN IN BLACK: I was just giving you this information

WOMAN IN WHITE: Yes?

WOMAN IN BLACK: You might not want to sit there

WOMAN IN WHITE: Why not?

WOMAN IN BLACK: You have all those shopping bags and I am getting off next stop.

WOMAN IN WHITE: I don't understand

WOMAN IN BLACK: I meant so you won't have to stand up for me

WOMAN IN WHITE: But I'm on the inside

WOMAN IN BLACK: Of what?

WOMAN IN WHITE: I don't have to stand up for you is what I mean.

WOMAN IN BLACK: Unless you decide to

WOMAN IN WHITE: But whyever would I do that?

(WHITE *looks at* BLACK *then away. Another pause*)

WOMAN IN BLACK: This was not an assault of any kind!

WOMAN IN WHITE: I don't think I implied it was.

WOMAN IN BLACK: Interesting comment on the times though, isn't it?

WOMAN IN WHITE: What?

WOMAN IN BLACK: Trying to be nice, considerate, thoughtful and it's taken as an assault?

WOMAN IN WHITE: Look, I really and truly am sorry if I offended you. You just took me a little by surprise is all. And I startled. That's all it was.

WOMAN IN BLACK: I was speaking for your own good.

WOMAN IN WHITE: Of course.

(*Another pause*)

WOMAN IN BLACK: Got a lot of bargains in those bags?

WOMAN IN WHITE: (*Chuckling*) Matter of fact I do . . .

WOMAN IN BLACK: (*As if a circus barker*) "Bankrupt Bargains from Macy's of Herald Square"

WOMAN IN WHITE: (*Smiling only slightly*) Uh . . . right . . . right . . .

WOMAN IN BLACK: Towels? . . . Lap robe? . . . Warm . . . woolly . . . underwear?

WOMAN IN WHITE: (*Hesitantly, subtly shoving bags a little away from* WOMAN IN BLACK*'s feet*) Well . . . towels—

WOMAN IN BLACK: White? . . . Thick? . . . Soft? . . . CLEAN?

WOMAN IN WHITE: Yes, of course clean—they're new . . .

(*Another pause, a little more awkward than the ones before.* WHITE *pushes bags farther away.*)

WOMAN IN BLACK: And what kind of time do you have?

(WOMAN IN WHITE *frowns a little then looks at wristwatch.*)

12:52 . . .

WOMAN IN BLACK: Seiko?

WOMAN IN WHITE: (*sliding sleeve over watch*)

Yes . . .

WOMAN IN BLACK: Perfect isn't it?

WOMAN IN WHITE: (*Putting hand with watch into her pocket*) My watch?

WOMAN IN BLACK: The time. For a one o'clock luncheon I mean. I *always* have a one o'clock luncheon. When I can.

(*The train now screeches to a stop.*)

Oh! We're here!

(WOMAN IN BLACK *now jumps up, announcing like conductor*)

"FORTY-SECOND STREET!"

(*Turns to* WHITE)

    You out to lunch too?

(*She starts into aisle. She has a slight limp.*)

    Come on!

(*She does a little tap shuffle, singing.*)

    "Let's beat our feet
    On 42nd Street!"

(*She turns to* WHITE)

    Well, aren't you coming?

WOMAN IN WHITE: No. I'm not out to lunch . . .

WOMAN IN BLACK: No?

WOMAN IN WHITE: No

WOMAN IN BLACK: Then why should I be?

(*And she sits back down.*)

WOMAN IN WHITE: I rarely ride the subway at all, actually. But I couldn't get a cab. And I'm very late!

WOMAN IN BLACK: (*Singing*) "For a very important date?"

WOMAN IN WHITE: No. Just late.

WOMAN IN BLACK: Terrible neighborhood besides! Right?

(*Sound of train starting again. A pause.* WOMAN IN BLACK *looks around.*)

    Nobody else seems worried about it though. They all got off. Now we're in here solo! Express!

(*Slowly, uneasily,* WOMAN IN WHITE *starts looking around.*)

WOMAN IN WHITE: I—I see—

(*A pause*)

WOMAN IN BLACK: So where *do* you get off?

WOMAN IN WHITE: Uh—next stop—

WOMAN IN BLACK: 59th? Then I will too. Know a good cafe up there?

WOMAN IN WHITE: No! . . . Uh, no . . . I don't . . .

WOMAN IN BLACK: Nothing? You never eat out up there?

WOMAN IN WHITE: Look, do you mind? I have a headache.

(*She turns away, resting head in hand.*)

WOMAN IN BLACK: You're going to eat home then? Your apartment? With your husband? You have a husband don't you? You look like you do.

WOMAN IN WHITE: Listen, I don't care to have a conversation just now, all right? As I said, I have this headache.

(*She shifts farther away; looks out window.*)

WOMAN IN BLACK: Like I was assaulting you again!

WOMAN IN WHITE: (*She gets idea: Takes book from purse, opens, starts to read.*) I . . . I just want to read my book.

(*A pause*)

WOMAN IN BLACK: You live on 59th street?

WOMAN IN WHITE: Will you *let me alone?*

WOMAN IN BLACK: Okay. Okay. I just asked a question. What's wrong with you anyway?

WOMAN IN WHITE: NOTHING is wrong with me! Except I have a headache. And I want to read my book.

WOMAN IN BLACK: And you don't want to talk to me!

WOMAN IN WHITE: That's right! I don't!

WOMAN IN BLACK: Because I'm a stranger?

WOMAN IN WHITE: No—

WOMAN IN BLACK: You're afraid to tell me where you live.

WOMAN IN WHITE: I told you where I live.

WOMAN IN BLACK: You told me your subway stop. The rest is confidential, right? Your address, your husband? Your kids? You have some don't you? Teenagers—thirteen, fourteen would be their age? I imagine you with kids and a husband—everybody together at home with you—

WOMAN IN WHITE: Will you *stop* this?

WOMAN IN BLACK: Because I don't seem right in the head.

WOMAN IN WHITE: I didn't say that!

WOMAN IN BLACK: It's what you were thinking though. I'll give you an example:

WOMAN IN WHITE: That's it: let me out!

(WOMAN IN WHITE *suddenly stands up.*)

Just LET ME OUT OF HERE!

(*She tries to shove past* BLACK *but* BLACK *now jumps up too, blocking* WHITE.)

WOMAN IN BLACK: *I* stood up recently. On the "*C*" train. And suddenly I just started

(*Screaming*)

SCREAMING!

WOMAN IN WHITE: (*Blanching*) Oh no! Here we go—

(WOMAN IN BLACK *steps into aisle.*)

WOMAN IN BLACK: And the woman next to me said: "You're crazy! YOU ARE CRAZY IN YOUR HEAD!" And I said, "The truth of the matter is:

(*She addresses* WOMAN IN WHITE, *confidentially.*)

I am hemorrhaging inside. There is blood running down my legs! GET ME TO A HOSPITAL LADY! GET ME TO A DOCTOR!

(*Takes a step into aisle, then like waitress placing order*)

"AND ONE CUP HOT SOUP BREAD BUTTER WHISKEY DOWN!

(WOMAN IN WHITE *now bolts past her, into aisle backing away,* WOMAN IN BLACK *in pursuit.*)

I AM HEMORRHAGING INSIDE!"

(WOMAN IN WHITE *backs up against double doors of subway,* BLACK *pinning her there, hands on each side of door, growing confidential again.*)

"You're crazy!" The woman on the "C" train said to me as all the blood ran down my legs!

WOMAN IN WHITE: (*Whispering*) You *are* crazy!

WOMAN IN BLACK: (*Whispering too*) "Help!" said the woman next to me.

WOMAN IN WHITE: (*Whispering, looking around out of corners of her eyes*) Help—help—!

(*She tries to duck out but* WOMAN IN BLACK *blocks her. She tries to duck other way,* WOMAN IN BLACK *blocks her.*)

WOMAN IN BLACK: "Stop trying to run out!" I said. "Can't you *see* I am hemorrhaging inside? Can't you see *I* need help?" That's what I said to her.

WOMAN IN WHITE: HELP!! HELP!!

(WHITE *now turns and tries desperately to open the double-doors.*)

WOMAN IN BLACK: (*Very calm, whispering in* WHITE'*s ear*) "Stop
that!" I said. "Those doors could fly open and you'd be
killed!"

(WOMAN IN WHITE *now suddenly turns, shoves* BLACK, *knocking her
backwards, running to exit door to next car, trying to open it.* BLACK
stumbles, gets up, runs to WHITE, *grabs her, pinning her against door by
her shoulders, stopping her exit.*)

WOMAN IN BLACK: A woman died last week!

WOMAN IN WHITE: (*She slumps, defeated, against door, sobbing.*) Oh,
God . . . oh God . . .

WOMAN IN BLACK: Not to worry! It's *not* the woman I was telling
you about!

(*She grows compassionate, relaxing her grip.*)

Don't cry. A million differences between women besides.
See, she got the door open and ran out. But that train had
stopped. A local. Not like now. Besides that was days ago.
And I really *was* hemorrhaging that day. Pouring blood at
that time. But I didn't mean her any harm . . . she was just
scared I guess . . .

(*A pause*)

You scared?

(*Another pause.* WOMAN IN WHITE *nods very slightly.* BLACK *comforting:*)

Don't be. We're "A" not "C." I keep telling you that. Why
exaggerate, hallucinate, prevaricate, or hang gloom in *here?*
There is nothing in the world to be afraid of. We are "A"
for effort Express!

(*She smiles, warmly, takes a step away from* WHITE *then turns back,
smiles, goes toward seat, indicating it.*)

Look, why don't you just sit down?

(WHITE *looks at her, then at seat.*)

Biting, spitting, defecating in public places, smelling to high heaven—I don't do that. Or spreading rotten stuff like TB. Or AIDS. Or being nigger. Or anything antisocial in behavior like that. I'm not going to hurt you.

(*She smiles at* WHITE.)

Can't you see I'm harmless? Just a person—

(*She smiles more broadly.* WHITE *is studying her*)

Another woman . . . railing it . . . uptown . . .

(*She now turns profile view, in posture reminiscent of* WHITE, *and poses for* WHITE *to appraise her. In spite of herself* WHITE *starts smiling.* BLACK *turns to her.*)

Look, all I wanted was the name of a small cafe for lunch, right?

(WHITE *nods.*)

And then I wanted the time of day? And to warn you I'd be getting off so you wouldn't have to move those bags?

(WHITE *nods.*)

Not one bad thing has happened, now has it?

(WHITE *shrugs, then shakes head.*)

Didn't harm you, molest you, steal from you, assault you in any way. Only touched you once: to stop you from getting hurt! True or false?

WOMAN IN WHITE: (*Hesitantly, very softly*) True—I guess—

WOMAN IN BLACK: Of course true! So? Why stand there swaying in the breeze?

WOMAN IN WHITE: I—I don't know exactly—

WOMAN IN BLACK: You don't have to stand up for me! I've been telling you that for miles.

WOMAN IN WHITE: It is pretty silly, huh?

WOMAN IN BLACK: You said you had a headache.

(*Indicating seat.*)

Why not sit down and close your eyes and enjoy the ride? I'll let you know.

(WOMAN IN WHITE *hesitates a moment.*)

WOMAN IN WHITE: I—I guess I will— (*She now slides back into inside seat.*) Thank you.

(WOMAN IN BLACK *settles into her seat.*)

WOMAN IN BLACK: Don't mention it. But, if the name of any small cafe happens to pop into your head somewhere between here or there or uptown a ways, mention that?

WOMAN IN WHITE: Of course—

WOMAN IN BLACK: (*Fantasizing it*) Bistro type—brick walls, red checked tablecloth, fireplace burning bright—

WOMAN IN WHITE: (*Imagining it*) Sounds dreamy . . .

WOMAN IN BLACK: It is—

(*Sound [slightly surreal] of subway screeching to momentary halt. Lights on train blinking off then on immediately. Sound of train lurching on.*)

WOMAN IN BLACK: Oh dear.

WOMAN IN WHITE: (*Turns to* BLACK) What's wrong?

WOMAN IN BLACK: I am beginning to bleed somewhere. Something just ruptured.

WOMAN IN WHITE: (*Not comprehending*) What?

(WOMAN IN BLACK *throws one arm out across the front of* WOMAN IN WHITE *to grab the window ledge. This traps* WOMAN IN WHITE *in her seat. With other arm* WOMAN IN BLACK *grabs pole bracing herself.*)

WOMAN IN BLACK: I'll let you know when blood is about to spurt and make puddles on the floor.

WOMAN IN WHITE: What are you saying?

WOMAN IN BLACK: So you can move your bags. All right?

(WOMAN IN BLACK *looks straight ahead.* WOMAN IN WHITE *looks at her terrified.*)

WOMAN IN WHITE: Oh God! Let this be a dream!

WOMAN IN BLACK: INSIDE HEMORRHAGE IS ON THE WAY!

(*The train races on.*)

BLACKOUT

END

STARS

A TEN-MINUTE PLAY

Romulus Linney

CHARACTERS

HE
SHE

PLACE: Manhattan.

TIME: The present.

A penthouse terrace. A summer night. Stars.

(HE *and* SHE, *drinking wine.*)

SHE: Stars.

HE: Great penthouse.

SHE: Like the party?

HE: Very much.

SHE: Like me?

HE: Very much.

(*Pause.*)

SHE: When people. (*Pause.*) What I mean is. (*Pause.*) Do you think suicide is more anger or sorrow?

HE: I have heard both.

SHE: I met a man named Norwood in Southampton at a club called The Dunes. It went out of business but that was the afternoon it opened, and my husband and I came from a rental on Shelter Island to a party in the bar and he left me there.

HE: What for?

SHE: My husband is very effective.

HE: I know that. You know I know that.

SHE: Drink, kiss. "Enjoy yourself." Off talking to a client.

HE: He's very effective.

SHE: So there I was. Five o'clock Saturday afternoon, Hamptons, smiling and bored. Norwood Struther wore a blue linen blazer, a red and yellow tie, silly and snappy. He didn't say a word. Men liked him, slapped him on the back, called him Squeaky, kidded him about being a bachelor, fondly, but with some kind of something else about it, I couldn't tell what. Well, I was so sick and frustrated with my husband, mad at the world and my utterly asinine position that summer in the Hamptons, hello, there, Norwood, you squeaky bachelor, how are you, say something, and he did. He did have this stutter and high weird voice. I was desperate. "Bartender, tell my husband I've gone to the movies." I was in Squeaky's bedroom in half an hour. He lived right on the beach, million dollar real estate Bridgehampton. Bedroom whole side wall open to the sea. God. God, you could hear the surf roaring and pounding. Wonderful. Kissing, hugging. He undressed me. Grand. But it took him a while to undress himself. It took me a while to notice it, then to see that he was choking, face red as a lobster, mortified, in that ravishing home, in our beautiful bed by the sounding sea. He had a very small sexual organ. Tiny.

HE: Oh.

SHE: He tried to apologize. I kissed him and said stop, it didn't matter.

HE: Did it?

SHE: Of course. He wouldn't talk to me afterwards. Mumbled something about reality I couldn't understand, stuck his head under a pillow, like a little boy. I had betrayed my husband—again—this time with a poor wretch lying next to me in abject misery. Outside on the beach, we could hear the surf pounding. The sea, powerful and potent, alive with cruelty and beauty. There was even moonlight, gorgeous, ravishing, and me and Norwood in that bed.

HE: By the sounding sea.

SHE: And my husband, who hoped I liked the movie.

HE: What does this have to do with suicide?

SHE: Look at the moon.

HE: All right.

(*Pause.*)

I'm in a bar on Columbus Avenue. I meet a woman who says she's a schoolteacher. We have fun, a really good time. She takes me home. It's good. I leave about eleven, she's looking at me like I'm an angel from heaven. Four o'clock in the morning, my telephone rings. It's her, sounding terrible. Help! Right now! So I go back to her apartment and she is looking at me like I'm a demon from hell. "What's the matter?" "Did you call me on the phone?" "When?" "Right after you went home." "No." "You swear?" "I swear." "Oh, my God, my God!" "What happened?" "What a fool I am! What a *fool* I am!" *"What happened?"* "Well," she said, "about eleven o'clock a man whose voice sounded I thought just like yours called me. You, I thought it was you, said you had a way of making us both some money right now but you needed two hundred dollars first, and didn't have any cash, did I? Yes. Would I lend it to you. Oh, I had such a good time with you, I liked you so much, so I said yes, I have that, come get it. You said, no, you wanted me to meet a man and give it to him, with whatever else he asked for. 'What?' I said. You told me to go to a children's playground off Central Park West at midnight, and just sit in a swing and wait. You hoped I would do this for you. I was speechless, and God help me, I was excited. I got the money and went. There were shadows of people at the playground,

coming and going in darkness, there for sex. I was frightened
and disgusted with myself and terribly, terribly alive. He was
wearing a cowboy hat. When he came up to me and when I
saw it wasn't you, I was horrified and thrilled. I gave him
two hundred dollars and he pulled on his belt and I knelt
down and gave him sex. He thanked me and was gone, leaving me there on my knees. I felt—well—debased but delivered. Then I thought, was that really like you? What if it
wasn't you who called me? Was it? Oh, tell me the truth! We
did meet in a bar but you were decent, weren't you? You
wouldn't do that to me, would you? But who else could
have? Nobody knew about us. It has to be you!" "No it
doesn't," I said. "It could be somebody in the bar." "Oh," she
said. "But I don't go there often. I don't!" "Sometimes?"
"Well, yes." She thought a minute. "That man, with the
cowboy hat, he could have heard us, heard I was taking you
home." "Right." "But that means it was somebody who
knows me, my phone number, and everything." "That's the
only other possibility." "Oh, God," she said. "I don't know
what to believe. Was it some man who's been watching me
in that bar? Or was it you? Who did that to me?"

SHE: Do you expect me to believe this?

HE: It's true.

SHE: *Was* it you? You sent some man to do that to her for two
hundred dollars? Which he kicked back to you?

HE: No.

SHE: Then who was it?

HE: I never knew. If she does, I never did.

SHE: It was you.

HE: Probably. But it wasn't.

SHE: I believe it was.

(*Pause.*)

HE: Did you keep up with Norwood?

SHE: I read about him, in a Long Island newspaper, two years later. In that beach house, with majestic surf and the ravishing moonlight, with two big pistols, one at each side of his head, both at once. Paper said there was nothing left of his head but the top of his neck.

HE: Point of the conversation.

SHE: Yes.

HE: Two years later?

SHE: About.

HE: It was the day after.

SHE: A week.

HE: A day.

SHE: A day.

HE: I steal her money. You laugh at him. Point of the conversation?

SHE: Did she die?

HE: Oh, no.

SHE: You saw her again?

HE: We married.

SHE: Still?

HE: Still.

SHE: You told me that awful story about your wife?

HE: She's in there now.

SHE: You're not going home with me?

HE: Not tonight.

SHE: Do you like your wife?

HE: Very much.

SHE: Then why are you here?

HE: Why are you?

SHE: I wish I knew.

HE: The moon.

SHE: Those stars. I'm shaking.

HE: I don't feel very good either.

SHE: I'm really upset.

HE: So am I.

(*Pause.*)

SHE: 555-5492.

HE: 555-5492.

SHE: Mornings.

HE: OK.

SHE: OK.

HE: Stars.

SHE: Bright.

HE: Hard.

SHE: Cold.

HE: Still.

SHE: They never change.

HE: They never will.

(HE *holds out his hand to her.* SHE *takes it, presses it, gets up and leaves.*
HE *looks at the stars and shivers.*)

A SERMON

David Mamet

A SERMON was written as a companion piece for a 1979 Chicago revival of *Sexual Perversity in Chicago.* It featured Cosmo White and, later, W. H. Macy, directed by Sheldon Patinkin.

CHARACTER: *Clergyman*

In September 1939, a dentist in Viceroy, Louisiana, placed a human tooth into a jar of Coca-Cola and let it stand overnight. The next morning Hitler invaded Poland. A man has a deaf yak. The yak cannot hear. It grew up deaf. And this man speaks to it: "How are you today, King?" "Bow wow," says the yak one day. Bow wow. And the next day the yak goes "moo." (*Pause.*) The animal has no *idea* of its responsibilities. It knows that something is required of it; it knows that it should make a *sound,* but it has no idea what that sound is supposed to be. Life is like that. I feel. If it were not one thing, it would surely be another. It is, however, one thing. Though it is by no means the *same* thing. Although it's always something of that nature.

And kindness starts at home. You cannot beat your pets and come quick on your wife and pretend you forgot to take the garbage out and go be nice to whales. It's not *right,* it's transparent, and it makes you *look* bad, too.

Our most cherished illusions—what are they but hastily constructed cofferdams restraining homosexual panic.

Let's talk about love. (*Pause.*) Love. My golly, it sells diapers, don't it!

Love is the mucilage that sticks the tattered ribbons of experience—the stiff construction-paper Indians and pumpkins of experience—to the scrapbook of our lives.

And there may be many *kinds* of love:

Love may be the Rocky Coast of Maine, with boats and salt spray gooshing up and you all cozy in the rented cabin.

All the others have gone down. Gone down to Boston, gone back to New York. His hands are pressing into the small of your back. His breath is hot upon your shoulder. You have come to write and he has forced the lock. You've never *seen* this man, he followed you home from the pier. But do you care? You care very much. You whack him with the cover of your typewriter. Whack, whack, whack. Whack, whack, whack. Whack, whack, whack. You hit him on the head. And he gets off, he pulls his trousers up and leaves. (*Pause.*) You go back to work. You're typing. "September 18th. Today dawned bleak and sere and I was up to see it. Surely there must be an end to time . . ."

You look down to read back your sentence to yourself. What do you see but weak and colorless impressions. Your ribbon has run out. Oh well, that's a fair excuse to go up to the Lodge to share a cup of coffee with the Kind Old Woman who runs the resort.

You open the door. You breathe in the cold, life-giving spray. The Old Man from the Pier hits you on the head with an oar and he jumps on your bones. And this time he has brought his friends.

And what of Death? (*Pause.*) What *of* it? That's my question. All of us are going to die, but nobody believes it. And if we did believe it we would not go to the office. We would call in sick.

Everybody's talking about "Death." Nobody's been there. Yes, yes, yes, there is a rash of testimony to the effect that Ms. So-and-So or Mr. Whossis once was dead for thirty seconds, or something, and it was just like going through a car wash.

You lay back and it is warm and wet outside. But you feel nothing. Whiirrrr, whiirrrr, and here comes the soap. And everything clouds over. Then you hear a hum. And that must be the brushes. Everything goes white, then black, then white again. You feel a buffeting. There is a wall of water/It cascades over the windshield, wetting all, and driving off the sludge, the salt, the road dirt, and the soap. Until you're clean. You're clean.

Then comes the hot wax. Analogous in the experience of death to—what? (*Pause.*) *Exactly.* Hot wax coursing for a mere half-dollar more with ten bucks worth of gas. (Well worth it) making your car shine. Shine on. Shine on, my car. (*Pause.*)

Five youths dressed in coveralls drop upon you like ministering angels, rub your imperfections out and then move on. You'd better *tip* them, though, cause you'll be back this way again! There you go. Out into traffic. And how *proud* you feel. And why not? (*Pause.*) This is death. You've been there *before,* you say . . . well, you're going there again.

And sickness. Is it real?

And suffering? (*Pause.*) Are they real? (*Pause.*)

Yesterday a man was going to the supermarket. There he went. Upon some errand. His head full of news or gossip. *Fiscal* problems . . . (They are never really far away . . .) He turned the corner and he trod upon the mat which would open the door, and he walked on. The door, however, some of you have already guessed, did not open. Not a jot. (*Pause.*) He slammed right into it and broke his nose.

His blood flowed. As many times may happen, attendant upon a sharper blow to that area—particularly such a blow to one un-used to violent contact—he began to cry. (*Pause.*)

Many who had seen his accident were laughing at the picture that it made. And then we heard him cry. And then he turned, and then we saw the blood. (*Pause.*)

"I've broke my nose," he rather oinked. "I've broke my nose, and you think it's funny." (*Pause.*) He could not think of what to say; a phrase which might instill in us, the spectators who deigned to ridicule his pain, shame or remorse. His mind searched for a curse. (*Pause.*) "Fuck you," he said. (*Pause.*) Fuck you.

What is required of us? To whom do we owe allegiance, and is this a laughing matter, or should we just mope around as if the dog died?

This is a good question, and in conclusion, let me say the following:

A traveler is in the desert. He has lost his way. He has no water. And he is near death. Far off he sees a mountain. In the distance. Far away. Ice encapsulates its top and flows in freshets down its sides, and becomes springs and rivers. Cool, fresh water, redolent of trout. Clean, unpolluted, there for all to drink, to bathe in, to enjoy. And he knows it is a mirage. (*Pause.*) There *is* no mountain there. There is but desert. But he trudges on toward it in any case. (*Pause.*) Whom should we identify with in this story? (*Pause.*) How many thought the trout? It's not the trout. It's not the trout at all. We've *all* been down. We've all been at the end of our rope. We all know what it is to call on powers—and let's pray that they exist—far greater than ourselves; to call out, "Lord . . . Lord, this world of yours sucks *hippo* dick, I just can't hack it anymore." And what answer was forthcoming? (*Pause.*) Exactly.

Therefore, let's smile. Let's slap a silly grin on our face that says to all the world, "Yes, I see what's going on, but I'm pretending not to notice. I see the misery . . . the pain . . . the hopes frustrated in our daily lives . . . the fear of loneliness . . . the fear of death . . ." I'm going to skip to the end of this list ". . . and through it all I *smile,* and I say, with the prophets: 'Lo, this world has been the same a great long while. It all shall be the same a hundred years from now—probably sooner.'" (*Pause.*)

And that's it.

Therefore be well. Peace to you. Be very kind to one another in your daily lives. And clean up when you're done.

Good evening, and Amen.

SHASTA RUE

Jane Martin

SHASTA RUE was originally produced by Actors Theatre of Louisville in November 1983. It was directed by Jon Jory; the set was designed by Paul Owen; the costumes were designed by Marcia Dixcy; the lighting was designed by Karl Haas; the stage manager was Richard A. Cunningham. The cast was as follows:

MAMA   Theresa Merritt

A fifty-year-old black woman in a flowered summer cotton dress made vague with age. Over the dress she wears a beauty contest sway reading Miss Prettybelle Kentucky. In her hair is a gold bead tiara. In one hand she carries a golden scepter, and in the other, several slightly wilted long-stem yellow roses. She is a plain woman with a mountainous energy that contains elements of the traditional Southern tent revival.

MAMA: So what you think's wrong with this picture? (*Adjusts her tiara.*) Yeah, that's right, Miss Prettybelle Kentucky. Struck three to four million citizens of this here Commonwealth dumb with admiration. Uh-huh! The considerable number who was dumb already jes' got theyselves struck dumber. Yes, yesssssss! Oh, I got the beauty! My big ol' daughter Shasta Rue, she got it for me. "Don't cry, Mama." "I ain't cryin', Shasta Rue." "Cryin' make you wet an' ugly." "Ugly already, missy, so I'll jes' get wet." "You cryin' at the TV, Mama?" "No, jes' cryin' for the sheer life of it, honey." Sittin' in the trailer, drinkin' flat Falls City beer, watchin' the Dukes, licken' on a taffy apple, switchin' them channels an' jes' cryin' all over my miserable low class life. "Hold on there, Mama." "Say what?" "Miss Kentucky Pageant." "Uh-huh." "Looky them beauties. All them white beauties." "Reasen is, ain't enough black people got them a bathin' suit." Yes, yessssss! Me an' Shasta lookin' on the beauties. Lookin' at all that fine horse flesh. Chilled me to the bone, baby. Made us mean, you know? Gave me an' Shasta the blood lust for straight bourbon whiskey. Oh black Jesus, didn't we knock it back! Didn't we drain the cup? Yes. Oh yes! Ol' Shasta she got down to pantin', started in sighin', started in rockin', rockin' back to front, way she does. "How come you didn't be no beauty, Mama? How come you ain't the Monroe County contestant, huh? How come you ain't up there doin' the sugar-sweet bird calls of the Kentucky cardinal in your apricot one-piece bathin' suit, huh?" "Cause first, God made him the pretty. Then he make him the plain to make the pretty shine, an' then he made us, Shasta Rue, to give them plain folks a laugh on Saturday night."

Then Shasta she bang on the table. She's a big strong girl, Shasta, an' she yell, "An' you made me, didn't you, Mama? You give me my poundage and my six-foot-one an' my hand can close up over a tea pot so y' can't see it, didn't you, Mama?" "Yes, I did do that!" An' she yells, "Butcha lef' out m' glory, lef' out my beauty, lef' out my swim suitabil-ity." An' I stood up like Moses on the Mount, an' I point at the TV beauties an' I holler, "*They* got it. They got it all!" An' she yells, "Let's git it!" And we do! We haul ass outta that trailer over to Loco Boys' pickup an' we hotwire that sumbitch, and drive eighty million, lead-footin' bumpity-squealin', lay-rubber miles-an-hour downtown. An' we kill that Kentucky Lucky half-pint dead on the way, singin' "Amazin' Grace" and "Deep Soul Kisses" and yellin' about them beauties, tears running down our faces, and then we see it. See where they got the pageant. Loomin' up. All shiny like a jewel box. Name up in lights. Search lights criss-crossin'. Shasta rockin', doin' little whoops. "Hit them brakes!" she yells. An' I do, I slam 'em. I bang 'em and we go smashin' our heads through that pick-up windshield like a kiss through Kleenex, an' we're bleedin' an' cryin', and we're outta the pick-up, an' this shrimped-up tuxedo door-man says, "Y'all cain't go in there." An' I stomp on's foot and Shasta rips off his li'l blond toupé an' we wipe off the blood wif it an' we're through that lobby eatin' usherettes on the

way an' Shasta she hauls open these big ol' oak doors an'
there it is! Yes, Lord, there it is! We in the theatre with the
Miss Kentucky Prettybelles pageant.

An' there's them beauties straight in a line, rainbow dresses
and 'lectric bouquets, smile-to-smile like one big long
picket fence, an' they waitin' on the envelope for they fate
to be delivered by one a' them. A.C./D.C./Emcees.
An' ever' single one a' them ding-dong beauties is blonde.
Look like a police lineup for Palomino ponies. White folks
must jes' kill them brunettes at birth. An' Shasta she goes
crazy! Sound come through her throat like an ash from a
volcano, an' the rivers dry up, an' all the dogs and cats turn
to stone, an' all over town the trees start glowin' in the dark
an' Shasta an' her mama start down that aisle, pickin' up
speed, an' it's downhill, gettin' steep, rollin', roarin', and
there's ushers step up and we blow 'em away, poppin' up,
goin' down, poppin' up, goin' down, an' we speedin', and we
fly over this pit, this fifteen-foot hole an' the audience is
screamin', and then there we are, we up there, we up there
with the beauties.

An' Shasta stops, an' the audience it stops, an' the man with
the envelope he stops, an' the big clock on the balcony it
stops, an' it's grave-closin', low moanin', down deep, well-
water quiet. An' Shasta spreads her arms, she lets out her
wing span, an' her eyes bug out and she say in this deep bass
voice, "I come for my beauty." An' they all still smilin' but
they got pee-pee seepin' outta the corners of their eyes.
An' then Shasta she throw her head back an' crows like a
rooster, an' we're amongst 'em like bears in a hamster hutch.

Oh, there's bouquets flyin', an' strips of chiffon like a bliz-
zard, an' falsies floppin' out like burger patties. Store-bought
eyelashes gettin' stuck on boobies an' ol' Shasta, she stuff
two fuck-me pumps in the emcee's mouth and kick his
Miami-tan ass right into the orchestra pit. I got this one

blonde beauty by her prissy French-braids and I'm hootin', "Gimmie that uptown wig you Baptist bitch!" And then, right from up on this high place, clear like a tornado alert comes this voice sayin', "Y'all hold on there Batman, you and Robin back your blackness off!"

I look up and Shasta she looks up, and there she is, lightnin' zappin' off her tiara, radiation round her head, Miss Kentucky, last year's model, got her gown on, got her crown on, got her sash on, oh so white looks like she been bleached once a day since creation, an' she got crimson red hair like the Grand Klan Dragon just set her to fire, and them neon blue eyes flashin' on and off, blinkin' and winkin', and baby sparkles like fireflies midst the hairs on her arms, and she say, "What you niggers want?" An' Shasta she shake her ham-fist up in the air, and she stamp on the floor an' she say, "I come for my mama's beauty!"

An' Miss Vanilla she walk her pretty perfume tallow-candle self down her red carpet paradise stairs 'til she nose-to-nose with Shasta Rue, an' she say, "Shit, honey, you want this raggedy crap, you can sure as hell have it. You can have the crown, the gown, and the chicken à la king. *You* can pull that parachute off them new Toyotas, dress like Scarlett O'Whatsit at the Kosair luncheon, an' chap your lips at the kiss-a-queen booth at the Twitchelltown Fair. You ain't chaos and confusion darlin', you the goddamned marines!" Then she turn to the multitude an' she say, "Y'all redneck trash, hesh up, you hear?" An' she lay that sash on me, gimme her rhinestone sceptor and gold bead tiara, an' then she smile on Shasta Rue and give her her ear bobs.

Lordy, it was lessez faire! An' the three of us walk on out, hand-in-hand like ol' Hubert Humphrey's wet dream a' racial equality, an' the Red Sea parts an' we under the marquee with them searchlights goin' and I say, "Thank you, Miss Pale," an' she say, "You entirely welcome, Aunt

Jemima," an' she unzip her strapless aquamarine dot-sequin formal an' she say, "They ask you where I gone, Sweet Ebony, you tell 'em I gone to Houston to the Spoon Gravy debutante ball." An' she walks off down Third Street naked as a jaybird in her lime green heels, an' that white pickaninny's whistlin' "Dixie." Lemme tell you one thing, it takes a real lady to walk bare naked through downtown Louisville after 'leven o'clock at night an' git home with two arms and legs. Yes, yesssssss!

Well, that's how Shasta Rue got me the beauty. White missy lay it down like it was spit or ol' gum, but I know better. Beauty beats smart. *Beauty* is the *life*. *Smart's* jes' talkin' about it. Uh-huh. See, now I got the beauty an' *you* ain't got shit. You want it, you go hunt some up for y'self. Ain't that right, Shasta Rue? Yes it is, it's right.

BLACKOUT

FERRIS WHEEL

Mary Miller

SETTING

The setting is two folding chairs placed side by side or a small bench. The motion of the ferris wheel can be created by the movement of the actors . . . gradually leaning forward going up . . . leaning backwards going down. The safety bar in front of them should be mimed when necessary.

Note: The bulk of the play should run as almost two separate monologues with the characters seldom relating to one another until they have to.

CHARACTERS

JOHN and DORIE: They can be any age as long as they are close to the same age. However, the play becomes more poignant if they are a little older and rather average looking.

TIME: Late afternoon. The present.

The stage is two folding chairs—or a small bench. A woman is seated with her arms outstretched in front of her, her fist clenched, her feet planted firmly on the ground and her eyes shut.

A man enters. He looks down at the woman and then behind him and then back at the woman. He then starts to sit next to her . . .

JOHN: Excuse me. Excuse me? I hope I'm not . . . crowding you . . .

DORIE: (*flustered/embarrassed*) No.

(*He slides into the empty seat next to her and takes hold of the "bar."*)

JOHN: I would have taken another seat but the line is too long to let anyone ride by themselves.

(*She nods but doesn't respond.*)

JOHN: . . . They force you to be a couple whether you want to or not . . . not that I mind. I mean it's a pleasure.

(*He looks at her, sitting bolt upright and perfectly rigid.*)

JOHN: Are you comfortable?

DORIE: Just fine. Whoops . . . we're off.

(*She squeezes her fist tighter, clenches her eyes shut and presses her feet to the floor.*)

JOHN: Are you all right?

DORIE: I'm fine.

JOHN: Are you sure?

DORIE: Couuuldn't be better.

JOHN: But you're not looking?

DORIE: No. Heights. I'm frightened of heights.

JOHN: And you ride a ferris wheel?

DORIE: Just once a year. On my birthday.

JOHN: Happy birthday.

DORIE: Thank you.

JOHN: You're welcome.

(*He looks at her gripping the bar.*)

JOHN: Your knuckles are turning white. Are you sure this is good for your circulation?

DORIE: What doesn't kill me makes me stronger, type of thing.

JOHN: So you do this in lieu of a birthday party with cake and ice cream?

DORIE: Oh no, I have that too, when I get through. Like a reward.

JOHN: But you go through this first.

DORIE: My Daddy started it and I keep it up.

JOHN: He was frightened of heights?

DORIE: Oh no, he just believed you should do something that frightens you at least once a year. Builds character. Strengthens moral fiber. You ought to try it sometime.

JOHN: I am riding.

DORIE: No, doing something *you're* frightened of, this doesn't count if you're not frightened of heights. I had this cousin once who tried to pretend like she was frightened of small places until she got locked in the attic during a thunderstorm. Lightning struck that house and burned it to the ground.

JOHN: Now she's frightened of fire?

DORIE: No sir, she's dead. You can't go messing with things like this.

JOHN: Truth is stranger than fiction.

DORIE: Don't you know it. Once I had this art teacher named Miss Thumb, who was missing two fingers. She used to say to paint all you needed were your ten good fingers and she'd hold up eight.

(*She demonstrates and then grabs for the bar.*)

DORIE: Whooopppss!!

JOHN: (Are) you all right?!

DORIE: I'm fine. (*pause*) . . . You're not from around here?

JOHN: No. Passing through, saw the wheel and drove on over. That's my little red car down there.

(*He points. She starts to look and stops.*)

DORIE: I'll take your word for it. (*pause*) You know it's funny running into a man like yourself riding a ferris wheel alone.

JOHN: (*embarrassed*) I used to do this as a kid . . . but you get older . . .

DORIE: Nonsense, you're never too old. My Momma always said you're only as old as you feel. Of course some days I feel like I'm a hundred. . . .

(*Suddenly they both jerk forward in their seats . . . and stop still.*)

DORIE: Oh my God? What happened?

JOHN: Looks like we stopped.

DORIE: Why?

JOHN: We seem to be stuck.

(*He leans forward to look.*)

DORIE: Don't do that!!

JOHN: Do what?!

DORIE: Don't move! You're rocking the car. Please don't rock the car.

JOHN: I'm sorry. They're probably just making an adjustment. We'll be moving . . . (*They do not move. He looks at her.*) . . . any minute.

DORIE: Yes. (*panic growing*) We should be . . . rolling? Any . . . minute . . . ?!

JOHN: Would you care for a cigarette? Calm your nerves.

DORIE: Me? No. I don't smoke. Do you?

JOHN: Not if you don't want me to.

DORIE: No, it doesn't bother me.

(*He starts to light up.*)

DORIE: When I was younger I saw this demonstration with an invisible man, where they hung this sack off his windpipe and said it was an exact duplicate of the human lung tissue. Then they put this lit cigarette in its plastic mouth and we watched the smoke slowly trickle down into the lung sack. And all of a sudden it started popping and bubbling—disintegrating right in front of our very eyes 'til it was nothing but a brown dripping glob hanging off that clear plastic windpipe. They said that's what happens to a tiny layer of your lung every time you take a puff. So I don't care to smoke myself, but if you want to, go right ahead.

(*He looks at the cigarette in his hand, changing his mind.*)

JOHN: I was thinking of giving it up. Now would be as good a time as any. Right? . . . Do something you're frightened of . . . sure? Why not?

DORIE: Once you do, it's best not to take it back. Remember my poor dead cousin . . .

JOHN: I don't need a cigarette.

DORIE: Good.

(*He pats his chest pocket where his cigarettes are, then starts twitching his shoulder, drumming his fingers on his leg impatiently . . . leans over, looks down.*)

JOHN: It must be mechanical.

DORIE: (*newly panicked*) Mechanical?! We could be up here for days!

JOHN: No.

DORIE: It is possible.

JOHN: Anything is possible . . .

DORIE: Oh God.

JOHN: Why don't you open your eyes?

DORIE: I'm frightened of heights!

JOHN: Just lean back and look up.

DORIE: Lean back . . . and . . . look . . . up!?

JOHN: Like in a field, on your back, looking up. Nothing scary about that.

DORIE: Leaning back, looking up? Lean back and look up. (*She does.*) Yes. (*looking up*) Oh God, it's going to rain. What are we going to do if it rains?! This thing will rust over solid and we'll be stuck up here forever!

JOHN: It's not going to rain. My knee locks up when it rains and it's fine. See.

(*He moves his knee.*)

DORIE: Don't move!

JOHN: I'm sorry.

(*He looks at his pocket where his cigarettes are.*)

DORIE: So much for my luck. I should have checked my horo-scope.

JOHN: We're going to be . . . all right. (*referring to having quit smoking*) I'm going to be . . . OK? (*He looks away from his pocket and pats his chest.*) This isn't so bad.

(*Uneasily, he takes a deep breath.*)

DORIE: . . . Bad. I knew today was going to be bad when the cream in my coffee curdled up like a relief map of the Hi-malayas.

JOHN: It's easy. (*struggling*) This is easy.

DORIE: You know, like the kind of maps we made back in high school . . . out of flour and salt water? Of course my mother never would let me cook.

JOHN: I could have quit a long time ago. (*pause*) So, how long has it been?

(*He feels in his pants pockets.*)

You wouldn't happen to have any gum, would you? Juicy Fruit? . . . Doublemint?

DORIE: Gum? No . . . My grandmother never allowed it.

JOHN: Neither would mine.

DORIE: She thought it was tacky. Bad for your teeth.

JOHN: . . . a waste of money.

DORIE: . . . socially incorrect.

JOHN: (*as if to himself*) She grew up during the Depression . . . always kept her money in a black leather purse pinned tightly under her arm.

DORIE: (*to herself*) My family has always been socially correct, even at the most incorrect political times.

JOHN: When she died, that was the first time I'd ever seen her without that purse.

DORIE: My cousin made her debut during the Vietnamese War.

JOHN: I thought without that purse, she wasn't going any place.

DORIE: My sister was a Nixonette during the Watergate Convention.

JOHN: Not Heaven . . .

DORIE: We got our first color TV the day Kennedy was shot . . .

JOHN: . . . not Hell . . .

DORIE: . . . spent the rest of the week watching his funeral . . .

JOHN: . . . they say her house is haunted . . .

DORIE: . . . in black and white . . .

JOHN: . . . I know what she's looking for . . .

DORIE: . . . on a *color* TV!

JOHN: . . . that damn *purse!*

DORIE: (*to him*) So, I doubt I have any gum. But you're welcome to look.

(*She hands him her black leather purse and he jumps.*)

JOHN: NO! No. I can wait. (*pause*) So . . . Seriously. How long has it been?

DORIE: Five minutes.

JOHN: Just *five* minutes! (*to himself*) And I'm already starving. I'm going to blow up like a blimp.

(*He unconsciously starts moving his leg and tapping his foot.*)

DORIE: (*without looking down*) What are you doing?!

JOHN: Nothing.

DORIE: You're moving.

JOHN: I'm not moving.

DORIE: You're twitching.

JOHN: Twitching?

DORIE: (*pointing down/looking up*) Your leg. It's going like a house of fire. Are you nervous? . . . Or is this some sort of warning signal before you break into a full uncontrollable fit?

JOHN: I am not breaking into a fit!

DORIE: A nervous twitch, wouldn't you know it!

JOHN: I'm not twitching! Look. (*She doesn't look.*) Don't look. See . . . (*He holds his hand out in front of him.*) . . . Steady as a rock. (*His hands start to shake, he grabs for the bar.*) Oh God.

DORIE: Oh God. What if they make us climb out on a ladder?! (*panic*) I can't climb out on a ladder. I'm going to be sick.

JOHN: Just take a deep breath. It's mind over matter. Just breathe. Breathe.

(*They both breathe together, she a deep breath and he like he's smoking an imaginary cigarette.*)

JOHN: (*breathing*) Better?

DORIE: (*breathing*) Better.

JOHN: It's all will power. (*He closes his eyes*) Visualization. See a stream. A peaceful . . . quiet . . . winding stream . . .

(*smiling*) . . . draw it into your mouth . . . taste it . . . feel it going down . . . hitting you here. (*He hits his chest.*) Cooouugghhh!! (*He opens his eyes, sits upright.*) You wouldn't happen to have a Tic Tac . . . Lifesaver . . . cracker . . . ?

DORIE: I wish you'd quit mentioning *food*. That's like talking about going to the bathroom in a moving car riding down the highway.

JOHN: I hadn't thought about the *bathroom*.

(*He crosses his legs.*)

DORIE: Just promise me one thing, promise me you won't eat me.

JOHN: Eat you?

DORIE: It happens. I've read about it. "Snowbound in the Andes." "Shipwrecked on a Desert Island." Two people stranded together and one eats the other. Instead of falling in love you have to worry about being dinner.

JOHN: I am not that hungry.

DORIE: Of course, I could stand to lose a pound or two . . . but I never lose it where it counts—it drops out of my face and I look like a cadaver with hips.

JOHN: I feel fat. Do I look fat? I am putting on weight and I'm just sitting here!

DORIE: Nonsense. You're thin.

JOHN: I used to be thin.   DORIE: I used to be thin.

(*During the following he starts picking lint off his jacket and biting his finger nails.*)

DORIE: In high school, I was so thin when I wore panty hose I pinned them to my bra. That kept my panty hose up and my bra down.

JOHN: But you filled out nicely.

DORIE: (*embarrassed*) Thank you.

JOHN: (*distracted*) A regular beauty pageant contestant.

DORIE: I was once. But I didn't win.

JOHN: The prettiest girl doesn't always win. (*He bites at a nail.*)

DORIE: Of course not. If looks were all that counted *anybody* could win.

JOHN: I bet you won Miss Congeniality.

DORIE: Me? Oh no. She was incredible. She had a way of making friends . . . getting coffee—smiling and greeting—always saying you're prettier than she was; and let me tell you, that is *one* sure fired way to make friends at a beauty pageant contest. Why the night of the finals she came fully equipped with vaseline for your teeth, double stick tape for your bathing suit, needles, thread, a walking medicine cabinet for headaches and cramps, everything from dental floss to Dr. Scholls. I voted for her. You can't let that much talent go unrewarded. . . .

JOHN: . . . and she was a cousin.

DORIE: Would that she were! We would have been proud to have her in our family tree.

JOHN: I'd have thought anybody as . . . ah . . . as . . . *chatty* . . . as you would have won Miss Congeniality. (*He spits out a nail.*)

DORIE: That's just my breeding. My mother always said it was our social obligation to be entertaining.

JOHN: Don't have to feel any obligation on my account.

DORIE: No! You're easy to talk to. I could talk to you all *day*.

JOHN: (*reacting, he bites his finger*) Ouch!

DORIE: You are going to bite those nails clear down to the nub if you're not careful.

JOHN: It's just a . . . hangnail.

DORIE: I had this roommate in school once who got gangrene from an infected hangnail. Nearly had to have her finger cut off . . .

(*Takes his hand out of his mouth, starts feeling for his cigarettes.*)

JOHN: (*recalling*) You said, that cousin of yours—who broke this pact . . . Died, didn't she?

DORIE: Deader than a door nail. They say that poor little body was charred beyond . . .

JOHN: STOP! I'll pay you a *hundred* dollars if you don't say another word.

DORIE: I could never take money from a stranger. My mother always told me . . .

JOHN: (*interrupting/loosening his tie*) Is it hot up here? Do you feel hot? I feel *hot* . . .

DORIE: No.

JOHN: How can you feel anything? You haven't stopped talking since we sat down. I'm sorry. It's my fault. (*pause*) Five minutes?! It's only been five minutes! They say when you die your life flashes in front of you in five minutes. I never believed that was possible before now.

DORIE: I'm sorry. I'm boring you.

JOHN: You're not boring me. It's just . . . (*He pats chest.*) I've been smoking ever since I was twelve. They'd give me a dollar for the collection plate at church and I'd fish out change—enough for a pack. God got the bulk of it but He's getting even now.

DORIE: No, you are right. I do talk too much. I always have. Especially when I'm nervous . . . or scared. Sometimes I get so wound up I can feel myself floating up over my body and I just want to slap myself silly saying . . . "Shut up. Shut up. Shut up." (*pause*) Like now. I'm sorry.

JOHN: It's OK.

DORIE: No, you see my greatest flaw is . . . I just want people to like me. I'm about the only person I know who thought Sally Field's acceptance speech at the Academy Awards . . . "You like me! You like me!!" . . . had real depth. I understood what she meant. But sometimes what we do has the exact opposite results.

JOHN: I like you.

DORIE: How can you tell, you keep twitching and biting and picking . . .

JOHN: . . . and listening. Sometimes when I listen to you I forget about smoking.

DORIE: You're teasing.

JOHN: No. I do . . . like you . . . and . . . ah . . . I don't even know your name.

DORIE: My name is . . . Dorien. But people call me Dorie.

JOHN: Pleased to meet you . . . Dorie. I'm John.

(*He holds out his hand to shake hers and as she does, she briefly looks down and regrabs the bar.*)

DORIE: Oh my God.

JOHN: Just look up. Look up. (*She does.*) Better?

DORIE: Yes. (*pause*) I'm sorry about the smoking.

JOHN: No, I was planning on giving it up . . . sometime . . . sooner or later. Maybe. (*longingly*) Nasty habit. A manner of keeping your distance with those . . . little . . . perfectly round . . . white cylindrical three and a quarter inch cigarettes . . . Oh God.

DORIE: But I bet your wife will be happy.

JOHN: I'm not married.

DORIE: (*surprised*) No?

JOHN: You?

DORIE: (*embarrassed*) Me?! No! No. . . . But . . . you? . . . I assumed . . .

JOHN: No, divorced. Traveling salesman . . . only she couldn't take the traveling so *she* moved on.

DORIE: I'm sorry.

JOHN: (*covering*) Yeah, well, you get used to being alone. You get over it. You adjust.

DORIE: Isn't that the truth. Why, I don't even mind eating by myself anymore. Not as long as I have something to read. Newspaper, magazine, those little bitty sugar packets they set at the table, the ones with the history of each state written real tiny on the back. You can learn a lot eating alone. The state flowers. The state birds. . . .

(*Suddenly he leans over and kisses her on the cheek.*)

DORIE: What did you do that for?

JOHN: I don't know . . . I thought if I kissed you, you'd stop talking for a minute.

DORIE: Oh.

(*She looks at him. He leans over and kisses her on the lips.*)

DORIE: I wasn't talking.

JOHN: No. My lips. I had to do something with my lips.

DORIE: So you didn't mean anything personal by it. It was just, sort of, reflex action?

JOHN: No. It wasn't totally reflex. I enjoyed it.

DORIE: You did? Oh . . . ah . . . (*nervous/flustered/she starts talking again*) Did I tell you I have an aunt who lives in Dublin,

GA., semi-related to Kim Basinger? You remember the
movie *The Natural* . . . Well, she was in it . . . Kim . . . not
my aunt . . . and when they started (filming) . . .

(*He leans over and kisses her again, on the lips.*)

DORIE: Lips itching for another cigarette?

JOHN: No. Partially.

DORIE: But not wholly?

JOHN: I wanted to see if I enjoyed it as much the second time as
I did the first.

DORIE: Did you?

(*Their lips almost touching when . . . suddenly they both jerk back in
their seats.*)

DORIE: What was that?!

JOHN: Looks like we're moving.

DORIE: (*She looks down.*) Oh God! (*She grabs the bar and shuts her
eyes.*)

JOHN: Won't be long now. (*looking*) They're letting us out one by
one.

DORIE: You don't think we'll go around again?

JOHN: No.

(*They jerk again in their seats.*)

DORIE: They'll probably close it for good.

(*They jerk in their seats, and stop.*)

JOHN: This is us.

(*They both raise their arms up and let go of the "bar."*)

DORIE: Yes.

(*She then suddenly embarrassed jumps out, extends her hand in a formal good-bye.*)

DORIE: It . . . it . . . has been a pleasure.

(*He takes her hand.*)

DORIE: (*newly flustered*) Yes. Well . . . you better get going . . . and have that cigarette, I wouldn't want you to get in any trouble kissing every girl in the park just so you can make it through the day without smoking . . . Look at me I'm running off again and I am safe on the ground. I don't know what's the matter with me . . . I better get going.

(*She lets go of his hand and starts to walk away. He hollers out to her.*)

JOHN: Dorie, you coming back next year?

(*She stops and looks at him.*)

DORIE: It is a tradition. And you know, my family, we're keen on tradition.

(*She exits right. He looks after her, smiles but doesn't follow. He takes out a cigarette, puts it in his mouth, hears thunder clap and, thinking better of it, puts the cigarette back in his pocket and exits left.*)

END

YESTERDAY'S WINDOW

Chiori Miyagawa

YESTERDAY'S WINDOW premiered at New York Theatre Workshop (James Nicola, Artistic Director) in April 1996. It was directed by Karin Coonrod; music by Fabian Obispo; the set and lighting was designed by Darrel Maloney; the costumes were designed by Myung Hee Cho; the stage manager was Anne Marie Paolucci. The cast was as follows:

WOMAN	Dawn Akemi Saito
SEPTEMBER	Lenora Champagne
DELIVERY MAN	Bonny Daye

YESTERDAY'S WINDOW can be performed by itself or as an epilogue to *Nothing Forever.*

CHARACTERS

When accompanying *Nothing Forever,* this play should also be performed by the same cast of three multicultural actors.

WOMAN: Asian American, in her thirties.
SEPTEMBER: Six years old. Played by a non-Asian woman in her thirties.
DELIVERY MAN: African American

A large window structure with white curtains.

Dreamy lights on WOMAN.

WOMAN: I awake from a dream, confused by the ambiguous line
that separates what could have been and what is. In this re-
curring dream, I am alone in a big empty house. There is an
open window with a lace curtain wildly dancing with the
wind. If I step through it, on the other side is yesterday. I
know this. I can take back every word I regret. I can meet
the daughter I never had. But something is not right. I
named her September, didn't I? She must be somewhere in
the house. How can I forget this? There is no need to go
through the window. I stay here. On this side. With September.

(*Lights up on* SEPTEMBER. *End of the dream.*)

SEPTEMBER: Why don't I ever see baby pigeons? Why are all the
pigeons in the world grown up?

WOMAN: Maybe they are hiding somewhere until it's safe.

SEPTEMBER: Do you think baby pigeons are rainbow striped?

WOMAN: I don't know.

SEPTEMBER: Do you hide until it's safe?

WOMAN: Sometimes.

(*Lights change.*)

SEPTEMBER: What's this?

WOMAN: An apple.

SEPTEMBER: I don't think so.

WOMAN: Oh? What is it then?

SEPTEMBER: I call it a ruby.

WOMAN: How would you communicate with the man selling fruits on Sixth Avenue if you call his apples rubies?

SEPTEMBER: He is calling my rubies apples!

(*Pause.*)

WOMAN: Would you like a slice of ruby now?

(*Lights change. A knock on the door.* MAN *enters.*)

MAN: Pizza delivery. One medium with sausage and mushroom. Twelve-fifty.

WOMAN: I didn't order any pizza.

MAN: What did you order? Pad Thai? Chirashi? Bibimbap? Cheeseburger?

WOMAN: I didn't order anything.

MAN: Why not?

WOMAN: I'm not hungry now.

MAN: But the food exists. You don't expect all the McDonald's to close just because you are not hungry right now, do you? And what about later? What will you do when you are finally famished and there is no pizza man? Where will you be then?

WOMAN: I have Corn Flakes at home.

MAN: That is absolutely not the point. You can't stay in your apartment and ignore the fact that out there are Cap'n

Crunch, Fruit Loops, Cheerios, and Special K. You are not allowed to be content with Corn Flakes. That's selfish. Anti-social. Anti-American.

WOMAN: My daughter likes Corn Flakes.

MAN: I like peanut butter and SPAM sandwiches on Wonder Bread, but do I insist on eating that when there is so much to tend to? What about just plain good American pork chops?

WOMAN: How much?

MAN: Huh?

WOMAN: How much do I owe you for the pizza?

MAN: Twelve-fifty.

(WOMAN *hands* MAN *the money.*)

MAN: Yeah, well, OK.

(MAN *exits. Lights change.*)

SEPTEMBER: When I'm sad, I know I can step through that window and the other side is yesterday.

WOMAN: You liked yesterday better?

SEPTEMBER: I don't remember. But I'll do something this time so I won't be sad today.

WOMAN: Why are you sad today?

SEPTEMBER: Because it's raining.

WOMAN: Would you like a slice of ruby?

SEPTEMBER: Yes, please.

(*Lights change.*)

SEPTEMBER: Tell me a story.

WOMAN: Some years ago, I went away to the country with some friends. We were all dreamers. There was a lake in the woods. It was summer. I liked to take a walk around the lake when the sky was on the edge of orange and gray.

SEPTEMBER: Pink and beige.

WOMAN: One early evening, I was alone at the lake. Then I heard someone jogging behind me. I looked back, feeling a little fearful of encountering a stranger. Maybe dangerous. But it was a boy, about fourteen years old, wearing a white T-shirt and blue shorts.

SEPTEMBER: A yellow T-shirt and blue and white striped shorts.

WOMAN: I felt relieved that it was just a boy. He jogged past me, turned around up the hill, and began jogging toward me. I noticed then he wasn't a boy anymore. He was about my age.

SEPTEMBER: Still wearing the same clothes?

WOMAN: Yes. He jogged past me, and I heard him turn around again and begin jogging toward me from behind. As he was passing me I said, "Excuse me. Do you have the time?" The man stopped, looked at his watch, and said, "It's half past fireflies." He was an older man this time. I walked out of the woods into the field covered with fireflies.

SEPTEMBER: Stars!

WOMAN: Yes. Covered with stars.

(*Lights change.*)

WOMAN: Would you like some pizza?

SEPTEMBER: That's not pizza.

WOMAN: What is it then?

SEPTEMBER: I call it Immie.

WOMAN: How would you communicate what you want to the pizza man on the corner?

SEPTEMBER: I'll say "May I please have one slice of Immie with pepperoni?"

WOMAN: What is pepperoni?

SEPTEMBER: (*Sadly.*) I don't remember.

WOMAN: Would you like a slice of Immie now?

SEPTEMBER: Yes, please.

(*Lights change. A knock on the door.* MAN *enters.*)

MAN: Delivery.

WOMAN: What are you delivering?

MAN: What do you want?

SEPTEMBER: I want a Oooyamyam. A big one.

MAN: You can't always have what you want.

WOMAN: Well, what do you have?

MAN: I have a video tape of that movie you remember seeing on TV when you were a teenager, but can't remember the title or any other significant information so you thought you could never find it again. I have that. I have your favorite earrings you lost eight years ago. You were sure they were in your apartment, and looked and looked, but never found them. I have those. I have the first love letter from your ex-husband.

WOMAN: How much?

MAN: Twelve-fifty. Each.

WOMAN: I'll take everything you have. When will you be back for another delivery?

MAN: Tomorrow.

(*Pause.*)

WOMAN: Why are you so lonely?

MAN: I don't know.

(MAN *exits.*)

SEPTEMBER: I don't know.

(*Lights change. In the following section,* SEPTEMBER'*s voice floats between that of a child and an adult's.*)

WOMAN: I thought I figured out the puzzle. September was supposed to be the missing piece of my life. But already, September has her own puzzle to figure out. I don't even recognize it. It's made of alien languages and images. I am filled with worry that she will grow up missing pieces of her life.

SEPTEMBER: Which is better? The moon or oatmeal cookies?

WOMAN: Oatmeal cookies.

SEPTEMBER: Why? What's in the moon?

WOMAN: I don't know.

SEPTEMBER: You don't know. How many moons have you seen?

WOMAN: I've seen the moon many many times.

SEPTEMBER: And you still don't know. How can you live with yourself?

WOMAN: I don't think there are raisins in the moon. Sometimes you have to figure things around what you don't know. Please, September. Stop looking at the moon. You'll be lost. Have some oatmeal cookies.

SEPTEMBER: You look at the moon.

WOMAN: That's why I'm lost.

SEPTEMBER: You don't mean it.

WOMAN: I don't mean it.

SEPTEMBER: What should we do to find out what's in the moon?

WOMAN: The thirteenth night of September is called *Kuri Meigetsu*, the chestnut moon, in Japan. You are supposed to reserve that night for moon-watching. The sky is always clear on the thirteenth night of September.

SEPTEMBER: Where is Japan?

WOMAN: The other side of the moon.

SEPTEMBER: The same moon?

WOMAN: Yes. Let's roast some chestnuts and watch the moon this year. You and me.

SEPTEMBER: Are we looking for answers?

WOMAN: Yes, my love.

(*Lights change. A knock on the door.* MAN *enters.*)

MAN: Delivery.

WOMAN: What are you delivering?

MAN: Let's see . . . I have moons. They come in red, white, and blue. I also have oatmeal cookies.

WOMAN: Oatmeal cookies.

MAN: What flavor?

WOMAN: . . . Oatmeal flavor.

MAN: I don't have that.

WOMAN: What?

MAN: I have oatmeal cookies in pineapple, carrot, and spinach flavors.

WOMAN: Well . . . Maybe not today.

MAN: You are not buying anything then?

WOMAN: Not today.

MAN: Tomorrow?

WOMAN: Yes, maybe.

MAN: Promise?

(*Pause.*)

WOMAN: Why are you so lonely?

MAN: It's not me. Anyway, it's time now. I'm going.

(MAN *exits.* WOMAN *calls after him.*)

WOMAN: Wait. Let me see the moons.

(*Lights change.* SEPTEMBER *speaks in a child's voice throughout.*)

SEPTEMBER: It's time now. I'm going.

WOMAN: Where?

SEPTEMBER: Jupiter.

WOMAN: Where is that?

SEPTEMBER: The other side of the window.

WOMAN: I don't understand.

SEPTEMBER: It's time to go to sleep. When you awake, ten years
have passed. You haven't even organized the pictures from
your trip to Italy. Where would you find the forgotten
time? Pickled in a jar on your kitchen counter? What should
you do with the pictures of tainted memories? Books you
never read. Postcards from faraway friends you never answered. A homemade apple pie you meant to bake one day.
You open an old shoe box under your bed and out fly dusty
moments of your life you never meant to keep. In ten more
years these moments will grow moss and give you a soft bed.
There are no answers. Just sleep.

WOMAN: There is so much I don't understand.

SEPTEMBER: Yes, I know.

WOMAN: Will you be back?

SEPTEMBER: Yes. In eight thousand years. So will you.

WOMAN: May I have this dance?

(*Music. They waltz. The wind dances with the curtain on the window. Black.*)

END

TWO ECLAIRS

Joe Pintauro

SETTING

Loft or apartment. MARK has taken up sculpting huge flight forms, as if his unconscious is working on some sort of escape plan. Absurdly large, the wing is perhaps several times larger than MARK himself and is all too obviously present on stage. His wing is a delicate skeleton. It may resemble a gigantic balsa plane model. Or, it may be a more fantastic wing form.

CHARACTERS

MAUD: *Over eighteen*
MARK: *Over eighteen*
BETH: *Eighteen or under*

(MARK *is fitting large sheets of foil or colorful paper to the wing as* MAUD *enters, dressed in executive clothes, carrying groceries and her attaché case and keys from the door she just opened.*)

MARK: Hi. (MAUD *plops down case and places shopping bag on the table.*)

MAUD: Hey, you've gotten far with that thing. I'm impressed. (*Kisses* MARK, *who is engrossed in work on the model. She hangs up her jacket and starts removing groceries from the shopping bag.*) I did something wonderful today. You'll be proud of me. Mark?

MARK: You sold the Twin Towers.

MAUD: Much better.

MARK: Really? Much better? Makes an airplane wing look silly no doubt.

MAUD: There's nothing creative about real estate, but it'll pay the rent until you . . . (Whoops)

MARK: Get a job?

MAUD: Did I say get a job? I consider this wing your job.

MARK: You do, eh?

MAUD: It'll do till the muses stop picketing the building.

MARK: Maybe I *should* get a job. (*She imposes herself into his arms.*)

MAUD: You're an artist. It's like being a little God.

MARK: You'll take any old shit from me.

MAUD: Tell me you love me.

MARK: What's the wonderful thing?

MAUD: Did I tell you I've had dreams of flying?

MARK: In airplanes?

MAUD: (*opening arms*) In the nude. I'm asleep, and suddenly air's
blowing on me so I open my eyes expecting to see the fan
and instead I'm two thousand feet *up* looking down at a
bridge. The East River's down there, and I'm headed toward
the Atlantic. (*simulating flying*) And suddenly. . . . Why? Am
I? Not faaaalling? Oh-ma-god, how do I stay *up*? Got to will
myself to be *up*. Gotta fly or I'll fall. And I squeeze every
ounce of *willpower-ohmagod*-if I weaken I crash. So I throw
my *soul* and *body* into staying-*up*. Aaaaand I veeeer to the
left . . . I'm goin' toward Queens. Oh-ma-god, I'm *flying*
over Queens. There's Aqueduct Race Track, Jamaica Bay, and
suddenly, oh . . . I'm over the *ooooocean* and it's *gloooorious*,
so I dive down. (*confidence*) I become acrobatic. I can do it. I
swoop down and skim the water. I'm . . . spray in my face,
I'm . . . a speedboat kissing the water so I shoot up straight
like a rocket, five, ten thousand feet *up* through the hole in
the ozone, past the sun, till I'm up with a whole new bunch
of stars, in a totally new nighttime . . .

MARK: Was that the wonderful thing? The dream?

MAUD: No. But that dream gave me the confidence to *do* the
wonderful thing. Today, I bought two eclairs for our dessert,
and . . .

MARK: That's wonderful?

MAUD: What's wonderful is that Beth . . . is gone. We have this
place all to ourselves. That's wonderful.

MARK: How did all this happen?

MAUD: I said, Beth, you're my sister. Mark and I love you, but when we said a few days, we didn't mean eight months . . . and you've got to get out for your own sake more than ours, that it's all workspace up here, one bedroom, one bathroom and it's not healthy to sleep on a couch and share a bathroom with a married couple, and it's not easy for you to work with my kid sister around all day.

MARK: She's out most of the time . . .

MAUD: Well, I was trying to make a good case out of it.

MARK: But she never bothers me.

MAUD: But eight months, she's gotta go. You're the one who said so . . .

MARK: Alright. When is she leaving?

MAUD: Okay. This is what will surprise you. I said tomorrow.

MARK: Good for you.

MAUD: It was like flying, once I got started it all just came out of me and when she asked . . . "When?" it flew out of my mouth like Vaseline. (MARK *is about to explode. He can't fake it.*)

MARK: Where the hell is a kid her age gonna go on such short notice?

MAUD: Huh?

MARK: She's quiet, she just . . . amazes me how she's so invisible here. She must change her clothes in the damn closet.

MAUD: Markie. . . .

MARK: I've never *once* had to wait for the bathroom. I've had to wait for *you* . . . (*pointing a finger with violently accusatory force*)

MAUD: She's my mother's problem.

MARK: I don't give a good god damn about your shit-face mother . . .

MAUD: Huh?

MARK: Your mother's the problem here. . . . You're driving me crazy I . . . am going crazy very well all by myself here twenty-four hours a goddam day. I can't finish this thing. What in the damn. Dang . . . Goddam . . . Sonofabitch . . . (*He tears the foil or paper off his wing, punching it into balls.*) am I supposed to *do* here all day . . . ?

MAUD: Mark . . . ?

MARK: . . . Wait to die? The woman doesn't even make noise when she runs the fucking water . . .

MAUD: I can't believe this.

MARK: She's like an *angel* around here. Oh God.

MAUD: (*stunned*) She's a very good kid . . .

MARK: Go away. Go outside. Go for a walk. Please. . . . Forgive me. (MAUD *just stares at her husband, confused by his reaction. She stiffly walks to a spot on stage where she takes a moment to think.*) . . . I'm not saying what you did was mean . . . or wrong. The girl has to go sometime. I know that as well as you do, but it's *dropping* it on me . . .

MAUD: You had sex with her. You had sex with my sister.

MARK: Oh for heaven's sake, no.

MAUD: You're lying.

MARK: . . . Jesus.

MAUD: God help me.

MARK: Take it easy. This is like lightning.

MAUD: I . . . don't know . . . I . . . I don't know how I'm going to . . . to live.

MARK: Oh please.

MAUD: I'm afraid to be all alone. Oh God, I'm falling, Mark.

MARK: Don't start your catastrophic thinking. C'mere. (*He becomes physically affectionate, caring.*)

MAUD: I'm losing my breath.

MARK: Breathe. (*She's torn between breaking away from his touch and needing him to physically balance her.*)

MAUD: I feel I'm gonna die in a minute, Mark.

MARK: You're just feeling very strong feelings. They won't kill you.

MAUD: Do you love her?

MARK: Don't torture yourself.

MAUD: Tell me and get it over with.

MARK: She loves me.

MAUD: So we are going to break up you and me?

MARK: C'mon . . .

MAUD: Don't play with me, if you're gonna push a knife into me stab me all at once all the way; are we gonna break up?

MARK: We're discussing it.

MAUD: Who? You and she?

MARK: Right.

MAUD: Discussing your relationship with me?

MARK: *All* our relationships.

MAUD: (*Makes a dash for the closet. Pulls out suitcase. Madly starts packing.*) Gotta go. Gotta . . . get outta here. (MARK *tries to stop her, to hold her.*)

MARK: Now please, don't panic.

MAUD: No. No. Don't touch me.

MARK: People get through these things. Our friends have all been through this . . .

MAUD: Not me.

MARK: What?

MAUD: Not with my family.

MARK: What are you saying?

MAUD: They've . . . they've finally killed me, finally killed me! Keep the place.

MARK: Huh? You're being irrational . . .

MAUD: I can't talk straight. Don't care. (*She grabs the dish liquid and the bakery box.*)

MARK: You can't just leave in a minute. (*key sound in door.*)

MAUD: What's that?

MARK: She's here. Go in the bedroom.

BETH: (*enters*) Hi. (*Kisses* MARK, *walks over to kiss* MAUD) Where are you going?

MAUD: Into the bedroom.

BETH: With dish liquid?

MAUD: Oh. Here. (MAUD'*s coordination is so confounded that she hands* BETH *the bakery box instead of the dish liquid.*)

BETH: What is it?

MAUD: Oh. Have one. (*Exits, still clutching the dish liquid.*)

BETH: Did you talk to her?

MARK: Yeah.

(BETH *opens the bakery box and pulls out an eclair, sits, and starts eating it. These eclairs may be a little larger than usual. Suddenly she giggles with a mouthful, offering the other eclair in its box to* MARK. MARK *stares, outraged.* BETH'*s smiles evolve quickly to a bland sadness and the mood goes straight to Hell. Music kicks in, such as Carly Simon's "I Get Along Without You Very Well."* MARK *starts disassembling the wing. Lights go down.*)

END

THAT MIDNIGHT RODEO

Mary Sue Price

THAT MIDNIGHT RODEO premiered at the Circle Repertory Company Lab in April 1990. Mary Beth Easley directed the following cast:

CINDY	Colleen Quinn
BO	Scott Rhymer

CAST

CINDY: 20s, national contender for the barrel racing championship at the National Finals Rodeo.
BO: 20s, her husband, calf roper, trainer.

SETTING

Present. Kitchen, with a screen door, in a small farmhouse near Wheaton, Missouri.

At Rise: Around dawn, summer, Monday morning.

BO *and* CINDY, *both sleepy and the worse for wear, sit at the table drink-ing coffee.*

CINDY: I've wanted this since I was nine.

BO: You shouldn't be drinkin that coffee.

CINDY: Nobody from Missouri ever won the National Finals.

BO: It's too strong.

CINDY: Not just barrels. Nothin. Is it six yet?

(*Pause*)

BO: It ain't gettin light.

CINDY: It will get light.

(*Beat*)

BO: Who's gonna run Sonny?

CINDY: You think I didn't ask somebody to see about Sonny? You think with the National Finals eleven weeks away and Fargo coming up ten days from now and Oklahoma City next weekend, I didn't make arrangements? You think it didn't cross my mind?

(*Beat*)

Did you want to run him?

BO: You want me to?

CINDY: You said he don't need to adjust to a man rider this close to the big money. Didn't we talk about this?

BO: All I asked was who, darlin.

CINDY: Jannie said she'd do it. Till the weekend.

BO: She'll ruin his mouth.

CINDY: She's all right.

BO: You ever ride that bay?

CINDY: I finished in the money in Little Rock on that bay summer before last.

BO: How long did it take you to get him stopped? Memphis?

CINDY: That horse had a rock mouth before Jannie ever got a-hold of him.

BO: Sonny'll be just like that time you can ride him again.

CINDY: We've been out all summer and I don't even know who's doin what around here right now. Who else can I get?

(*Beat*)

I'll have her use a hackamore.

BO: Sonny's too wild for a hackamore.

CINDY: I ran him with it when Chip had to pull his wolf teeth.

BO: Jannie ain't.

CINDY: All she has to do is work him on the first turn so he doesn't run it too wide and keep him from cutting in too close on the third barrel when he's coming home. You told me that yourself.

(*Beat*)

Do you want to run him?

(*Beat*)

We gotta go.

BO: It ain't light.

CINDY: It's almost six. They said they wanted me in there by seven-thirty.

BO: You weren't supposed to drink anything.

CINDY: They said food.

(CINDY *checks a sheet of paper.*)

BO: You aren't going to Springfield with a pot of coffee on your stomach.

CINDY: It says here, food.

BO: She told us liquids, too.

CINDY: She did not.

BO: Are you sure?

CINDY: Half a cup of coffee won't hurt.

BO: People choke on that anesthetic. Bob Mitchell's sister died right in the dentist's chair. Wisdom teeth. Never woke up.

(CINDY *dumps out the coffee.*)

CINDY: I'll drive in by myself.

(*Pause*)

BO: Maybe that'd be the best.

(*Beat*)

I'll run Sonny for you if you want me to.

CINDY: Just make sure Jannie uses the hackamore. And tell her to hold tight on that second barrel. I don't think she's been on him since he broke the record in Fort Worth.

BO: Why don't you wait till tomorrow and you can go in on an empty stomach?

CINDY: They don't even put you to sleep.

BO: Yes, they do.

CINDY: That lady explained the whole thing.

BO: They put you to sleep.

CINDY: You didn't pay a bit of attention.

BO: Do you think it's like a colt? All curled up inside you?

(*Pause*)

CINDY: I'll leave the truck at my sister's.

BO: Don't be that way.

CINDY: You can get a ride in with Ricky or somebody and pick it up.

BO: What are you going to tell your sister?

CINDY: If you want your truck, you know where it will be.

BO: It's our truck. This is our place. Sonny is as much mine as he is yours.

CINDY: I found him.

BO: I broke him in.

CINDY: I finished him off.

BO: I loaned you the three thousand dollars to buy him when everybody said you were crazy.

CINDY: I paid you back the first summer I took Sonny out.

BO: You don't have to pay somebody back after you marry them.

CINDY: Sonny is the best barrel horse I'll ever have. He'll never be this good again. I'll never be this good again. I'm already an old lady.

BO: Twenty-six ain't that old.

CINDY: Martha Long was eighteen when she won last year and there's little girls fourteen and fifteen coming right up behind me with their Daddies haulin them anywhere they want to go. Don't cost those kids a dime. I have to do this now.

BO: I know that.

CINDY: I can win.

BO: I know.

CINDY: I'll be goin into the National Finals a good two thousand dollars ahead of anybody else, if Sonny keeps winnin like he is now and if we win the Finals—$125,000 is a lot of money. We can train. Maybe start a school. We already talked this out. Martha Long got those Tony Lama ads and that Wrangler's commercial. Maybe I could get something like that.

BO: I don't want your picture up all over the place.

CINDY: We need the money.

BO: I'll quit. I've lost money all summer.

CINDY: It just takes ropers longer to develop, Bo. We can get you a real good horse with the National Finals money.

BO: There ain't nothin wrong with my horse. Don't go.

CINDY: You said you'd hold my hand.

BO: I said I'd provide for my family, too. For better or worse.

CINDY: You said me for better or worse. Not family.

BO: This isn't right.

CINDY: Bye.

BO: Wait.

CINDY: Don't worry about it.

(BO *grabs her arm, gently.*)

BO: I said wait.

CINDY: You said a lot of things.

(BO *holds her.*)

BO: Come here.

(CINDY *fights tears.*)

CINDY: The last time I went to the dentist, the novocaine didn't work.

BO: OK.

CINDY: And once I got my finger stuck for a blood test and I swear to God it bled the rest of the day. I swear to God it did.

BO: It's OK.

CINDY: What if I can't have any more?

BO: Have this one.

(*She pushes him away.*)

CINDY: You said anything I thought was right.

BO: I didn't think it would be like this.

CINDY: I didn't even have to tell you about it. I could have just taken a little trip someplace.

BO: I want you to have it.

CINDY: You never said that before.

BO: You can run Sonny next year.

CINDY: You know I can't.

BO: We can figure something out.

CINDY: We'll lose everything.

BO: No we won't.

CINDY: We still owe money on every single thing we have, except Sonny.

BO: A lot of people have babies they can't afford.

CINDY: I don't want it.

BO: Don't say that.

CINDY: Not if it costs me the National Finals.

BO: Don't say that!

CINDY: I've spent my whole life getting to where I am now. We've spent our whole life together getting me and Sonny into the big money and now we're almost there and I'm not going to let a couple of nights in the back of the truck when we weren't careful at all keep me from having what I've worked for ever since I was a little girl.

(*Beat*)

BO: Where do you think it will go?

CINDY: I don't know.

CINDY: Do you think it's saved?

CINDY: You ain't stepped inside a church since we got married.

BO: Do you?

(*She gets ready to leave.*)

CINDY: Pick up your truck at my sister's.

BO: Do you think it's saved?

CINDY: They ain't takin it out of you. They ain't askin you to spread your legs and let them stick some cold metal in and scrape out the start of a life.

(*Beat*)

I don't know if I can go through with it or not, if you won't go with me. I don't know what I'll tell my sister. But I'll sure as hell find somebody to hold my hand.

(*Beat*)

I won't bring a child into this world when we don't have five hundred dollars between us. We've spent it all on me and Sonny and we can't back out now. I won't bring up a kid to be as broke as my family was all the time. Not if I can help it.

(*Beat*)

And I won't have a baby knowing that it kept me from doin the one thing I ever really wanted to do. I'm afraid I'll kill it.

BO: No.

CINDY: I'm afraid I won't love it.

BO: Stay here.

(BO *kisses her.*)

CINDY: Maybe I'm wrong. I've chose wrong before.

(CINDY *steps through the door.*)

BO: Wait! Cindy! Wait.

(CINDY *turns around and looks at him. A long moment.*)

END

THE SPIRIT IS WILLING

Nicole B. Quinn

THE SPIRIT IS WILLING premiered at Actors & Writers, in Olive Bridge, New York, in October 1994. Carol Morley directed the following cast:

BARBARA   Elizabeth Benedict
JOHANNA   Mary Louise Wilson

PLACE: A New Age Expo

TIME: The present

Lights up on three BOOTHS bearing signs:

"SPEEDY DEMON REMOVAL: Visa and Mastercard accepted,"
"CLASSICAL PALMISTRY," "COSMIC SINGLES CON-
NECTION"

CONSUMERS, *carrying pentagram inscribed helium balloons, pennants,*
and sundry freebies, straggle across the stage, singly and in small groups,
stopping at one or more of the booths, throughout the play.

BARBARA MANNING, *a comely, upscale reporter in her middle years, talks*
into a mini tape recorder.

BARBARA: . . . Everything from EST to witchcraft. There's even
    an expert on "UFO abduction phenomenon." One hold-
    over from the sixties, a local Swami, who once made his liv-
    ing writing for *Hustler,* now offers workshops in "Sex as a
    Doorway to Divinity." . . .

(JOHANNA, *a handsome woman of about Barbara's age, moves out of the*
center booth.)

JOHANNA: Barbara?

BARBARA: (*turns in confusion*) Yes?

JOHANNA: (*menacing*) I know your past.

BARBARA: (*startled*) Excuse me?

(JOHANNA *crosses to her.*)

JOHANNA: It's John Biddle . . . Johanna now, Muncie, Indiana? You look fabulous. Just eyes or whole face? How's your mother?

BARBARA: (*confused*) Johanna Biddle? It sounds familiar.

JOHANNA: John. We went out twice, senior year. Once for fun and once so you could mock me in front of the entire class. Remember?

JOHANNA: (*recognition dawns*) Not "little Biddle"?

JOHANNA: Not anymore. I had it snipped.

BARBARA: My God!

JOHANNA: I thought I was, until you dashed my dreams. Just as well, really. The experience prepared me for the rest of the size queens who tip the scales at meat over motion. (*He indicates the recorder.*) Could you turn that off? I'm not anxious to become one of the curios you collect on this hunting expedition.

(BARBARA *clicks off the recorder.*)

JOHANNA: So, tell me, Barbara, are you still a self-centered bitch?

BARBARA: Do I detect a note of bitterness?

JOHANNA: Take it as a compliment, sweetie. Some of us actually admired you for it. Even in grammar school, you were the only one who got to see foreskins without having to bare any skin yourself.

BARBARA: You remember more about me than I do.

JOHANNA: Because I studied you. It must have been very lonely being Barbara.

BARBARA: I see you've taken a degree in amateur psychology.

JOHANNA: Paranormal psychology actually.

BARBARA: You're joking.

JOHANNA: No, I'm not.

BARBARA: But I heard that you became a lawyer.

JOHANNA: So I did.

BARBARA: Do you practice?

JOHANNA: Only numerology and tarot.

BARBARA: Male lawyer turned female gypsy. What a story.

JOHANNA: A little too "true confessions" even for you, dear.

BARBARA: Did you have any children?

JOHANNA: Three. Two girls and a boy.

BARBARA: And are you their father or mother?

JOHANNA: Father. Surgical technology hasn't come that far yet.

BARBARA: So, you were gay.

JOHANNA: No, I was a woman trapped in a man's body. Now I'm gay.

BARBARA: (*shocked*) You changed your sex to become a lesbian?

JOHANNA: I changed my sex to become a woman. Consequently, men have never turned me on.

BARBARA: Oh . . .

(BARBARA *backs away involuntarily.*)

JOHANNA: Don't worry, dear, you're no longer my type. Too socially correct, too waspy, too mean. Tell me, is your husband still fucking the starlet?

BARBARA: (*Direct hit.*) I see I should have attended some of those high school reunions. Muncie's not as dull as it used to be. What else do you divine in my aura?

JOHANNA: I needn't divine anything about you. I follow your byline, dear. And since that charming bit of exhibitionism on

Lifestyles of the Rich and Famous, your daily existence has become an open tabloid. Why are you here, Barbara? To ridicule and humiliate?

BARBARA: To inform.

JOHANNA: Meditation and past life regression don't seem quite your beat.

BARBARA: I'm curious.

JOHANNA: Anxious to find out how many peons you had beheaded, or the acreage of your plantation?

BARBARA: (*Hostile*) Something like that.

JOHANNA: That was judgmental of me, wasn't it? I do apologize. I'm operating on out of date information. For all I know you might be very enlightened.

(JOHANNA *bursts out laughing.*)

BARBARA: Now what?

JOHANNA: I was trying to imagine you with a titanium pyramid on your head.

BARBARA: Do you honestly believe in any of this New Age hype?

JOHANNA: If you sift through enough crap, you might find a few genuine spiritualists here.

BARBARA: And how does one tell the real from the fake?

JOHANNA: Basic instinct. And I don't mean dykes with ice picks. But then I don't suppose your exposé has room to embrace simple truths.

BARBARA: Such as?

JOHANNA: Ordinary people living plain and exemplary lives amidst chaos and confusion. Using their gifts, with little fanfare, for the well-being of others.

BARBARA: So this iconographic display is not a parody of itself, and these gurus are not gold-digging merchants masquerading as Messiahs?

JOHANNA: That's not what I mean at all. There are definitely those here who enlighten their pockets as they hawk the New Age version of the dashboard Jesus. But behind all the acting and the artifice, the seeming charade of it all, there are also those who see things, terrifying things unappeased and dangerous, lurking in the dark. And if you seek with unveiled eyes, Barbara, you just might see those angels.

BARBARA: Tell me, John, do you see them?

JOHANNA: Everyday. Just as one sees God. With the mind and the heart.

(JOHANNA *moves upstage.* BARBARA *watches her in confusion before talking into her recorder.*)

BARBARA: Academics, who now study the new age, consider it a kind of fundamentalism for liberals, "wherein consciousness is numbed, not raised." This trade show, marketing products targeted for human potential, has attracted some twenty-one thousand shoppers to the Hilton Convention Center over a three-day period. From tribal drums to crystals, this buffet of spiritual consumerism . . .

WOMAN'S VOICE: (*voice of an old German woman*) Bebe?

(BARBARA *stops in her tracks.*)

WOMAN'S VOICE: Bebe?

BARBARA: Who said that?

(*Lights up on the center booth.* JOHANNA, *head thrown back, speaking in the thin German voice.*)

JOHANNA: You mother saying you not wanting to be Jewish.

BARBARA: This isn't funny.

JOHANNA: In the war I pretend I'm not, you know?

JOHANNA: Stop it.

JOHANNA: I joined the German Army. It was the only way I know how to stay alive, Bebe. One day you go to work and at night you return to find a rubble heap with only lifeless limbs, the remnants of humanity. Every night, in the barracks, I was afraid I might talk if I slept. Some word in Yiddish, a Kaddish for so many dead. I didn't dream for three years. This is why I always am telling you what a luxury sleep is.

BARBARA: (*shock*) Nana?

JOHANNA: It is so hard to decide what is right, Bebe. Do we choose to protect the one, or rise together and fight for the many? These questions plague me, like waking nightmares, even now.

(JOHANNA*'s head drops to her chest.*)

BARBARA: Nana?

(JOHANNA *raises her head, looking around in curious bewilderment.*)

JOHANNA: Was I doing that lampshade on head thing, or just having wild sex with strangers?

BARBARA: Why are you doing this?!

JOHANNA: My, my, my, what's got your knickers all wet?

BARBARA: Had to be after high school. You certainly could have exacted your pound of flesh with that tasty morsel. What are you planning to do with it? Sell it to the tabloids? "Barbara Manning hides Jewish heritage to become prom queen." Limited potential for character assassination these days, I'm afraid.

JOHANNA: Dear Barbara, one always has something dark and dirty to drive an ambitious little engine. But please don't measure me by your warped, albeit expensive, yardstick.

BARBARA: You don't understand. You have no idea what it's like to listen to disparaging remarks, uttered only because no one suspects. An insider's view of hatred. Knowing they despised Jews, made sleeping in their houses, sharing their trite little secrets, and fucking their sons that much more enjoyable. In this country power comes from fitting in. Having that always impressive membership to an all-WASP country club. Even if it is only as a Mrs. somebody or other.

JOHANNA: Funny, that's what I was taught to believe about being a man. But the most powerful day of my life was when I chose to give up my membership. Because it just wasn't for me. Now, I am sorry if I've upset you. This session, of course, is gratis. But next time, you pay. Just like everybody else.

(JOHANNA *begins to move offstage.*)

BARBARA: John?

(JOHANNA *turns to face her.*)

BARBARA: I'm really not all Jewish. My father's not, you know.

JOHANNA: I don't care.

(JOHANNA *moves away.*)

BARBARA: John?!

(JOHANNA *turns back, slightly menacing.*)

JOHANNA: Yes, Barbara?

BARBARA: Was it real? Nana I mean.

JOHANNA: You want guarantees on the ephemeral. Was it real? Is love real? Can you see it, taste it, wrestle it to the ground and keep it from consuming you? No matter how much we comprehend the emotion, once infected we are its servants. Catering to its whims, humbling ourselves before its awesome need, the victims of its passions. The flesh is so weak, Barbara. Nothing but a decaying vessel. Was it real? Look around you. Do you see them? All those murky essentialities not yet manifest, slithering in the recesses of your reality, seeking form, eager to worm their way into existence. And you, Barbara, are the receptacle of that dormant slime. Through you it oozes into being. You simply allow it to happen, you vapid vain little creature. Was it real? Am I?

(*Huge, oily black wings unfurl from behind* JOHANNA's *back, stretching to a resplendent span, as she swoops toward a terrified* BARBARA.)

BLACKOUT

END

THE BATTLE
OF BULL RUN ALWAYS
MAKES ME CRY

Carole Real

THE BATTLE OF BULL RUN ALWAYS MAKES ME CRY premiered in the Ensemble Studio Theatre Octoberfest, 1995. Sara
Chazen directed the following cast:

DONNA	Ann Talman
LINDA	Sara Smarr
AMY	Camilla Enders
PATRICK	Kevin O'Keefe

CHARACTERS

DONNA: 34, single, successful, lonely, funny.
LINDA: Donna's friend, married, with a toddler.
AMY: Donna's friend, also married, practical.
PATRICK: 35, Irish American, single, well dressed, attractive.

(*A coffee shop.* LINDA *and* AMY *are awaiting* DONNA, *who enters, frazzled.*)

DONNA: Hi, I'm sorry, I just, oh God what a thing. I got pulled over! By a cop! And he noticed my emissions sticker was expired and I'm like oh God what's that going to be, like another seventy-five-dollar thing? So I started crying!

LINDA: You did?

AMY: Good move.

DONNA: Yeah, I know. But it wasn't even like I had to try.

LINDA: Was he cute?

DONNA: (*Disappointed.*) No.

LINDA: (*Disappointed.*) Oh, too bad.

DONNA: So I said to him that I was on my way to pick up my little girl, Enid. It just came out of my mouth. So, of course he knows I'm lying. I can tell. Because no one has a little girl named Enid.

AMY: Right.

LINDA: What'd he do?

DONNA: He softened.

AMY: Oh good.

DONNA: Yeah, and told me I should get the emissions thing done and that he'd let me go this time.

AMY: Great!

DONNA: But it freaked me out, let me tell you. That and . . . you know I keep having dreams about Sai Baba.

LINDA: Who?

DONNA: Sai Baba. He's a guru of some sort. They chant for him in Norwalk and places. The guy, who came to clean my rug, Gary? I assumed he was, you know, a pod, and then he picked up one of my Alan Watts books and started talking about it and kundalini and stuff and then he mentioned Sai Baba. *But* the weird thing *is* . . . they think he's God. Really God. "The avatar" is what Gary said, which I guess means God. And every night since then, I've had these dreams where I'm someplace, doing something, then all of a sudden people are chanting or talking about Sai Baba. I tried to get one of his books, but they were out.

LINDA: Oh, for God's sake!

DONNA: Well, I'm not saying I'll convert . . .

LINDA: For God's sake, for God's sake, for God's sake! Tell us about your date!

DONNA: Oh . . . my date . . .

LINDA: Yes, your . . .

DONNA: My . . . You want to hear . . . ?

LINDA: My God, yes! I got a babysitter so I could meet you!

AMY: We want to hear . . . We're here to hear.

DONNA: Well, it's a thing, let me tell you.

LINDA: What happened?

(PATRICK *crosses to opposite* DONNA, AMY, *and* LINDA. *He is good-looking and well dressed. He stands, waiting to meet someone. During the play,* DONNA, AMY, *and* LINDA *can see* PATRICK, *and he can see them, though he interacts only with* DONNA.)

DONNA: Well! We met at the movie theater. And he looked really cute.

AMY: Yeah?

LINDA: No, he's really cute.

DONNA: Right. So he was there, really cute. And I thought, "Oh God." You know?

AMY *and* LINDA: (*three syllables*) Yeaaaaah.

DONNA: So we saw the movie, and then we went . . .

LINDA: Wait wait wait. I did not *not* get a babysitter to hear a summary. Start from the beginning. Did you have popcorn. Did he pay for it.

DONNA: I had popcorn. He did not pay for it.

(LINDA *and* AMY *react visibly negatively.*)

He had bought the tickets.

(LINDA *and* AMY *take this in and give him a few points.*)

So we saw the movie . . .

LINDA: Which movie.

DONNA: *Dark Rain.*

(*We see* PATRICK *seated at the movie.*)

AMY: That's supposed to be really sad . . .

DONNA: Oh, it is. It's really *really* sad.

LINDA: Is it sad?

DONNA: No, it's *sad.*

LINDA: It has that really cute, that . . .

DONNA: Yes. And he *dies.*

AMY: Oh.

DONNA: Alone, in a prison in Istanbul, like a thousand miles from his girlfriend, who really loves him. I was like, distraught.

(PATRICK *hands a napkin to an invisible person next to him.*)

AMY: Did you cry?

DONNA: Yes! Plus I was so tense, from the date thing.

LINDA: Did he cry?

DONNA: No. Actually. He was sort of smirking.

LINDA: Oh, I don't like that. Did he notice you were crying?

DONNA: Yes, he gave me a napkin.

LINDA: That's good.

DONNA: Then after the movie as we were walking to the restaurant he started talking about politics.

AMY *and* LINDA: (*sympathetic, been there.*) Oh . . .

DONNA: And then, over dinner? The Civil War.

(PATRICK *is now at dinner, holding forth about the Civil War. We see his lips move, but we cannot hear him.*)

AMY: The whole war?

DONNA: One battle in particular.

LINDA: Well, he was probably trying to impress you.

DONNA: Don't people understand how totally unimpressed I am with people trying to impress me?

LINDA: He probably wanted you to think he's smart.

DONNA: Would I be eating with him if he weren't smart? Have I eaten with a man who is not smart?

LINDA: Well, he doesn't know that.

AMY: So, what happened?

DONNA: He talked for about forty-five minutes about this one particular battle.

LINDA: Which one?

DONNA: Oh, like it would mean something to you.

LINDA: Well . . .

DONNA: Anyway, I can't really say which battle. I was feigning. I was sittin' there thinkin' "Cat food, kitty litter, broccoli, I'd like to fuck this guy . . ."

(PATRICK and DONNA lock eyes for a moment.)

DONNA: And he's like blah blah blah Shiloh, blah blah blah Lee.

(During PATRICK's speech, DONNA crosses to him and joins him at a dinner table.)

PATRICK: . . . then Chamberlain, who was really a remarkable person, a professor of classical language at Bowdoin . . . he had asked for a leave to go fight, they said no, so he asked to go to England to study and then joined the army instead . . . he served throughout the war, and at Gettysburg had the job of holding the flank at Little Round Top. This is all in Shelby Foote's book.

DONNA: (to AMY and LINDA) Like I'm gonna read Shelby Foote's book, you know?

PATRICK: The Union had set up artillery on the ridge. Of course if you can turn the flank and get behind the Yankees . . .

DONNA: (feigning) Right . . .

PATRICK: Anyway, Chamberlain had withstood several charges, he was running out of men and ammunition, but at the next charge he made a countercharge with bayonets and the South freaked and didn't try to take Round Hill after that. He got the Congressional Medal of Honor. One person *can* make a difference.

DONNA: (*to* LINDA *and* AMY) Why do they do that? Why do they talk to me about the Civil War?

AMY: Did you see that documentary?

DONNA: Are you talking about the Civil War?

LINDA: (*to* AMY) Yes.

AMY: Did you see that part, that letter . . .

LINDA: Please, I'll go hysterical crying.

AMY: This army officer knows he's going to die in the next battle, and he writes his wife . . .

LINDA: I can't listen to this! I'll start sobbing!

AMY: The most beautiful letter . . . I cried.

LINDA: I sobbed.

AMY: I boo-hooed. I couldn't watch the rest of the show, I had to lie down.

DONNA: Well, why couldn't he talk about something like that about the Civil War? Why did he have to go on and on about a battle?

AMY: Because men think *out* (*makes a gesture with her hands indicating the outside world*) . . . *in* (*gesture meaning inner life*). Women think *in* (*gesture*) . . . *out* (*gesture*).

DONNA: Oh . . .

LINDA: No, that's true.

AMY: So the reason they think of you last, after all the stuff that's out there in the world, is because they think of themselves last, and you and your relationship with them is part of them.

DONNA: That's why they like military history.

AMY: Right.

DONNA: Because it's all *out*. (*gestures*)

AMY: Right.

LINDA: What happened next? I have a two-year-old, I need to live vicariously here.

DONNA: So then I said to him . . . (*to* PATRICK) Are you nervous because you know I want to sleep with you?

(PATRICK *stares at her*)

AMY *and* LINDA: (*They turn towards one another and squeal, at once horrified and thrilled.*) AAAAAAAHHHHHH!

LINDA: You didn't.

AMY: Oh my God.

DONNA: Naaah, I didn't have the balls. What I really wanted to say was. (*To* PATRICK) Shut up and kiss me! Just please *God* shut the *fuck* up and kiss me! (*To* LINDA *and* AMY) But instead I just said (*to* PATRICK) I'm not really a Civil War fan. Per se.

(PATRICK *looks hurt, and moves the food around on his plate with his fork. To* LINDA *and* AMY.)

Then he was sort of hurt, I could tell, and he sort of moved the food around on his plate. And I started to think, I'm such an asshole, you know, here's this guy taking me out, trying to talk to me, okay, so it's about the battle of Bull Run, whatever, but I can't even be nice to him. And here I am, I'm thirty-four, I haven't had a boyfriend since . . .

LINDA: Ron . . .

DONNA: Ron, who was . . .

LINDA: Unkind.

DONNA: Unkind . . . I need to be more . . . I need . . . I don't know.

AMY: Now, why do you want to date Patrick?

DONNA: What?

AMY: I mean, aside from that he's cute.

DONNA: Well. He looks like my father. A *lot*.

(LINDA *and* AMY *take this in.*)

And we have a lot in common. Weird things. And, when I look in his eyes I feel like I'm falling down a long tunnel towards ancient Celtic mysteries.

AMY: Wow. Okay. That's a good reason.

LINDA: Did you tell him that thing? That we talked about? About how you've got all this stuff going for you, a career, and a nice place to live, and now you're really ready for a serious relationship, and looking forward to it? You know, really strong and confident and knowing what you want, but letting him know that you want something more than just a fling?

DONNA: Oh, right. The thing. Right. Okay. (*to* PATRICK) You know, Patrick, actually, over the past year it's become sort of clear to me that, well, I have this career, that is going well, and I have a nice home and friends, but the truth is that, without, you know, someone to share it with, it can be really . . . really . . .

(*She starts tearing up.*)

. . . lonely and . . . empty.

(*She cries outright.*)

Really lonely.

(*She sobs.* PATRICK, *a little stunned, hands her a napkin.*)

I'm sorry.

(*She wipes her eyes.*)

I have to go to the ladies room.

(*She gets up and crosses back to the table with* LINDA *and* AMY. *She sits between them, resting her elbows on the table, and crying into the napkin. To* LINDA.)

It didn't really go how we planned.

AMY:	LINDA:

(AMY *and* LINDA *both rub/pat her back.*)

Ooooh.	No.

DONNA: It just gets very lonely when they talk about the Civil War.

AMY:	LINDA:

(AMY *and* LINDA *both rub/pat her back.*)

Ooooh.	I know.

DONNA: Or politics.

AMY:	LINDA:

(AMY *and* LINDA *both rub/pat her back.*)

Ooooh.	I know.

DONNA: Or books.

AMY:	LINDA:

(AMY *and* LINDA *both rub/pat her back.*)

Ooooh.	I know.

DONNA: Because they're lecturing! And you don't want a lecture. You want back and forth.

(*She makes a back and forth gesture.*)

LINDA: I know. That's the thing.

DONNA: That's the thing. You want the back and forth.

AMY: You want back and forth.

DONNA: That's the thing.

LINDA: Then what happened?

DONNA: I stayed in the ladies room a while. There were some other women there and we chatted, you know, about the toilet paper.

AMY: That must have been a nice break.

DONNA: It was.

(*She crosses back to* PATRICK'*s table.*)

The Battle of Bull Run always makes me cry.

PATRICK: That's all right. Do you want to go for a walk?

DONNA: (*Noticing that he's paid the check.*) Yes.

(*They leave the restaurant and start to stroll.*)

Do you ever think there's just so much that we don't understand? Like, my cat? Kitty? She's been staring at this cat next door, for like two years. But I never let her out, so all she can do is stare at him from the deck. Sometimes I sing the theme from *Romeo and Juliet* when I see them doing this. Anyway, I had problems with her, pee problems. It's a long story, but I decided it was time for her to be able to go outdoors. So I got her all her shots, which cost like two hundred dollars. And then I had to keep her in till the shots kicked in and then the very day she was finally okay to go outside, I came home from work, thinking, okay this is *the* day Kitty gets to go outside and I see Woody, the cat from next door, on my

path. And what's at my door but a tiny little freshly killed
bird. Like a present. Which he had never done before, in the
whole two years I've been there. But my question is, how
did he know? How did he know that this was the day, the
first day in the two years I've been there that she could come
out? Then I realized: this is *much much* bigger than we think.

PATRICK: What is.

DONNA: Courtship. I mean, forget trying to analyze it. Because
most of it will always remain completely . . . mysterious.
And we should just honor the mystery. (*To* LINDA *and* AMY.)
Do you think men do that, and women sort of don't? Honor
the mystery?

AMY: (*thinking about it*) Maybe.

DONNA: Why is that?

LINDA: What'd he do then?

DONNA: He . . .

PATRICK: (*Thinks it's funny.*) Where's your coat?

DONNA: (*Knows it was dumb.*) I didn't wear one. I always do that.

PATRICK: (*takes his raincoat off*) Here.

(*puts the raincoat on her, and buttons it*)

DONNA: You'll get wet.

PATRICK: It's okay.

DONNA: Thanks.

PATRICK: My pleasure.

LINDA: What'd he do?

DONNA: He . . .

PATRICK: (*Offers her his arm*)

LINDA: What?

DONNA: It's hard to describe.

(*She takes his arm.*)

AMY:	LINDA:
Tell us!	Tell!

DONNA: He gave me his coat. And he buttoned it up.

AMY:	LINDA:
Oooooo.	Oooooooh.

LINDA: That is so hot.

DONNA: And then he gave me his arm, and he walked me home. And he was quiet the whole way.

LINDA: Uncomfortable quiet, or nice like you're in a bubble together quiet?

DONNA: Bubble together.

LINDA: Then, when you got to your place, what did he do?

PATRICK: Goodnight.

(*He kisses her.*)

DONNA: He said, "goodnight" and kissed me.

LINDA: How was the kiss?

(DONNA *taps* PATRICK *on the shoulder.* PATRICK *kisses her again.*)

DONNA: Very nice. It was a very nice kiss.

LINDA: You had a nice date.

DONNA: Did I?

AMY: Yes.

LINDA: No, you did.

DONNA: I did. I had a nice date.

END

GAS

José Rivera

For Juan Carlos Rivera

GAS was first produced by the Magic Theatre in San Francisco, California (Mame Hunt, Artistic Director) in November 1993, as part of an evening of one-acts by José Rivera called *Giants Have Us in Their Books*. It was directed by Roberto Varea; the set design was by Lauren Elder; the costumes were designed by Chrystene Ells; the lighting was designed by Jeff Rowlings; the production stage manager was Lisa Larice. The cast was as follows:

YOUNG MAN   Sean San José Blackman

CAST

CHEO

TIME: Start of the ground offensive of the Persian Gulf War.

PLACE: A gas station.

(A car at a gas station. CHEO *stands next to the pump about to fill his car with gas. He is a working-class Latino. Before he pumps gas he speaks to the audience.)*

CHEO: His letters were coming once a week. I could feel his fear. It was in his handwriting. He sat in a tank. In the middle of the Saudi Arabian desert. Wrote six, seven, eight hours a day. These brilliant letters of fear. This big Puerto Rican guy! What the fuck's he doing out there? What the fucking hell sense that make? He's out there, in the Saudi sand, writing letters to me about how he's gonna die from an Iraqi fucking missile. And he's got all this time on his hands to think about his own death. And there's nothing to do 'cause of these restrictions on him. No women, no magazines, 'cause the Saudis are afraid of the revolutionary effects of ads for women's lingerie on the population! Allah would have a cow! There's nothing he's allowed to eat even remotely reminds him of home. Nothing but the fucking time to sit and think about what it's gonna be like to have some fucking towelhead—as he calls them—run a bayonet clean through his guts. He's sitting in the tank playing target practice with the fucking camels. Shooting at the wind. The sand in all the food. Sand in his dreaming. He and his buddies got a camel one day. They shaved that motherfucker clean! Completely shaved its ass! Then they spray-painted the name of their company, in bright American spray-paint, on the side of the camel, and sent it on its way! Scorpion fights in the tents! All those scenes from fucking *Apocalypse Now* in his head. Fucking Marlon Brando decapitating that guy and Martin Sheen going fucking nuts. That's what fills my brother's daily dreams as he sits out there in the desert contemplating his own death. The Vietnam Syndrome those people are trying to eradicate. His early letters were all about that. A chronicle. His way of laying it all down, saying it all for me, so I would know what his last days, and months, and seconds were like. So when he got offed by an Iraqi missile, I would at least know what it was like to be in his soul, if just for a little while. He couldn't write to save his life at first. Spelled everything totally, unbelievably wrong. "Enough": e-n-u-f. "Thought": t-h-o-t. "Any": e-n-y. But with time, he started to write beautifully. This angel started to come out of the desert. This singing angel of words. Thoughts I honestly never knew he had. Confessions. Ideas. We started to make plans. We start to be in sync for the first time since I stopped telling him I loved him. I used to kick his fucking ass! It wasn't hard or nothing. That's not bragging, just me telling you a simple truth. He was always sick. Always the first to cry. He played drums in a parade back home. He couldn't even play the fucking instrument, he was so unco-ordinated. Spastic. But they let him march in the parade any-way—without drumsticks. He was the last guy in the parade, out of step, banging make-believe drumsticks, phan-tom rhythms on this snare drum—playing air drum for thousands of confused spectators! Then he got into uni-forms and the scouts. But I knew that bullshit was just a cover anyway. He didn't mean it. Though after he joined the army and was in boot camp, he took particular delight in coming home and demonstrating the fifty neat new ways he learned to kill a guy. One day he forgot he weighed twice my weight and nearly snapped my spine like a fucking cu-cumber! I thought, in agony, "where's my bro? Where's that peckerhead I used to kick around? The first one to cry when he saw something beautiful. The first one to say 'I love that'

or 'I love Mom' or 'I love you.'" He never got embarrassed
by that, even after I got too old to deal with my fucking little brother kissing me in front of other people. Even later, he
always, always, always ended every conversation with, "I love
you bro," and I couldn't say, "I love you" back, 'cause I was
too hip to do that shit. But he got deeper in it. The war
thing. He wrote to say I'd never understand. He's fighting
for my right to say whatever I want. To disagree. And I just
fucking love how they tell you on the news the fucking
temperature in Riyadh, Saudi Arabia! Like I fucking care!
And a couple of times the son-of-a-bitch called me collect
from Saudi! *I said collect!* And I told him if Saddam Hussein
didn't kill him, I would! He told me about troubles with his
wife back home. He'd just gotten married a month before
shipping out. He didn't really know her and was wondering
if she still loved him. My brother always loved ugly women.
It was a thing with him. Low self-esteem or something. Like
he couldn't love himself and didn't understand a woman that
would. So he sought out the absolute losers of the planet:
trucker whores with prison records who liked to tie him up
and whip him, stuff like that. I honestly have trouble contemplating my little brother being whipped by some trucker
whore in leather. Love! He didn't know another way. Then
he met a girl who on their first date confessed she hated
spiks—so my brother married her! This racist looked him in
the eye, disrespected his whole race to his face, and my
brother says, "I do." Last night somebody got on TV to say
we shouldn't come down on rich people 'cause rich people
are a minority too, and coming down on them was a form
of racism! And I thought, they're fucking afraid of class war-
fare, and they should be! And the news showed some little
white punk putting up flags all over this dipshit town in California and this little twirp's story absorbed twenty minutes
of the news—this little, blond Nazi kid with a smile full of
teeth—and the protests got shit. And this billboard went up
in my town showing Stalin, Hitler, and Hussein, saying we

stopped him twice before we have to stop him again! This
billboard was put up by a local newspaper! The music, the
computer graphics, the generals coming out of retirement to
become media stars, public hard ons. And we gotta fight
NAKED AGGRESSION—like his asshole president should
come *to my fucking neighborhood* if he wants to see naked aggression! I never thought the ideas in the head of some
politician would mean the death of my brother and absolutely kill my mother. I'm telling you, that woman will not
survive the death of my brother no matter how much she
believes in God, no matter how much praying she does. But
I keep that from him. I write back about how it's not going
to be another Vietnam. It's not going to be a whole country
that spits on you when you come back. That we don't forget
the ones we love and fight for us. Then his letters stopped. I
combed the newspapers trying to figure out what's going on
over there, 'cause his letters said nothing about where he
was. He wasn't allowed to talk about locations, or troop size,
or movement, 'cause, like, I was going to personally transmit
this information to the Iraqi fucking Ministry of Defense! I
thought about technology. The new shit Iraq has that was
made in the United States, shit that could penetrate a tank's
armour and literally travel through the guts of a tank, im-
molating every living human soul inside, turning human
Puerto Rican flesh into hot screaming soup, the molecules
of my brother's soul mixing with the metal molecules of the
iron coffin he loved so much. I couldn't sleep. My mother
was suicidal. Why wasn't he writing? The air war's continuing. They're bombing the shit out of that motherfucking
country! And I find myself ashamed. I think, "yeah, bomb it
more. Level it. Send it back to the Stone Age. Make it so
every last elite Republican Guard is dead. So my brother
won't get killed." For the first time in my life, I want a lot of
people I don't hate to die 'cause I know one of them could
kill the man I love most in this fucked up world. If my
brother is killed, I will personally take a gun and blow out

the brains of George Herbert Walker Bush. And I'm sick.
I'm sick of rooting for the bombs. Sick of loving every day
the air war continues. Sick of every air strike, every sortie.
And being happy another Iraqi tank got taken out and
melted, another Iraqi bunker was bombed, another bridge
can't bring ammunition, can't deliver that one magic bullet
that will incapacitate my brother, bring him back a veg-
etable, bring him back dead in his soul, or blinded, or
butchered in some Iraqi concentration camp. That the Iraqi
motherfucker that would torture him won't live now 'cause
our smart bombs have killed that towelhead motherfucker
in his sleep! They actually got me wanting this war to be
bloody!

(*Beat.*)

Last night the ground war started. It started. The tanks are
rolling. I find my gut empty now. I don't have thoughts. I
don't have dreams. My mother is a shell. She has deserted
herself and left behind a blathering cadaver, this pathetic
creature with rosary beads in her hands looking up to
Christ, and CNN, saying words like "Scud," "strategic inter-
ests," "collateral damage," "target rich environment"—words
this woman from a little town in Puerto Rico has no right
to know. So I fight my demons. I think of the cause. Blood
for oil. I NEED MY CAR, DON'T I? I NEED MY CAR
TO GET TO WORK SO I CAN PAY THE RENT AND
NOT END UP A HOMELESS PERSON! DON'T I
HAVE A RIGHT TO MY CAR AND MY GAS?
AND WHAT ABOUT FREEING DEMOCRATIC KU-
WAIT?!

(*Beat.*)

So I wait for a sign, anything, a prayer, any sign, I'll take it.
Just tell me he's okay. Tell me my brother's gonna kill well
and make it through this alive. He's gonna come home and
he's gonna come home the same person he left: the spastic

one who couldn't spell . . . the one who couldn't play the drums.

(CHEO *starts to pump gas. As he pumps the gas, he notices something horrifying. He pulls the nozzle out of the car. Blood comes out of the gas pump.* CHEO *stares and stares at the bloody trickle coming out of the gas pump.*)

BLACKOUT

END

DUET FOR BEAR AND DOG

Sybil Rosen

For David

DUET FOR BEAR AND DOG premiered at Actors & Writers in Olive Bridge, New York in October 1995. It was directed by Shelley Wyant; the production stage manager was Brian MacReady. The cast was as follows:

WOMAN	Gigi Buffington
MAN	David Smilow
BEAR	Carol Morley
DOG	John Seidman
SHE	Nina Lvovna

Empty stage. A stepladder can serve as a tree. WOMAN *and* MAN *enter.*

WOMAN: (*Two-way radio noises.*) 203, this is 364. What's your 20?

MAN: 209 north above Kerhonkson. What you got?

WOMAN: Bear up a tree on Main Street in Woodstock.

MAN: I'm on my way. How'd it get there?

WOMAN: Would you believe, a little rat dog?

(*They exit.* DOG *chases* BEAR *onstage. She goes up on ladder.*)

BEAR: Oh, shit.

DOG: (*Triumphant.*) Aha! I'm a dog! I'm a dog! (*Pisses on tree.*) Take that, you rottweilers, you shepherds, you labradors! Up yours, you pachyderms and raptors and primates! You can cut off my balls, but I'm still a man! I'm a dog!

BEAR: Ah, the call of the wild. Are you finished?

DOG: (*Over.*) Cousin to the wolf, brother to the jackal, helpmate of the *homo sapien*—!

BEAR: Oh my God.

DOG: I'm a dog. And you—are mine!

BEAR: You're nuts! (*She growls, takes bluff swipe at him.*) I never ate a dog before, but there's always a first time. I had a pig once. It was a bad year. I'm not scared of you.

DOG: Then what are you doing up a tree?

BEAR: It's called instinct. You wouldn't know about that.

DOG: Very funny. What I lack in instinct, I make up for in finesse. They're coming for you.

BEAR: (*Panicked.*) Who? Who's they?

DOG: I don't know. Some guys got called.

BEAR: Who called them?

DOG: The one I belong to. Who belongs to me. (*Sings.*) "Fish gotta swim, birds gotta fly, I gotta love one man till I die—" She does nails. And facials.

BEAR: That explains the ribbon. (*Laughs as* DOG *rips ribbon from head.*) You guys have a curious thing with these humans. I bet you have a name.

DOG: (*A sore point.*) What's it to you?

BEAR: I knew it. Look, I got lost. I took a wrong turn. Just let me get down. Who knows what they'll do to me?

DOG: I don't know. Put you in a zoo maybe. (*Finds this hilarious.*)

BEAR: Don't laugh! I have a cousin that was captured by these circus people. Last thing I heard he's walking a tightrope and wearing a tutu.

DOG: You got what you deserve—plundering those garbage cans, sucking up to Dumpsters.

BEAR: Oh? I've seen your handiwork. You and your kind. You're not above delving into garbage.

DOG: I don't do garbage. I'm a lapdog. I get cashews by hand.

BEAR: (*Hungry.*) Cashews?

DOG: Yeah. And chocolates. Potato chips. Raspberries even.

BEAR: Raspberries?

DOG: I'm highly evolved.

BEAR: The little red ones? The nubbly kind you roll around on your tongue?

DOG: Whatever.

BEAR: (*Swoons.*) I love those. It was a dry year for raspberries. Blueberries too. That's why I had to go to Dumpsters. Did you ever eat a diaper?

DOG: What do I look like?

BEAR: Oh, spare me. You guys are notorious shiteaters. Me, I'm basically a herbivore.

DOG: What about the pig?

BEAR: Like I said, it was a bad year. Okay, I admit I'm not above a fish or two. When they're running. How about you? You like fish?

DOG: (*Shrugs.*) Only to roll on. (*Looks around, sees something, growls at* BEAR.)

BEAR: Hey! Quit that! What's the big idea?

DOG: (*Growling.*) She's coming. I gotta make it look good. Could be some cashews in it. (*Growls more.*)

(SHE *speaks with a thick Russian accent.*)

SHE: Good boy, Boris.

BEAR: Boris?

DOG: Shit!

SHE: Keep up there. They come soon. Good boy, Boris.

BEAR: (*Mocking.*) Good boy, Boris!

DOG: (*To* BEAR.) Shut up!

SHE: My God, that is big bear! Look at that behind. Is big as Kremlin.

BEAR: I take that as a compliment. And this is just August. I have to put on fifty more pounds before I den and birth my babies.

SHE: Would look good, lying on floor in den, yes?

BEAR: No.

DOG: There's a thought.

BEAR: Shut up, Boris!

SHE: In Russia, we have bears. Brown bears. They drink vodka and come down chimney at Christmas time.

(MAN *and* WOMAN *enter.*)

BEAR: Oh God, they're here.

WOMAN: There it is.

MAN: Jesus. Nice bear.

WOMAN: What do you think? One hundred fifty pounds?

MAN: Easy.

SHE: You come for bear?

MAN: Yes ma'am. Garth McGowan. Department of Environmental Conservation. You the woman that called?

(WOMAN *walks around ladder, checking out* BEAR.)

SHE: Yes.

MAN: That the dog?

SHE: That is Boris.

BEAR: (*To* WOMAN.) What are you looking at?

MAN: What happened?

SHE: I am in shop, making motion circles on face of customer. With cucumber facial. I make myself. And I am telling how I leave in Russia bad husband and mother of rotten heart—

MAN: Ma'am? Excuse me, we—

SHE: Wait! I tell you. So Boris is barking. Yip, yip, yip, yip, yip.

DOG: That's not how I sound.

MAN: (*Appreciatively.*) Damn dog.

WOMAN: I'll get the equipment. (*Exits.*)

SHE: I look. Oh my God. Staring in window—is bear. Standing on legs, with paws on window. Like this. (*Demonstrates.*) First I think is bad husband from Russia, come to finish me. I am shaking in booty—

MAN: These are brown bears, ma'am. They're very docile.

SHE: What means docile?

MAN: Gentle, timid, shy.

(WOMAN *returns.*)

SHE: I should marry one. You are married?

MAN: Yes ma'am.

SHE: Why do I know that?

WOMAN: (*To* MAN.) Let's go, let's go—

MAN: Ma'am—

SHE: Let me finish story. Please. I jump. (*Demonstrates.*) Bear jumps. (*Demonstrates.*) I go to close door. Out goes Boris. Yip, yip, yip, yip, yip. Bear goes up tree. I make phone call. Customer gives big tip. End of story.

MAN: Got it.

SHE: What you do now?

MAN: First we'll dart the bear. Tranquilize it. Then when it's on the ground, we'll take some data, pull a tooth—

SHE *and* BEAR: A tooth?

MAN: Yes ma'am. That's how we age them.

BEAR: Ouch.

MAN: Then we'll give it some ear tags, put it in the trap we brought, take it to the mountains, and let it go.

SHE *and* BEAR *and* DOG: (*Surprised.*) Oh. That sounds nice.

MAN: Yes ma'am. It'll be a lot happier up there. So if you'll just stand back—You can call your dog off now.

DOG: (*To* MAN.) Wait a second. You don't get it.

SHE: Here, Boris.

DOG: Jeez. I treed that bear.

SHE: Boris. Come, Boris. Come to Momma.

DOG: (*Moping over.*) Times like this I wish I was a dingo.

SHE: Sit.

DOG: Shit. (*Sits.*)

BEAR: It's your own fault. You gave in. For the easy bone and winter hearth. For the soft bed and the cashews.

DOG: We didn't give in! It wasn't like that at all. Hell, it was *our* idea, we thought of it. They had scraps, for God's sake. These human beings. Just laying around. They couldn't eat everything. You know how big a mastodon is? It seemed like a good idea. It *was* a good idea. It still is. I could do without the ribbon.

BEAR: You call that evolutionary? I call it quits. Adaptation? Please. Let's not mince words. You capitulated. You should have been out there with us. In the Pleistocene. Working out the kinks of hibernation. Fine tuning the fecal plug. Learning how to give birth in our sleep.

DOG: So sue me.

(*Bam!* WOMAN *fires the dartgun.* MAN *sets a stopwatch.* BEAR *starts.* DOG *barks.*)

WOMAN: Bulls-eye.

MAN: Good shot.

WOMAN: Are you timing?

MAN: (*Nods.*) I give it sixty seconds max.

SHE: Boris. Stop. What is wrong?

BEAR: (*Beginning to slow down.*) What do you know? I have a dart in my ass.

SHE: What happen now?

MAN: It'll come down. Watch.

(BEAR *begins to get very loose and woozy. Her tongue goes in and out.*)

BEAR: I hear bees. Back and forth between nectar and hive. Follow the buzz to the succulent grubs, socked away in the waxy comb, swimming in sweet honey. Rip the hive, the paper breaks like an egg. Bees zing around my head. Sting my nose. I don't feel them. I don't feel anything. Roll the grubs on my tongue. Stinging berries dipped in sugar—

(*She falls slowly down ladder to the ground.*)

WOMAN: Bingo.

MAN: (*Stopping watch.*) Fifty-two seconds.

(*They go to* BEAR. SHE *and* DOG *go too.* DOG *sniffs at* BEAR.)

SHE: Is hurt?

WOMAN: No. It makes a big boom, but they're very limber. They have a lot of fat to cushion them.

SHE: It and me both. Is sleeping?

WOMAN: Not exactly. More like immobilized. Now if you could just step back, ma'am, until we're finished—

SHE: It will wake?

WOMAN: No. We just want to move as quietly as we can around the bear. If you could back up ten feet. When we're done, you'll have a chance to touch it. If you want. And the dog too, ma'am, please.

SHE: Boris. Come.

DOG: Smells like a dream I had once. One of those where your paws gallop and your jowls blow. (*Demonstrates.*) Wish I could remember what I was dreaming about. Something about savannahs, and a fire, and bones, big as a house.

SHE: (*Sharp.*) Boris! (*Then quietly.*) Boris. Come.

(DOG *and* SHE *go to one side.*)

MAN: Nice bear.

WOMAN: It's a female.

MAN: Wonder if she's pregnant.

WOMAN: Hang on, honey. We're taking you home.

(*All freeze except* BEAR.)

BEAR: I follow the north side of the mountain, where the sun neither rises nor sets. Under two silver birches, below the sheltering rock, I squeeze myself into crevices an otter couldn't fill. My breath heats the den, steam rises from my fur, making weather under the earth. I sleep the long sleep, in a cradle of soil. And dream of babies, pushing out of me, cubs small as kittens, fat as flesh, eyes awake. They know the continent of my body. They find their way in the dark, to force their mouths upon me, and suck and purr and thrive. Until the unseen days lengthen and the wild crocus pushes through the snow. Then I awaken, newborn and ageless, and take my young into the still white world.

END

PHONE SEX
AND A DUMB SHOW

Steven Sater

PHONE SEX AND A DUMB SHOW was first produced at Love Creek Productions, and was originally published in *Rockford Review.* It has since been incorporated as a scene within the full-length evening, *New York Animals,* which will premiere at the WPA Theatre during the 1996/97 season. The author wishes to thank Byam Stevens for his dramaturgical work on this script.

CHARACTERS

GRAY: Late 20's. So overtired that he is losing his will.
THE PEEPING TOM: Mid-to-late 40's. Congenial.

TIME & PLACE: The present, New York City, GRAY's apartment.

NOTES: We hear but do not ever see the PEEPING TOM.

I have littered this scene with "beat"s, because so many big decisions happen between the speeches.

GRAY *in his apartment. He's packing an overnight bag—not his—with clothes and toiletries, also not his. He hasn't slept and is unsure just what to pack. The phone rings.*

GRAY: (*Answering phone*) Hello.

PEEPING TOM: (*We hear but do not see him.*) Hello.

GRAY: Yeah? Who is it?

PEEPING TOM: It's me.

GRAY: Who?

PEEPING TOM: Me.

(*A beat*)

GRAY: Ken, I'm too tired for this.

PEEPING TOM: Not Ken. (*A beat; playfully*) Guess again.

(*A beat*)

GRAY: Who is this?

PEEPING TOM: Just me.

(*A beat*)

GRAY: Me, who?

PEEPING TOM: Just a fan.

(*No response*)

Now, what are you putting in that bag? Going away for the weekend?

(GRAY *jerks his head toward the window.*)

GRAY: Who *is* this?

PEEPING TOM: (*Leadingly.*) Who is anyone?

(GRAY *hangs up. Looks out again. Moves away. The phone rings.*)

GRAY: Oh, my God.

(*He speaks to the window.*)

I won't get it.

(*A long beat. The phone rings and rings. Finally, he answers it.*)

How did you get my number?

PEEPING TOM: Baby, come on. I've got your number.

GRAY: You are crazy.

PEEPING TOM: (GRAY *shouldn't call him crazy.*) Now, baby, don't be bad to Daddy.

GRAY: "Daddy"?! Jesus!

(GRAY *starts to hang up the phone.*)

PEEPING TOM: Don't hang up! I'll spank you.

(*A beat*)

GRAY: Spank me?!

PEEPING TOM: Oh, yeah. My hands are ready.

(*A beat*)

GRAY: (*Looking up and out the window*) Where are you?

PEEPING TOM: (*An immediate command; forcefully*) Look down.

(*A beat*)

GRAY: Look down?

PEEPING TOM: To your shoes. (*A beat*) Do it. (*A beat.* GRAY *looks down to his shoes.*) Good. Good boy. Now, look up. (*A beat.* GRAY *looks up.*) Yeah, good, baby. Now down. To your shoes. (GRAY *looks down again.*) Good. Now bring your hands along your thighbones. (*A beat*) Like you do it. (*A beat*) You know, like you do with him.

GRAY: (*Looking out the window again.*) What?!

PEEPING TOM: (*A forceful command*) Look down!

(GRAY *looks down.*)

GRAY: (*Meaning "It's impossible"*) You've seen us . . . ? No!

PEEPING TOM: (*After a beat, seductively*) Oh, yeah. I've seen you . . . Mm, hmm . . .

GRAY: But—

PEEPING TOM: Oh, baby . . .

GRAY: You—?

PEEPING TOM: Uh, huh . . .

GRAY: No!

PEEPING TOM: (*After a beat*) Baby, come on, let go. (*No response. A longer beat, then*) Baby, I had to call you; you just looked so good.

GRAY: Yeah, right.

(*A beat, then*)

PEEPING TOM: Baby . . .

GRAY: What?

PEEPING TOM: Make me good.

(*A beat*)

GRAY: No.

(*A beat; then*)

PEEPING TOM: No . . . ?

(*A beat, then*)

GRAY: No.

PEEPING TOM: "No, no, Daddy."

GRAY: (*With a laugh*) "No, no, Daddy"!

(*A beat*)

PEEPING TOM: There, isn't that better? Now let me unzip your pants.

GRAY: No.

PEEPING TOM: "No, no, Daddy." (*A beat*) Come on . . . Just a little.

(GRAY *hesitates.*)

PEEPING TOM: Baby, feel my hand. Feel it?

GRAY: Uhh . . .

(GRAY *sits down on his bed.*)

PEEPING TOM: That's it. Just relax . . . Lemme do it for you. Lemme rub it for you. Here. Lemme make it good . . . (*A beat*) Baby . . . Baby . . . I love you, baby . . . Daddy loves you, baby . . . (*A beat*) Baby, how is it for you? Is it good? (*No response*) Baby, tell me what you feel. You feel like—

GRAY: Like—I'm all alone.

PEEPING TOM: No, baby, I'm here. I'm with you.

GRAY: No, I'm—so alone.

PEEPING TOM: Baby . . .

GRAY: So . . . alone.

PEEPING TOM: No, baby . . .

GRAY: Frank's . . .

PEEPING TOM: Forget about Frank.

GRAY: Frank's . . .

PEEPING TOM: You don't need Frank.

GRAY: Frank's . . .

PEEPING TOM: I said forget about Frank.

GRAY: They took him.

PEEPING TOM: Huh?

(*A beat*)

GRAY: On a stretcher. He couldn't breathe. (*A silence*) God, I don't know. I'm so . . .

PEEPING TOM: What, baby?

GRAY: Alone.

(*A beat, then* PEEPING TOM *hangs up.*)

GRAY: (*Doubling over, receiver in hand.*) No. No. No. No. No.

(GRAY *hangs up the phone. The phone rings.* GRAY *won't answer it. The phone rings. A beat, then he picks up.*)

GRAY: Please don't.

PEEPING TOM: Baby, I— (*A beat*) What can I say to you . . . baby? (*A beat, then*) Look, I—well—I lost somebody too.

(*A beat.* PEEPING TOM *hangs up.* GRAY *sits a moment then breaks down in tears. He's crying as the lights fade to black.*)

END

WELCOME TO THE MOON

John Patrick Shanley

To James Ryan, for his friendship.

WELCOME TO THE MOON was first presented by The Ensemble Studio Theatre, in New York City, in the fall of 1982. It was directed by Douglas Aibel; scenic design was by Evelyn Sakash; costume design was by Michele Reisch; lighting design was by Mal Sturchio; sound design was by Bruce Ellman; the music director was Barry Koron; and the production stage manager was Teresa Elwert.

The company was as follows:

ROBERT JOY	Anne O'Sullivan
JOHN HENRY KURTZ	James Ryan
MICHAEL ALBERT MANTEL	June Stein

A lowdown Bronx bar. VINNIE, *an Italian guy in his early thirties, is sitting on a stool, nursing a beer.* ARTIE, *the bartender, a wasted old Irishman, sits in the corner, reading the paper.* Enter STEPHEN, *gaunt, dark-eyed.*

VINNIE: Steve?

STEPHEN: Vinnie! How are you?

VINNIE: Good! Good! How you been, man?

STEPHEN: Alright.

VINNIE: You look like shit. It's been three years, man. I've been sitting here counting.

STEPHEN: Too long.

VINNIE: Damn right it's too long. Artie, give Steve a beer.

*(*ARTIE *silently does so.)*

STEPHEN: Thanks. So where is everybody? This used to be the big hangout.

VINNIE: Everybody split a long time since. The Bronx is dead.

STEPHEN: Where'd they all go?

VINNIE: Upstate.

STEPHEN: How come you didn't go?

VINNIE: Guess I'm lazy. Got the job at the Post Office. It's good. And I just don't like upstate. Fuckin' Poughkeepsie. Fuckin' Nanuet. Gimme a break.

STEPHEN: You like the Bronx.

VINNIE: That's right.

STEPHEN: I like the Bronx, too.

VINNIE: Now that does not compute.

STEPHEN: What d'you mean?

VINNIE: You were the first one to go.

STEPHEN: It just worked out that way. I went in the army, and by the time I got out . . .

VINNIE: Yeah, I know. By the time you got out, time and tide had you by the balls, and you were on your way to who knows where. Anyway, why would you come back to the Bronx? The Bronx is dead.

STEPHEN: There's still some neighborhoods that seem okay.

VINNIE: The Bronx is like one a those moon craters, man. Another couple of years, they're gonna be sendin' astronauts up here. Guys from Houston 'ill be collecting rocks on Tremont Avenue. So how's Manhattan?

STEPHEN: Manhattan's all right. It's good. Exciting. Always a lot going on.

VINNIE: Uh-huh.

STEPHEN: Good museums.

VINNIE: Museums. Yeah, they're electrifying.

STEPHEN: I can walk to school.

VINNIE: Still in school! Ain't that some shit!

STEPHEN: Well, I wasn't in right along. There was the service. And then a lot of shitty jobs.

VINNIE: And then you got married.

STEPHEN: Yeah.

VINNIE: What is she again?

STEPHEN: A speech pathologist.

VINNIE: A speech pathologist. It sounds fuckin' hideous. I live with a speech pathologist.

STEPHEN: Very nice.

VINNIE: Sorry. I'm hungry. Artie, what do you got to eat?

ARTIE: Canadian bacon and cheese.

VINNIE: Gimme one. You want one?

STEPHEN: All right.

VINNIE: Two.

ARTIE: (*Puts sandwiches in a little oven.*) It'll take twelve minutes.

VINNIE: We're not going nowhere.

STEPHEN: Vinnie . . .

VINNIE: Yeah?

STEPHEN: Vinnie . . . It's good to see you, man. (*Starts to cry.*)

VINNIE: It's good to see you, too, man. Time goes by, and everybody goes away, and you see what you had.

STEPHEN: It's true.

VINNIE: You went out and stood on the corner, and everybody you ever knew was hanging there with you.

STEPHEN: You know . . .

VINNIE: It was your neighborhood. It was something to be inside of. You could do anything because you knew the fuckin' rules.

STEPHEN: You know, I think I left my wife.

VINNIE: What d'you mean, you think you left your wife?

STEPHEN: Things have been bad for a long time. I don't know why. School is driving me up the wall. I can't seem to . . . I can't seem to find . . . There's nothing left that I enjoy.

VINNIE: I'm sorry.

STEPHEN: Nothing happened. That's the really strange thing. I just told her I felt like going . . . coming to the Bronx, you know, the old neighborhood, and she said okay. And I walked out.

VINNIE: Don't sound final to me. You can go back.

STEPHEN: I don't think I can. I don't want to.

VINNIE: It's your life.

STEPHEN: We were . . . We're friends, Vinnie. I know I didn't call you for three years, and I know I didn't keep in touch much for years before that, but, we're friends.

VINNIE: Yeah.

STEPHEN: I don't really have any friends in Manhattan. I know people, but . . .

VINNIE: Shut up.

STEPHEN: Yeah.

VINNIE: Look, Steve. How do you feel?

STEPHEN: I'm all right.

VINNIE: Yeah?

STEPHEN: Yeah.

VINNIE: 'Cause when I got your call, I thought you might like to see some of the old crowd. So I phoned around. A couple of the folks should be here in a minute. Is that gonna be okay?

STEPHEN: Who?

VINNIE: Ronny.

STEPHEN: Ronny. Yeah, I'd like to see Ronny. How's he doing?

VINNIE: Bad. Ronny's always doing bad. Tried to kill himself.

STEPHEN: No!

VINNIE: Three times.

STEPHEN: Really?

VINNIE: Yeah. I make him come around. He comes to my house sometimes. A few beers. Whatever. To keep him from thinking.

STEPHEN: About what?

VINNIE: I don't know. But whenever he starts thinking about it, he goes right down the tubes.

STEPHEN: Who else?

VINNIE: Shirley.

STEPHEN: Shirley.

VINNIE: Shirley Dunbar.

STEPHEN: She's coming here?

VINNIE: Yeah. She should be here now.

STEPHEN: Bartender!

VINNIE: His name's Artie.

STEPHEN: Artie!

ARTIE: The sandwiches aren't ready yet. A little bell rings when the sandwiches are ready.

STEPHEN: Gimme a big glass of tequila.

VINNIE: What are you doing?

ARTIE: How many shots?

STEPHEN: Five.

VINNIE: Five!

ARTIE: Okay. One. Two. Three. Four. Five.

VINNIE: What are you doing?

STEPHEN: You don't know what you've done.

VINNIE: I guess not.

STEPHEN: Shirley's coming here.

VINNIE: So?

STEPHEN: You know she was my girlfriend.

VINNIE: She was your girlfriend when you were seventeen. Hey, you been seeing her on the sly?

STEPHEN: I haven't laid eyes on her since the day we broke up.

VINNIE: That was fourteen years ago.

STEPHEN: So?

VINNIE: So what are you doing?

STEPHEN: I'm trying to drink enough tequila to hold myself together.

VINNIE: What the hell are you talking about?

STEPHEN: Don't you understand? That's why my marriage is breaking up! That's why I can't make it through college! That's why I can't gain any weight! Can't sleep! Can't . . . live. I'm still in love with Shirley Dunbar! (VINNIE *bursts out laughing.*)

VINNIE: You're kidding me?

STEPHEN: I can't joke about it.

VINNIE: But it was fourteen years ago!

STEPHEN: Five thousand, one hundred and twenty-three days ago.

VINNIE: Wow.

STEPHEN: The day we broke up, I knew it wasn't over. I knew we'd have to meet at least one more time. I was crying. I could see that she didn't understand, didn't want to understand. The thing we had was big. I joined the service to get away. I couldn't stand seeing her walking down the street, knowing that she wasn't mine anymore. That's why I never came back to live in the Bronx! That's why I hardly ever called you! Why I hardly ever called anybody from the old days. You were all part of that time, the time Shirley and I were together. The only time in my life I was every really alive! (STEPHEN *downs the tequila at one toss, throws himself down on the bar, and begins to sob violently. The sandwich bell rings.*)

ARTIE: (*Serving sandwiches, apparently unfazed.*) Two Canadian bacon and cheese. You want mustard with those? (*Getting no answer, he shrugs and goes back to his paper.*)

VINNIE: I am impressed. Here I thought you were just another nice shaky guy looking for his roots, and you turn out to be Heathcliff. "I cannot live without my love, I cannot die without my soul!" Welcome to the moon. (*Spots something outside.*) Oh shit. Steve, Ronny's coming down the block. I know it's a lot to ask, but can you pull yourself together? It's just that Ronny is real easy to get depressed, and he is always trying to do himself in, and... Can you hear me? (STEPHEN's *crying has continued unabated.*) Oh well. Fuck it. (*Ronny, a very short, very depressed guy, enters slowly. Without breaking rhythm, he joins* STEPHEN *at the bar, strikes the identical pose, and commences to sob with equal violence. A moment passes like this.*) You know what you two guys need? Canadian bacon and cheese. (*The two stop crying, take the sandwiches, and start to chew. There is an occasional whimper.*) You want some mustard? Artie, give them mustard. (*They take mustard from Artie.*) That's it.

RONNY: Hi, Steve.

STEPHEN: Hi, Ronny.

RONNY: Long time, no see.

STEPHEN: Yeah. How you been?

RONNY: Bad. Real bad.

STEPHEN: Me too.

RONNY: Artie. Gimme whatever Steve's drinking.

ARTIE: He's drinking five shots of tequila.

RONNY: All right! Give us a round.

ARTIE: One. Two. Three. Four. Five. One . . .

VINNIE: Hey, Artie, could you count to yourself!

ARTIE: Okay. (*Whispers.*) Two. Three. Four. Five.

VINNIE: Ronny, you shouldn't be drinking a drink like that. You know how you get.

RONNY: You're right, Vinnie. (*Drinks it down; then to* STEPHEN.) I'm an attempted suicide. I've tried to kill myself three times. First time, I tied my feet to this big rock, and jumped in the Bronx River. But the water was only two feet deep. I stood there all day. I thought maybe the pollution would kill me. Buncha Spanish kids came and made fun of me. I finally went home. Then last year, I cut my throat. Right there. But I had to stop because it hurt. The third time, I threw myself in front of the A train, but the fuckin' thing broke down before it got to me. Lately I've been eating in all the restaurants that have health violations. That might do it. Who knows?

I've missed you, Steve. I wasn't much when you left, but I'm a total fuckin' disaster now.

STEPHEN: At least you've had the guts to . . . (*Starts to cry again.*)

RONNY: What's the matter with him?

VINNIE: He just left his wife.

RONNY: That's the mouth disease lady, right?

STEPHEN: Speech pathologist! (*Goes back to crying.*)

RONNY: Right.

VINNIE: You ain't gonna believe this, but he's still in love with Shirley Dunbar!

RONNY: Really?

VINNIE: He's been in love with her for fourteen years without seeing her.

STEPHEN: I can see her in my mind! (*Goes back to crying.*)

RONNY: Sure you can, man! Sure you can! I know what's the matter with him, Vinnie, and it's real bad.

VINNIE: What?

RONNY: He's obsessed, man! He's got his fuckin' self an obsession.

VINNIE: How do you know?

RONNY: I know. I want you to do me a favor, Vin. I want you to give me five minutes with him. Take a walk around the block. I can help him. I know about this.

VINNIE: You do?

RONNY: Yeah.

VINNIE: But Shirley's coming. I invited her. She should be here any minute.

RONNY: All the more reason, man. Gimme five minutes right now, before she gets here, to straighten him out. I can do it, Vinnie. Gimme the chance!

VINNIE: Alright. (*To* STEVE.) I'm going out for a few minutes, okay? (STEVE *nods through his tears. Exit* VINNIE.)

RONNY: Steve! Steve! You gotta listen to me, Steve. There isn't much time. I know how you feel. You love Shirley, right? Shirley don't love you, right? It's a tragedy, right? You don't have to tell me. I know it's a tragedy. I know . . . 'cause I got the same thing. I'm gonna tell you what I've never told anybody. And you gotta understand quick 'cause there's no time! I'm in love with Vinnie. That's right! And I always have been. But I know it can't work so I never told him. That's why I'm a suicide attempt. Because my life is ruined from loving someone who don't love me.

STEPHEN: Me too.

RONNY: I know! I know! And that's why I want you to commit suicide with me.

STEPHEN: You do?

RONNY: It's perfect! We both kill ourselves right now, and then they find us. The two idiots who are responsible! Will you do it?

STEPHEN: How?

RONNY: A really good way. Plastic bags. (*Pulls two plastic bags and drawstrings out of his jacket.*) We just put these over our heads and die.

STEPHEN: How long will it take?

RONNY: Not long! How much air could be in a little plastic bag?

STEPHEN: All right, I'll do it!

RONNY: (*Handing him a bag.*) We ain't got much time. We'll die quicker if we do exercise. That makes you breathe faster.

(RONNY *and* STEPHEN *don their bags, and do jumping jacks. Then they run up and down the length of the bar.* RONNY *urges* STEPHEN *along, shouting "Faster" and "Run" and such. They both grow weak.*) This is it! This is it! (RONNY *lays down on the bar, and* STEPHEN *lays down on the floor.* ARTIE *watches all this without concern. Enter* SHIRLEY, *blond, a little plump, big round eyes. She takes it all in and screams.*)

SHIRLEY: They got bags on their heads! (*Enter* VINNIE.) Everybody's got bags on their heads!

ARTIE: I don't have a bag on my head. (VINNIE *rips the bags off their heads. They are both a little dazed, but otherwise fine.*)

VINNIE: That was very immature, Ronny.

RONNY: Four times.

VINNIE: And Steve, I'm surprised at you.

RONNY: Four times.

STEPHEN: It really seemed like the right thing to do.

SHIRLEY: Is that you, Stephen?

STEPHEN: Shirley?

SHIRLEY: Hi.

STEPHEN: Hi. My hair's all messed up.

SHIRLEY: That's all right.

VINNIE: (*To* RONNY.) Are you okay?

RONNY: Yeah.

VINNIE: Why do you keep trying to kill yourself, Ronny?

RONNY: Do you really wanna know?

STEPHEN: You look great.

SHIRLEY: You too. You got great color.

STEPHEN: That's 'cause I was suffocating.

SHIRLEY: Oh.

RONNY: I'm in love with you.

VINNIE: You're what?

SHIRLEY: Did you hear what he said?

RONNY: I'm in love with you.

SHIRLEY: He said it again.

VINNIE: That's impossible.

SHIRLEY: Oh my God, he's a faggot!

STEPHEN: Shirley, I love you.

SHIRLEY: I never woulda guessed it! I knew Ronny was crazy, but a crazy faggot?

RONNY: I loved you ever since we were little boys. On the see-saw. Playing curb ball. I never said nothing cause I knew it would hurt your feelings and you wouldn't like me anymore. I figured it was easier just to kill myself.

VINNIE: I don't know what to say.

RONNY: What could you say?

VINNIE: I love you . . . too?

SHIRLEY: Oh my God, Vinnie's a faggot, too!

RONNY: You what?

VINNIE: I guess I love you, too.

SHIRLEY: And they're brazen! They're brazen faggots!

RONNY: Why didn't you ever say anything?

VINNIE: Why didn't you?

RONNY, VINNIE: I was afraid.

STEPHEN: Shirley.

SHIRLEY: You are straight, right?

STEPHEN: Yeah, I'm straight.

SHIRLEY: That's a relief.

STEPHEN: Shirley, I love you.

SHIRLEY: You do?

STEPHEN: Yes.

SHIRLEY: Still?

STEPHEN: Yes.

SHIRLEY: Why?

STEPHEN: I don't know.

SHIRLEY: It's been about a hundred years now you've been loving me.

STEPHEN: I know.

SHIRLEY: And I've never loved you.

STEPHEN: I know.

SHIRLEY: The old crowd's together again.

STEPHEN: Yes. (ARTIE *sings "When You Were Sweet Sixteen." He has a lovely tenor. The two couples look into each others' eyes with sweet sadness.*)

ARTIE: (*Singing.*) When first I saw the love light in your eyes
I dreamt the world held nought but joy for me
And even though we've drifted far apart
I never dream but that I dream of thee
I love you as I never loved before
When first I saw you on the village green

Come to me 'ere this dream of life is o'er
I love as I loved you when you were sweet
When you were sweet
Sixteen

(*The lights go down.*)

END

BRIGHTS

David Smilow

BRIGHTS premiered at the Harold Clurman Theatre in New York City, May 1995. It was directed by Diana Gold; the set and lighting were designed by Dan Kozan. The cast was as follows:

KAREN BARNES   Dora Maxine
FRED BARNES   Jon Sperry
VERA BROUSSARD   Emilie Devezac
RICHARD MEYERS   R. J. Carlson

(*The interior of a car.* FRED BARNES *drives. His wife,* KAREN, *is in the seat beside him. Behind her sits* RICHARD MEYERS, *while* VERA BROUSSARD *is behind* FRED. RICHARD *studies the back of* KAREN's *head.*)

RICHARD: First the honeymoon. Now a weekend in the country. Your life's pretty much the tits.

VERA: Except for their house guests.

RICHARD: What. That wasn't rude.

VERA: You were fine up to the tits.

KAREN: Actually, I've always liked that expression. You don't hear it much anymore.

VERA: Wait. Richard's usually good for a few items that shouldn't be said at all.

FRED: Jerk. (*He squints up at the rearview mirror.*) This guy's tailgating me. With his high beams on.

(KAREN *glances out the rear window.*)

KAREN: No, honey. It's just the two headlights.

FRED: They're those high-low kind. They've got to be. Look how bright they are. Ass.

KAREN: (*after a beat, to* RICHARD *and* VERA) Fred told me you're working on a screenplay together.

VERA: Between fights.

RICHARD: Vera and I basically have zero respect for each other, so we figured we'd be partners.

FRED: Why do people do this?

(KAREN *looks out the rear window again.*)

KAREN: Wow. He is pretty close.

FRED: We could be towing him, for God's sake. But here's Route Eight, so . . . (*He turns the wheel. A second later, the interior's flooded with light again.*) Oh, terrific.

(RICHARD *glances back.*)

RICHARD: Maybe you are towing him.

KAREN: Sweetie, don't let it bother you.

RICHARD: Personally, as an actor, I'm very comfortable being bathed in light. Of course it only seems to happen in the back seats of cars these days. Which is why I've been reduced to writing a screenplay.

VERA: Down, Simba.

RICHARD: Skating dangerously close to self-pity, am I? What the hell. That's what weekends are for. (*He leans closer to* KAREN.) So how come you're still Baumgarten?

VERA: Here we go. Off to the races.

RICHARD: (*to* KAREN) Am I being rude?

KAREN: No.

(RICHARD *gives* VERA *a smug "so there" look.*)

RICHARD: Then what's the story? You're just not a Barnes kind of gal?

KAREN: I married Fred, not his name.

RICHARD: I was wondering about that too.

VERA: Why don't you ask her how her last pap smear went, while you're at it.

(FRED's *gripping the wheel tighter and stares at the rearview mirror.*)

FRED: What does this idiot want?

RICHARD: What any idiot wants, probably. No-brainer job. Comfy den—maybe in the country. A wife to bore.

(KAREN *stiffens, then turns to face* RICHARD.)

KAREN: Have you ever been married?

RICHARD: Not to the right person.

VERA: Either time.

RICHARD: Well hell, all the keepers end up with Freds.

KAREN: If they're lucky.

RICHARD: Or figure that's as lucky as they're going to get. (VERA *mouths "Back off" to* RICHARD.) Fuck off? Oh, back off.

VERA: Christ, you met the woman less than two hours ago. Can't you keep the conversation neutral till we at least get out of Connecticut? Talk about the weather. Or pets.

KAREN: How about bad movies? We can all agree on some of those.

(*She smiles pointedly at* RICHARD, *who squirms.*)

RICHARD: Beautiful day, wasn't it? I saw an Airedale outside Zabar's with a parrot on its back.

KAREN: What was that one called . . . ? Oh yeah; *Dying's Easy.*

VERA: You saw that? God, nobody else did. Not even the producer.

RICHARD: Vera.

VERA: (*portentous announcer voice*) "*Dying's Easy* . . . Sitting through it's impossible." (KAREN *laughs.*)

RICHARD: Couple of goddamn sadists. (*He fumes for a few beats.*) It was a fucking job.

KAREN: And you figured that was as lucky as you were going to get?

(*She and* RICHARD *eye each other.* FRED *abruptly turns the wheel again. Again the bright light fills the interior an instant later.*)

FRED: Jesus God.

VERA: We've still got company, huh?

RICHARD: Chill, Freddy. You're getting that old I'm-a-goner look. (*to* KAREN) I've seen it every week for the last two years. But your hubby's a terrier. Mark my words, the day's going to come when he does beat me at racquetball.

VERA: Then what'll you do—find a new partner?

RICHARD: Hell no. I love Fred. He's everything I'm not. Polite. Reasonable. Employed. The man's a pussycat. Not to mention a totally open book. With Fred Barnes, what you see is what's really there.

(*All three look at* FRED, *who stares up at the mirror with genuine dread.* KAREN'*s disturbed.*)

KAREN: Honey, forget the car. We'll get to the house whether there's an asshole on our tail or not. (*to* VERA *and* RICHARD) Excuse me.

RICHARD: Hey, there's an asshole on everybody's tail.

VERA: (*under her breath*) She's sure got one behind her.

RICHARD: That's another thing. By now, most guys would've hit the gas and lost this prick. Not Fred. Nope. He's got his way of doing things, and that's that. Right now he's driving, which means he'd rather cross the whole damn country with this moron on his butt than do it any different.

FRED: (*to* KAREN, *shaky*) I swear I didn't want this to happen.

RICHARD: (*sotto voce, to* VERA) He must go to pieces if the magazine section's missing from the Sunday *Times.*

KAREN/VERA: Shut up.

KAREN: I'm sorry. I just wish you'd . . . shut up.

RICHARD: Fine. No problem. (*muses bitterly*) You know why people don't like me?

VERA: Absolutely.

RICHARD: It's because they can't stand me reminding them of the one thing I care about above all others.

VERA: Yourself.

RICHARD: The truth! It's too tough to swallow. And too dangerous to bring up. God forbid someone has to deal with a point-blank shot of honesty. Or an audience does. That's why the hell I'm not working.

KAREN: Maybe you're just not talented enough.

RICHARD: That's bullshit.

KAREN: Have *you* seen *Dying's Easy?*

FRED: No, no, no . . . (*He can't tear his eyes away from the rearview mirror.*)

KAREN: Goddamn it, Fred, would you please . . . ? (*She trails off, upset.*)

RICHARD: Ah. Now I get it. You know, I could never figure out why after forty-some-odd Thursday nights of racquetball, Fred never asked me to come meet his new fiancée. But it just hit me: he was afraid.

FRED: Oh Lord.

RICHARD: Afraid I'd stir you up—get you thinking about stuff best left tucked away.

KAREN: Like what?

RICHARD: The life you really wanted.

KAREN: (*to* VERA) Are all actors like this?

VERA: The ones who can't get work are.

RICHARD: What did you dream about when you were a kid? Growing up and finding a guy who'd fall apart when he was tailgated? I don't think so.

KAREN: Gee, this ought to be a terrific weekend.

RICHARD: You want heat. Light. *Size.* Something new to reach for all the time, even if you can't always get your hand around it. I know, because that's how I am. But you know what the difference is between us?

VERA: She's a human being.

RICHARD: I'm still grabbing at the world. You're settling for that cozy den—and a guy who'll sit in it.

KAREN: I love Fred!

FRED: (*distracted*) Huh? What?

RICHARD: Then you're in great shape. Because this is exactly how the ride's going to be for the next forty years. Smooth and steady and way too slow for the people with the brights.

(KAREN'*s shaken.* VERA *glances at* RICHARD.)

VERA: Nice work.

(FRED *suddenly screams at the rearview mirror.*)

FRED: Damn you!

KAREN: Will you stop it!?

FRED: It's them.

RICHARD: What, in the car behind us?

FRED: Who else can it be? Someone who just happened to take Nine G, Route Eight *and* Marconi Road the same time I did? No.

VERA: Are you saying this car's following us?

FRED: Following. Chasing. It doesn't really make much difference how you put it now.

RICHARD: (*a bit spooked*) You're nuts. Who'd chase you?

FRED: Them.

KAREN: Fred, you're scaring me. Why would people be after you?

FRED: Because of what I did.

RICHARD: Relax. They don't sic goon squads on people for having overdue library books.

FRED: (*to* KAREN) I didn't go to my Aunt Gussie's cottage in Vermont last summer. I was in Marseilles.

KAREN: France?

FRED: And Tangiers. I was . . . helping a friend, but something went wrong.

RICHARD: Christ, this sounds like something out of our goddamn screenplay.

FRED: All I had to do was pick up the package and drop it off someplace.

KAREN: A package. What was in it?

FRED: Money. Maybe drugs. They never told me what I was carrying.

VERA: "Never told you?" This was some kind of regular gig?

FRED: (*nods*) Since nineteen eighty. No, eighty-one; I remember. It was just after I got my Sears card.

RICHARD: Jesus.

VERA: You got paid and all?

FRED: They treated me like royalty. They really did. First-class flights. Five-star hotels. Always. And after, when they handed me my money, they'd say "Thank you so much, Mr. Barnes." I think that's why I kept doing it. I liked how it felt being Mr. Barnes.

(KAREN *looks at* FRED *as if for the first time.*)

KAREN: Mr. Barnes. (FRED *meets her gaze.*) What happened in Marseilles?

FRED: The delivery was supposed to be at a bakery. The back door. In an alley. Only nobody answered when I knocked, and when I turned around there were two kids standing there. Kids. They were built like a couple of Mike Tysons, but still, they really were only kids.

VERA: Who ripped you off.

FRED: No, that's just it. I fought back. And killed one of them.

RICHARD: Get the fuck out of here.

FRED: It wasn't a plan. I didn't hate the boy. My hands ended up on his throat, though. And I squeezed, and kept squeezing till his tongue flopped out and his slobber was all over my sleeve. When I let go, he dropped like a sack of sand. Finished.

(*Silence.* VERA *turns to* RICHARD.)

VERA: This is better than our screenplay.

RICHARD: Wait a minute. How do you know the jerk-off wasn't just passed out?

FRED: I know.

RICHARD: How!

FRED: I smashed his skull with a brick.

KAREN: Fred.

RICHARD: (*not wanting to believe*) Where'd you get the brick?

VERA: The other kid got away.

FRED: (*nods*) And told his people, who obviously found these people (*indicates the following car*) who found me. Found us.

RICHARD: What's this "us" crap? You're the Marseilles strangler.

FRED: But you're with him.

KAREN: My God.

VERA: I think I'm . . . Yeah, I'm definitely going to throw up.

RICHARD: Hold it, hold it. This is bullshit. Fred Barnes, drug mule to the stars? Bare-handed killer? Come on. This is a guy who can't win a stinking racquetball game in two years, for Christ's sake.

(KAREN*'s eyes seem to glow a little brighter.*)

KAREN: I think it could've happened.

RICHARD: Okay, even if it did, we're supposed to believe that out of all the cars in the world, this one's got the bad guys in it? No, sorry. I don't buy it.

KAREN: (*looking ahead*) Honey. Pufton Lane.

(FRED *turns the wheel sharply. Everyone looks behind them. An instant later the light floods the interior.* RICHARD *and* VERA *scream.*)

RICHARD: Stop the car! Stop the goddamn car!

FRED: You'd be dead before your shoe touched the ground.

VERA: (*to* RICHARD) You had to keep hocking him to invite us up to the country, didn't you?! Moron. Idiot!

KAREN: Fred, what are we going to do? The driveway's just over this hill.

FRED: I know, I know.

RICHARD: The driveway?! Fuck the driveway! Just go. Drive. Floor it!

FRED: We'll never be able to outrun these people.

(*He reaches under the seat and comes up with an antitheft club, which he holds weapon-like.*)

KAREN: You're going to fight them?

FRED: What else is there?

VERA: That's it. See you. Good-bye.

RICHARD: Shit, shit, shit!

(FRED *tries to smile at* KAREN.)

FRED: Some surprise, huh? I'm sorry.

KAREN: There's the driveway.

FRED: You do know I love you, right? (KAREN *nods, terrified—and a bit turned on.*) Hang on. (*He wrenches the wheel and slams on the brakes.*) Come on, you sons of bitches!

(VERA *and* RICHARD *scream and duck out of sight. But as* KAREN *and* FRED *whirl to face their pursuers, they're stunned.*)

KAREN: They kept going. (RICHARD *and* VERA *pop up. All four react with a jolt.*)

VERA: And *now* they turned their brights on. (VERA, RICHARD *and* KAREN *stare at* FRED, *still clutching his weapon.* KAREN *shows the beginnings of a smile.*)

END

R.A.W.
('CAUSE I'M A WOMAN)

Diana Son

R.A.W. ('CAUSE I'M A WOMAN) premiered at the Ohio Theatre as part of the T.W.E.E.D. New Works Festival in May 1993. It was directed by Lenora Champagne; the lighting was designed by Richard Schaefer; the production stage manager was Wendy Onlette. The cast was as follows:

RAUNCHY ASIAN WOMAN 1	Liana Pai
RAUNCHY ASIAN WOMAN 2	Lisa Ann Li
RAUNCHY ASIAN WOMAN 3	Kim Ima
RAUNCHY ASIAN WOMAN 4	Elaine Tse

Music: The First four measures of Peggy Lee's "I'm a Woman" repeated long enough to accompany the slides.

Slide: Exotic.
Slide: Submissive.
Slide: Chic.
Slide: Obedient.
Slide: Mysterious.
Slide: Domestic.
Slide: Petite.
Slide: Oriental.
Slide: **R.A.W.**
Slide: **R**aunchy
Slide: **A**sian
Slide: **W**omen

ALL: Fuck!

Music: Intro.

1: In a crowded room,
3: in a smoky place,
2: in a bar with no light,
4: a man walks up to me and says:

Slide: I love your eyes.

1: And I ask him "What is there to love about—"
3: My eyes.

2: That they have given earnest love to men.

4: And complex love to women.

3: That through them he feels the grace that God has lent me.

1: That they're slanted.

3: Making me a geisha.

2: Who will walk on his back.

4: Who'll have dinner on the table and dessert between my legs.

1: Who will give him the blow job of his life.

Music: Cause I'm a woman.

2: And he asks me:

Slide: Where are you from?

2: And I say:

1: From a place where I was neither black nor white.

3: Where I checked the box marked "other."

4: Where I made myself. Where I changed.

2: He responds:

Slide: I mean what country are you from?

2: Because he wants to hear:

4: I'm from a fishing village off the Yangtze river.

3: Where my mother was a shaman who taught me shiatsu.

1: Where my father made musical instruments out of fish bones and moss.

2: Where I invented tai chi.

Music: 'Cause I'm a woman. W-O-M-A-N.

3: He says:

Slide: I've never been with an Oriental woman before.

3: And I try to give him the benefit of the doubt.

4: I think "been with" that comes from "to be."

1: He wants to be with me.

2: He wants to know me.

3: He wants to fuck me.

4: He wants to see if my clit is sideways.
2: He wants to make me moan in ancient languages.
1: He wants me to bark like a Lhasa Apso.
3: He wants to wow me with the size of his non–Asian dick.

Music: *'Cause I'm a woman. W-O-M-A-N.*
   I'll say it again.

4: Then he says:

Slide: *I love Oriental women.*

3: And I want to say.
4: So do I.

Music: *'Cause I'm a woman. W-O-M-A-N.*
   I'll say it again.
   I got a twenty dollar gold piece that says
   there ain't nothing I can't do
   I can make a dress out of a feedbag
   and I can make a man out of you.
   'Cause I'm a—

Music: *Intro.*

1: I will not give you a massage.
3: I will not scrub your back.
2: I will not cook exotic meals using animal parts that aren't
   normally eaten.
4: I will not *not* get on top.
1: I will not be your Soon Yi.
3: I will not kill myself to save your son.
2: I will not light your cigarette afterwards.
4: I will not let you come without me.
1: I will not be your china doll.
3: I will not be a virgin.

2: I will not call you papasan.

4: I will not worship you.

1: I will not be your fetish.

Stop music.

4: But I will love.

3: And be loved.

2: Yes.

1: I will.

4: But not by a:

Slide: SWM
Slide: MBM
Slide: Bi-Curious F
Slide: Open-minded DJM
Slide: Separated HM with kids

[The slides and lines occur at the same time.]

Slide: East Asian scholar
1: Geek.
Slide: Vietnam vet
3: Psycho.
Slide: Ivy leaguer
2: Jock.
Slide: New Age philosopher
4: Granola head.
Slide: Long-haired musician.
1: Slob.

Slide: Looking for

Slide: Oriental Beauty
3: Slant-eyed slut.
Slide: Sexy Asian Gal
2: Manicurist with a bad perm.
Slide: Bi-Oriental F
4: Joan Chen lookalike for him and his wife.

Slide: Import from the East
1: Non-English-speaking babe with bound feet.
Slide: Vegetarian SAF preferably from Nassau or Queens
3: PC Chinese girl with a fast car.

Slide: of Inner Beauty
2: Who won't talk too much.
Slide: And Spiritual Strength
4: Has no ideas of her own.
Slide: Who is Graceful
1: Easy to flip over.
Slide: And likes to be wined and dined
3: Gets drunk on one glass of chardonnay.

[the slides go quickly, the lines overlap]

Slide: To show me exciting new horizons
Slide: Give me a first time cultural experience
Slide: Exchange sensual customs with
1: To do what the white girls won't do.
3: To act out his most exotic fantasies.
2: To let him come in my mouth and say "thank you."
4: To be his dominant-obedient, desirable-untouchable,
   autonomous-dependent, virginwhore.
ALL: **It hath made me R.A.W.**

ALL: R.A.W.
3: 'Cause I'm from New Hampshire. How exotic is New
   Hampshire?
ALL: R.A.W.
2: 'Cause I'm not even that good in bed, O.K.?
ALL: R.A.W.
1: 'Cause these are the kinds of creeps I end up going out with.
   Why?
ALL: R.A.W.
4: 'Cause how am I supposed to be a virgin and a whore at the
   same fucking time.
ALL: R.A.W.

4: Because I want to love.

3: And be loved.

2: Yes.

1: I do.

3: I had my first boyfriend when I was 15 years old Paul Rossman.

4: Built like a brick shithouse Paul Rossman.

3: He lived in the old part of town in an old Colonial house with his divorcée mom. Once I caught them dancing. She was drunk he was embarrassed I was glad I came in when I did.

2: Paul was six-feet-two inches of purebred whiteboy.

3: He had flaky chapped lips which he marinated in Vaseline kissing him was like licking a carburetor but we had a big love.

1: Huge it consumed me.

3: I was just 15.

2: It was early for love.

3: I had feathered hair parted in the middle.

4: It was early for sex.

3: I wore pink oxford shirts tucked into wide wale corduroys.

1: I was the only Asian in town I was a famous preppie.

3: Paul used to drive me home after field hockey practice "Don't bring him in the house!" Mom would say, "It stinks, I've been cooking daddy's food. It smells. It smells like kimchee." Mom fed me lasagne with Green Giant green beans as daddy's dinner reeked on the stove. "Don't eat the kimchee," Mom would say as she brought daddy's food to the table "You'll never have an American boyfriend." "I have Paul," I would say. "Kimchee smells terrible," Mom said. "It's not nice for Paul." But mom ate daddy's food. Mom ate kimchee. "How come you can eat kimchee?" She gave me green Jello for dessert. "Because daddy eats it too. You can't smell it if you both eat it." Mom was Asian. Daddy was too. I ate green Jello with little marshmallows in it and clean my breath was clean. My breath was clean for kissing Paul Rossman.

2: A beautiful woman should never have to beg for the love of a man but I. Have begged because I. Am not beautiful outside no I know. They called me plateface when I was a child not just to tease me because I was Chinese because I was Japanese because I was Korean Thai Vietnamese all wrapped up into one no I know. My face is flat and truly flat when I was a child. And company came we ate store-bought desserts off of white china dishes they measured seven inches across seven inches up and down and sneaking one into the bathroom I put one up to my face and seven inches all around it fit me. The plate fit my face like a glove. And my eyes are squinty. Small not almond-shaped like the pretty geishas but slits like papercuts tiny. My hair is straight flat not shiny like the girl on the macadamia nut bottle but dry I got a perm it helps but I hate the smell. I have trouble finding men you're not surprised no I know. I took an ad out in the personal ads Single Asian Female looking for Single Man of any race to love to care for to share bountiful joy with. Will answer all replies. I got a jillion replies a bouquet of hopeful suitors. I answered them all I said I would. It took days I found some nice ones. I arranged to meet them at convenient times in attractive places. The men came but they wore disappointed faces. I said I never promised you I was pretty. They said you said you were Asian—I assumed. I forgave them these men who were not so cute themselves. I held no grudge I let them off the hook. Outside I am ugly no I know. But I am beautiful in my heart yes God knows my heart is the home of great love. These men weren't beautiful inside or out. I missed nothing. I don't feel bad. This beautiful woman will never beg.

4: No one ever suspects me of being queer so its hard to score *dates* they're so *innocent* these women I mean get a *clue*. A hand on her thigh when we're sitting next to each other, a finger down her back as I stand behind her, a kiss on her neck instead of her cheek and they think "She's so warm." I'm so warm I'm *hot* somebody *notice* me Jesus *Christ!* What's a girl gotta do to get some attention from the same *sex* these days stick my tongue down her throat and say "and I don't just mean that as friends"? I mean a goodlooking girl should not have to spin her own bean as often as I do. And I know what it is I know what it is no one thinks the nice little oriental girl likes to DIVE FOR TUNA. Likes to MUNCH MUFF. Likes to EAT HAIR PIE but I do I'm telling you I do. I've had plenty of guys as lovers and I can tell you that getting RAMMED that having someone's ROD IN MY FACE didn't really do it for me I like girls and as soon as I can get one TO LOOK AT ME like a woman I'll probably be . . . I don't know, maybe really happy. There was this woman at work she wasn't even my type physically but she was really funny I loved the way she used her hands the way she touched things. I wanted her hands to touch me I thought they would feel really good. So I flirted I asked her out I tried to kiss her she said wait. *Wait.* Are you saying you're gay? She was shocked she was embarrassed she said she had no idea. Why would a cute Asian girl have to be queer? I mean am I more cute than Asian? Am I more Asian than queer? And should I even bother asking myself these questions if she wasn't willing to let me be all of them?

1: Looking back I'm surprised we managed to love each other at all when the whole relationship was based on what we were not, who we were never going to be, what we weren't going to ask of each other. We were not a classic Korean couple. You did not pick me up from my mother's house in Queens in your top-of-the-line Hyundai. I did not kiss you on the cheek and tell you I had a nice time. In fact, we met in a dingy nightclub where you were dancing on the bar and I was shooting bourbon straight from the bottle. We took the subway to my apartment in Chelsea, fucked each other goodnight and I didn't have to tell you I had a nice time. I got involved with you *despite* the fact that you were a Korean man and I assumed that you made the same forgiveness of me. I grew to love your gentle wildness, your clumsy grace, your spirit your spirit. And I had leaned on the hope that there were similar things to love about me. I didn't want you to think of me as a Korean woman. Men who have been attracted to me for being Korean were interested in who I am only on the surface without knowing who I am not in the deepest part of my heart. I am not ashamed of the presence of my heritage on my face but I mourn shamefully for the absence of Korean in my heart. You and I had an unspoken pact—I wouldn't be Korean to you if you weren't Korean to me. We went to movies, we threw parties, we spent many sweaty hours in bed and then one otherwise nameless night while my breath was still heavy and your legs were still pressed against mine you looked at me and said *sarang hae*. I had never head it before. *Sarang hae.* You were telling me you loved me and I didn't understand what you were saying. *Sarang hae.* You asked me to say it. I couldn't say it. How could I use words that had no meaning to me to say what I knew in my heart. *Sarang hae.* The next time I say it I'll mean it.

3: I have had glimpses and tall moments of real love.
2: I can be recognized as a woman who has a beauty apart from good looks.
4: I can be cute Asian warm hot queer.
1: And I can love any man who can see what I am as clearly as what I am not.

3: Because I am not bitter.
2: I am not destructively angry.

4: I do not hold a grudge.

1: I am not jaded.

3: I am not fed up.

2: I am not without hope.

4: I am not too hurt to feel victimized.

1: I am not afraid to try again.

3: And I will eat kimchee and kiss you right afterwards.

2: And I will let you love me inside and out.

4: And I will stick my tongue down your throat because we *are* more than friends.

1: And I will spend sweaty hours speaking a language that we both understand.

3: And I will give you the benefit of the doubt.

2: And I will let you know me.

4: And I will have ideas of my own.

1: And I just may give you the blow job of your life, I mean it depends on the ones you've had before.

3: And I will love.

2: And be loved.

4: Yes by God—

1: I will.

3: 'Cause I'm a—

2: W.

4: O.

1: M.

3: A.

2: N.

Slide: That's all.
Music: That's all.

THAT'S ALL

JUDGMENT CALL

Frederick Stroppel

Spring training.

(*Three umpires—*JOE, FRANK *and* HARVEY—*are limbering up for the coming season. They do so by practicing their "safe" and "out" calls. Each has a particular style.* JOE, *a younger umpire, has a flamboyant, attention-getting style.* HARVEY, *the veteran ump, is low-key, self-assured.* FRANK *is introspective. He considers every call carefully before he makes it.*)

JOE: (*throwing his arms out wildly*) SA-A-AFE! SA-A-AFE!

HARVEY: (*a minimalist*) Safe!

FRANK: (*almost questioning*) Safe . . .

JOE: SA-A-A-AFE! (*switching now, jerking his thumb wildly*) OW-W-W-U-UT! YOU'RE OW-W-W-U-UT!

HARVEY: (*a sharp thumb jerk*) Out!

FRANK: (*still on safe, not sure of his hands*) Safe. Safe . . .

JOE: (*gives a strike*) STEEE-RIKE!

HARVEY: (*a different strike call; he leans forward on one knee, extends his palm*) Hi-eek!

FRANK: Out . . . !

HARVEY: Ball four . . .

JOE: SA-A-AFE!

(They go on like this for a few moments, creating a fugal counterpoint of umpirical music. But FRANK grows less and less confident with each call. HARVEY takes note of FRANK's demeanor.)

JOE: *(waves his arms)* NO PITCH! NO PITCH!

(As JOE wanders upstage, HARVEY takes FRANK aside.)

HARVEY: What's up, Frank? You seem a little tentative.

FRANK: I'm rusty, that's all. I haven't done this since October.

HARVEY: Hey, well, you can't walk away for four months and just expect it to all come back to you on the first day. That's why I stay busy. I like to keep those umpiring juices flowing.

JOE: *(waving his arms to the side)* FOUL BALL! FOUL BALL!

HARVEY: *(amused)* Look at the kid. He thinks he's gonna be a star. *(prompts JOE)* Tie goes to the . . .

JOE: *(whirls)* Tie goes to the runner! The runner! *(back to his calls)* STEE-RI-I-E-E-EKE!

(HARVEY laughs, shakes his head.)

FRANK: Had a busy winter, did you?

HARVEY: Sure. Well, you know, I worked the World Series again. My fifth. And then I went with the All-Stars to Japan. Got back in time for the Hot-Stove League. Hit a few baseball clinics, did one of those fantasy camps. Spoke at the Baseball Writers Dinner in New York. Spent two weeks at my umpiring school.

FRANK: That was your vacation, huh?

HARVEY: No such thing as a vacation. Even on my off days, I'd put on a videotape from last season and work on my calls. Can't let these goddamn millionaire players get ahead of you. I always have a copy of the rulebook sitting by my bed, winter or summer. It's the last thing I read at night, first thing I see in the morning. Nobody gets the jump on me.

FRANK: And how's Judy?

HARVEY: Judy's fine. Fine. (*beat*) Actually, she left me. But I think she's fine.

FRANK: Oh, I'm sorry to hear that . . .

HARVEY: So was I, but what are you gonna do? Said she had enough—couldn't take the grind anymore. I don't what grind *she's* talking about—I was the one doing all the traveling. (*to* JOE, *who is deep in umpire concentration*) Hey, Joe: First and second, one out, pop fly to shortstop . . .

JOE: (*signaling*) INFIELD FLY RULE! BATTER IS OUT! Runners advance at their own risk! (JOE *heads back upstage to work on his style*)

HARVEY: (*laughs*) I like that kid. He's crazy. And he idolizes me.

FRANK: So is this a trial separation or what . . . ?

HARVEY: (*dismissing the topic*) Oh, that's old news—yesterday's boxscore. How about you? Let me see your strike call. Come on. Show me what you've got.

(FRANK *shrugs, takes a crouching position*)

FRANK: (*unenthusiastic*) Strike.

HARVEY: (*critical*) Hmm.

FRANK: I know, it's not very decisive . . .

HARVEY: You look like you're afraid to pull the trigger. That's death in this business. You have to snap that strike. (*snapping his hand*) Hi-eeke! Hi-eeke!

FRANK: Maybe I've lost it.

HARVEY: Don't be silly. It's the first day of spring training. A couple of innings behind the dish, you'll be in midseason form. Yes, I think this is gonna be a big year for us. We're gonna break away from the pack early, establish ourselves as the

Number One Umpiring Crew in the American League. The
kid's coming along, Max will be back from his hernia oper-
ation next week, you're still my trusty first lieutenant . . .
and quite frankly, I feel like I'm at the top of my game. I'm
ready to take it to a new level. Got my eyes tested last
week—still 20-15, like an eagle. Did you see my call in
Game Four? The play at plate? Turned the whole series
around. Made the cover of *Sports Illustrated*. A money call, a
goddamn money call. It could very well have been the
defining moment of my career. What do you think?

FRANK: Actually, I didn't watch the Series last year.

HARVEY: (*astonished*) Didn't watch the Series? Were you sick?

FRANK: No, I just wasn't interested.

HARVEY: (*further astonished*) Not interested? Not interested in
the World Series?

JOE: (*argues with imaginary manager*) WHAT DID YOU SAY? BE
CAREFUL! YOU SAY THE MAGIC WORD AND . . .
(*throws imaginary manager out of the game*) THAT'S IT!
YOU'RE OUTTA HERE!

HARVEY: I don't know what to say to that, Frank. How could
you not be interested in the World Series? It's like not being
interested in Christmas.

FRANK: I did a lot of soul-searching this winter. Because, I don't
know, I feel like I'm missing something in my life. All I
know is baseball. I don't know what's going on in the world.
I don't read enough.

HARVEY: That reminds me . . . Hey, Joe—Do me a favor, run
over to the magazine stand and see if *Baseball Digest* is out
yet?

JOE: You got it, Harvey.

(JOE *runs off at full speed*)

HARVEY: There's supposed to be a big article about umpires in this month's issue. I wonder if I'm in there. I'd better be.

FRANK: (*goes on*) We live in such an insular little world here, we get so wrapped up in baseball, on this play and that pitch, that we forget the big picture, the vast, churning canvas of life around us. Look at what's going on in Bosnia.

HARVEY: What?

FRANK: The Serbs, Harvey. The ethnic cleansing. The rapes, the atrocities.

HARVEY: Yes, of course, but you know, that sort of thing goes on all the time.

FRANK: I know. All sorts of horrors and outrages happen every day—in Iraq, in Rwanda, in *America*—and we know nothing about them.

HARVEY: Do you feel better, now that you *do* know about them?

FRANK: It's not about feeling better. It's about . . . knowing. I stand out there on the field and I act like I know everything. But what do I really know? In my heart of hearts, can I say that I really know anything?

HARVEY: What got you started on this, Frank? I've always known you to be a predictable, unimaginative person up till now.

FRANK: (*grimly*) Remember last September, when I blew that call at second?

HARVEY: (*laughs*) Last September? You know how many games I've seen since . . . ?

FRANK: The Blue Jay–Oriole game?

HARVEY: (*remembers*) Oh. You didn't blow that call.

FRANK: I checked the tapes, Harvey, and I blew it. I didn't even see the play. I was screened out, I had no idea. I just said "Safe." "Safe." Because he *looked* safe.

HARVEY: So you guessed. We all guess.

FRANK: It was the *wrong* guess.

HARVEY: Okay, you were wrong. It was *last year*—put it behind you. I blow a call, it's forgotten by morning. Otherwise you drive yourself crazy.

FRANK: But it would have ended the game. The Jays would have won. A crucial game. Instead, the next batter, Ripken, hit a home run off Ashby, and the Orioles won. And it changed everything—the entire season.

HARVEY: Maybe. You don't know.

FRANK: It was the turning point. The Orioles got the wild card, the Blue Jays took a nosedive . . . And the guy was dead at second. I just blew it.

HARVEY: The breaks of the game. The Jays won two years ago, they'll win again.

FRANK: Ashby won't. Being that he's dead.

HARVEY: Dead? Really? When did that happen?

FRANK: I guess when you were in Japan.

HARVEY: Sorry to hear that. He was a good kid, that Don Ashby. Never beefed about a call, always kept his nose clear. What was it, drugs?

FRANK: Killed himself. A bullet in the head.

HARVEY: No kidding? See. I don't approve of tha. That's just a waste.

FRANK: He was depressed.

HARVEY: (*shakes his head*) People nowadays. How can you be depressed when you're playing the greatest game in the world, making all kinds of money? I don't get it.

FRANK: Harvey, he was depressed because he let everyone down, because he was hated and vilified by the fans, because he lost the most important game of the season. Because *I* blew the call.

HARVEY: Oh, so that's what this is about . . .

FRANK: I was screened out of the play, so now Ashby's dead. He's dead, and that's my fault.

HARVEY: Well, if you look at it that way, sure, it's your fault.

FRANK: How else can I look at it?

HARVEY: He was a grown man, he knew the pitfalls of being a reliever. You can't handle the pressure, don't get out there on the mound.

FRANK: He was just a kid, trying to make a living.

HARVEY: Baseball is more than a living. It's a game. And the game has rules and consequences, and you have to take the good with the bad. That's the beauty of it—sometimes you win, sometimes you lose.

FRANK: *We* never lose.

HARVEY: We never win, either. We just watch.

FRANK: We watch, and we decide the outcome of a life.

HARVEY: You can't think about that. You can't think about life and death when you're working a game. Think about the play. The play's the thing. The *only* thing.

FRANK: I'm not so sure I believe that anymore.

HARVEY: (*sternly*) Hey, I don't want to hear that kind of talk. That's loser talk. If you don't have the desire, I don't want you on my team.

FRANK: Maybe I don't belong on your team.

(JOE *returns with the* Baseball Digest.)

JOE: Here it is, Harv.

HARVEY: (*corrects him*) Harvey.

JOE: (*nods*) Harvey. Your picture's on the cover.

HARVEY: (*admires picture*) Look at that! "Play of the Year."

(HARVEY *mimics the photo, making an authoritative out call.* JOE *is impressed.*)

HARVEY: See, Frank? See what you missed? (FRANK *is still troubled*) Look—you can't beat yourself up over one questionable call. You can't always be right.

FRANK: But you should be! You have to be! There's no margin for error! I make a call against the home team, and maybe some disgruntled fan goes home and beats his wife. I punch out some broken-down player on an iffy third strike, and maybe his career is over. I guess wrong on a close play, and maybe the pitcher kills himself. I hold careers and lives in my hands—I can't afford to be wrong!

HARVEY: (*takes him aside*) Frank, Frank . . . My God, keep it down. You'll upset the kid.

FRANK: He should know. He should know the curse of absolute power. He should know the cost to his soul!

HARVEY: (*shaking him*) Frank! Stop it!

(FRANK, *spent, sits down on a bleacher seat*)

JOE: What's the matter?

HARVEY: Nothing. He's not used to this Florida sun. (*re: the magazine*) What do I owe you for this?

JOE: (*doesn't want money*) No problem.

HARVEY: (*flips through the pages*) Let's see . . . (*he finds the article, reads*) Aha. (*turns to* FRANK) Look who's one of the Top Ten

Umpires in the American League. It's you, see? See how important you are? You're number eight. And I'm number two. (*to* JOE) How about that, Joseph? You're working with two of the best umpires in the league.

JOE: Not bad.

HARVEY: And next year you'll be on that list. Goddamit, we're a great team. (*He puts his arm around* JOE) Come on, Frank. Group hug.

FRANK: Don't you ever feel it, Harvey? Don't you feel the awful responsibility, the thought that every decision you make can impact on so many people, can ruin their lives?

HARVEY: No, I don't. I don't allow myself to feel it. An umpire doesn't feel.

FRANK: But it's only human . . . !

HARVEY: So we're not human. Look at Joe, you think he's human?

JOE: I'm a fuckin' robot, man. All I care about is the game.

HARVEY: Exactly. The *game*. That's where your allegiance lies. That's all anyone expects of you.

FRANK: Is that all Judy expected?

(HARVEY *is caught short. He takes a beat.*)

HARVEY: Judy never understood baseball. I feel sorry for her. And that's *all* I feel. If you're saying I should have spent more time with her and less time with my vocation, with my life's work, then I say, let her go. I have my priorities. That's why I'm in the Top Ten! I'm Number Two! And next year I'll be Number One, goddammit! Number One! So let her go! The hell with her! (*composes himself*) Your trouble is, you've been away all winter, you forget what it's like to be out there between the lines, in that green world, and to know that every inning, every batter, every pitch, depends on *you*, on the clarity of your vision and the wisdom of your judgment. You hold all the cards, baby. There's no other feeling like it in the world!

FRANK: I'm an ordinary, unimportant man—Who am I to judge others?

HARVEY: Who are you *not* to judge? Who are you to stand by and let injustices go unredressed? You're an umpire! You took an unspoken oath! You have a moral obligation to seek out the truth and spotlight it, to say "This is good. This is not. That man is safe. That man is out." Especially in this ambiguous, crazy world today, people need someone to turn to, someone to stand up and clear away all the smoke and confusion, and point the way. That's you, Frank. You bring logic and order to an unruly, chaotic world. It's God's work, my friend. He's called you to do it. And do it you must! (*beat*) Now let me hear your strike call. Let me hear it!

FRANK: (*half-hearted*) Strike.

HARVEY: Come on, Frank. The bases are loaded, bottom of the ninth, Griffey's at the plate, count's three-and-two, Clemens goes into his windup, he brings it over the top, it's a fastball on the black, Griffey freezes, and you make the call . . . !

FRANK: (*blurts out*) Strike!

HARVEY: That's it! Again!

FRANK: (*louder*) Stri-i-ike!

HARVEY: You're goddamn right! (*does his strike call*) Hi-eeke!

JOE: STEEE-RI-I-IKE!

FRANK: (*feeling better*) Stri-i-i-ike!

HARVEY: See? That's all it takes. A little focus, a little heart. (*puts arms around* FRANK *and* JOE) What a team! The best goddamn umpiring team in the American League! Right?

FRANK: Right!

JOE: Goddamn right!

HARVEY: Let's do it, then! Let's go out there and kick some ass! (*starts calling*) Out!

FRANK: Safe!

JOE: FOUL BALL!

HARVEY: Balk!

FRANK: Ground-rule double!

JOE: YOU'RE OW-W-W-U-UT!

(*They keep practicing calls, once again slipping into a fugue for umpires.* HARVEY *and* FRANK *share a smile, and walk off together, still shouting out calls.*)

HARVEY: Ball four . . . !

FRANK: Take your base . . . !

(*They exit.* JOE *dusts off an imaginary plate, puts on his mask.*)

JOE: PLAY BALL!

(*Lights out*)

LOVE POEM #98

Regina Taylor

CHARACTERS

MARY
WIFE
EMMANUEL

N.B. Mary, the whore, and Mary, the wife, may be played by the same actress: underneath Mary's raincoat is the wife's housedress and apron.

TIME & PLACE

The tone is fifties film noir. A Hammett-like murder mystery.

EMMANUEL: I met her in an alley strewn with the refuse of the decaying city that I called home for the past thirty years. I had been following a trail of broken promises glittering like gold. Dropping behind me the wadded-up letters from loved ones who write from the shores of faraway continents. I am Hansel alone in the enchanted forest. (*Pause.*) The scent of her mixed with orange rinds, empty beer cans, dead roses, and pee-stained walls.

I met her in an alley behind the Singho Restaurant on 43rd and Seventh. Across from the 24-hour girly show. Butterscotch skin, a Pepsodent smile, and the eyes of a snake charmer.

I met her in an alley.

(MARY, *in platform shoes that attack and scrape the floor, crosses upstage.* EMMANUEL *watches her. She pauses but does not look at him. She exits. Lights out.*)

(MARY *sings a bittersweet Billie Holiday love ballad. Then:* EMMANUEL's *room.*
We hear ticking clock and static from the radio.)

EMMANUEL: I wake up in the middle of the night, my body bathed in her voice. Drowning in the sea of possibilities.

(*Ticking clock and static.*)

EMMANUEL: Four o'clock in the morning. From my window I can see her making her way across the Verrazano Bridge. (*He *turns off the radio.*) I will hound her footsteps. Haunt her waking days.

(*Lights out.*)

(*The radio blares a Screaming J. Hawkins love tune.
As* MARY *crosses and exits,* EMMANUEL, *following, crosses and exits.*
MARY *crosses back and* EMMANUEL, *close behind, crosses. They exit.
Light change.*)

EMMANUEL: I lost her in Central Park underneath the tunnel between the Delacorte Theater and the Met where I heard the muffled laughter from inside the Egyptian sarcophagus as Hamlet rowed across the lake dredging the waters for Ophelia's remains.

(MARY *enters and sits on park bench, her back to the audience.* EMMANUEL *approaches.*)

EMMANUEL: My name's Emmanuel.

MARY: What's it to me?

EMMANUEL: You've been haunting my dreams.

MARY: At least someone's getting some sleep. I'm an insomniac—thirteen years.

EMMANUEL: Your voice has washed me clean. Newborn.

MARY: Never wanted any children pulling at me for milk. They grow teeth. They want more. They always want more.

EMMANUEL: (*Takes out a knife and cuts himself across the palm.*) See, for you I bleed.

MARY: (*Laughs.*) Better save some. Someone may be hungry soon. Go on now—I'm no good at chitchat.

EMMANUEL: What's your name?

MARY: (*Laughs.*) Mary. Mary Magdalene. Now, shove off—you stink.

EMMANUEL: Maybe, but if I used a little Listerine and soap, maybe I could . . . You might find me bearable enough to . . .

MARY: To what—to what—?

EMMANUEL: To let me look upon you—

MARY: You want a look? You want a look? I'll give you the sixty-five-cent tour. (*She opens up her raincoat.*) This right here is where my father held me down and burned me with a frying pan when I was four for spilling Kool-aid on the carpet. This was from the three teen-age boys who took turns with my virginity when I was nine. This is from my first boyfriend. He was forty-three and I was twelve and pregnant with his child—right across the belly with the heel of his silver-tipped boots. This one here is my personal favorite—from a true admirer—he tried to carve his initials in my chest. And that there is a gunshot wound—close range. And these—let's just say that I've grown accustomed to the teeth of loved ones.

EMMANUEL: She displayed her jewel-encrusted body—

MARY: So what do you have to offer me—my sweet?

(*Light change.*
MARY *in spotlight—lip syncing.*
We hear MARY*'s voice over the radio, singing a Billie Holiday tune about the sacrifices of love.*)

(*As* EMMANUEL *cleans and puts together a gun. He loads in bullets.*)

EMMANUEL: I'll protect my love.

MARY: (*In spotlight.*) I carry razors behind my eyelids. I can debone a man in fifteen seconds and leave him bleeding in an alleyway—screaming out my name . . .

(MARY *lip syncs:*)

RADIO: (MARY's *voice*.) . . . How can he dream of me when I haven't slept in thirteen years? Tonight I will visit his bed . . .

(EMMANUEL *cocks the gun*.)

EMMANUEL: For my love . . .

(*Lights out*.)

WIFE: I am his wife. My name is Mary. We married when I was nineteen. A week after I graduated high school. He told my father he would protect me. And that was good enough for my dad. Since that day I've never looked at another. I had my first child that next year. And since, I've borne him seven more. I have stretch marks all over my body. A boy grows inside me now. He sleeps.

He's never been cruel to me. He's never touched me—not mean. He works hard, he comes home, he goes to his room—he sleeps. We have separate bedrooms. He says that I disturb his sleep . . . I don't complain. I don't mind working. Since they've had cutbacks at his job. I would never complain to him. It's been over a year now since we stopped going out to movies or to dance. Who has time? He's tired—he says. He's tired. I don't complain. I found a job. I'm a waitress—I work double shifts—then come home, cook, clean, hold the children. It's very hard. Sometimes I don't sleep. And hard for him. I would never say . . . I never said one word. He says it's in my eyes. The words are in my eyes. My eyes cut him to the bone. I've never said . . .

He was a good father. A good provider. He was never cruel. He cheated on me once. He confessed. Down on his knees. He cried in my lap. What's to be said? I think . . . He didn't have to tell me. I didn't have to know. He didn't have to say—but he did.

He says I hold things back. Behind the closed lids. I carry razors in my eyes—he says. I wish that . . . Never mind. More and more—I don't sleep.

(*Lights up on* EMMANUEL.)

EMMANUEL: (*Reads from crumpled paper.*) "He's tired—he says. He sleeps more and more. He haunts this house." (EMMANUEL *walks in circles picking up pieces of crumpled paper.*) . . . Can't find my way back . . .

(*Lights up on* MARY.)

MARY: I am his wife. My name is Mary. I wish that . . . Never mind.

When I was eighteen. After school I would visit his room. He had a nice apartment in midtown, except it had no view—except for the alley. We would lie down on his bed. He would whisper love poems in my ear as I held his organ in my hand. That's all. He didn't touch me. He wanted me to be untouched when we married. I couldn't tell him—I didn't have the heart to tell him. I never told him—He didn't need to know.

(EMMANUEL *and* MARY *lock eyes.*
EMMANUEL *assembles gun and loads it.*)

MARY/WIFE: Tonight I will visit his bed.

END

BREAKFAST SERIAL

Megan Terry

BREAKFAST SERIAL premiered at the Omaha Magic Theatre in December 1996. Jo Ann Schmidman directed, as well as designed the set and lighting; Megan Terry designed the costumes and photographic projections; Yi Chong Noh was the production stage manager. The cast was as follows:

KORD   Erich Christiansen
JEFF   Ji Hyang Noh
MIKEY   Jeremy Arakara
ROYCE   Jo Ann Schmidman

CHARACTERS

KORD: a strong, clean-cut twenty-year-old man
JEFF: a boy of fourteen, played by a woman over eighteen
MIKEY: a boy of thirteen, played by a woman over eighteen
ROYCE: played by a woman over eighteen (This character is a woman masquerading as a boy of twelve.)

SETTING

A road and a small clearing in a grove of trees near a river

TIME

Early Sunday morning. The present.

(*A suburban road. Dawn.*)

(JEFF *walks along, shivering.* KORD *flies by on his motorcycle.* KORD *returns from the other direction, gunning his cycle, then stops. Looks at* JEFF.)

KORD: Where ya goin'?

JEFF: Get m' papers.

KORD: Wanna git there fast?

(JEFF *shrugs.*)

KORD: Hey, I'll get you to your papers, help you fold 'em. We deliver them on the bike, and then I'll take you to a party.

JEFF: On Sunday morning?

KORD: You like parties?

JEFF: I like parties.

KORD: Hop on.

(JEFF *hops on and they're off, fast.*)

(*A small grove of trees.* KORD *helps* JEFF *fold papers very fast.*)

JEFF: Where are we?

KORD: I come here to party.

JEFF: Girls coming?

KORD: (*Nods*) You party with your friends?

JEFF: We have Robitussin parties.

KORD: Cough syrup?!

JEFF: Better high than Scotch Guard.

KORD: Scotch Guard fries yer brains.

JEFF: We don't do that anymore. Save up for "robe parties."

KORD: What's the "robe" high like?

JEFF: (*Trying to act cool.*) Cross between booze and psychedelic.

KORD: Where'd you get your hands on acid?

JEFF: Richie's brother made some.

KORD: Fer sure?

JEFF: He said witches in the olden times got high by eating the mold off their old rye bread. They'd get higher than kites and then put spells on people. People'd come down with bad sickness, get mad at the witches, and then burn 'em at the stake or drown 'em in the river.

KORD: Platte River's right over that hill.

JEFF: Hey, I'm too far from home. My mom'll kill me.

KORD: We won't tell her, will we?

JEFF: Let's go. Some a my route get up early Sunday—they want the sports pages right away.

KORD: We'll go on your route right after you take off your clothes.

JEFF: What?

KORD: You heard me.

(JEFF *looks at* KORD *and flinches.*)

KORD: I told you to take your clothes off.

JEFF: I don't dig guys.

KORD: Me neither.

JEFF: Why'd you bring me here?

KORD: To make you take off your clothes.

JEFF: People don't get their Sunday paper they'll call the paper, then they'll call the cops.

KORD: Nobody's up.

JEFF: The old guys are up. The fishermen, they're up.

KORD: Maybe they'll come looking for you. Would you like them to see you tied up? Would you like them to see you tied up with no clothes on?

JEFF: What do you get out of this?

KORD: You. I got you.

JEFF: But you said yourself . . . you don't want me, in . . . in like in that way.

KORD: What way?

JEFF: SEX.

KORD: You want sex?

JEFF: No. God no. I don't want nothin' from you.

KORD: NOT EVEN THIS? (*He shows him knife.*)

JEFF: Who are you?

KORD: Who are you?

JEFF: This isn't funny anymore.

KORD: But it's fun.

JEFF: I'm going.

KORD: (*Slaps him*) Good clean fun.

JEFF: What do you want?

KORD: (*Slaps him again*) I got what I want.

JEFF: I gotta go. (*Starts to run*)

KORD: (*Grabs him*) You'll go when I tell you.

JEFF: You bastard. Let go of me.

KORD: You got a dirty mouth. You know what we do with dirty mouths? We fill them with dirt. (*Forces* JEFF's *head down on ground*) Take a big bite. Take a nice big bite of nice clean dirt. It'll clean out yer dirty mind.

JEFF: Don't hurt me. Please.

KORD: (*Kicks him*) I can't stand begging. Plead for your life like a man.

JEFF: I got money saved for college. If you let me go, I'll give it to you. All of it.

KORD: Take 'em off. I wanna see you do that.

JEFF: Then can I go?

KORD: Hey, you're late fer work. You better get started. Huh? Huh? (*Pokes him with knife*)

JEFF: I'm not gonna do it.

KORD: Oh no? How far do you think your blood can spurt? As far as you can pee? Let's see how far you can pee. Oh oh— you smell! I smell you from here. You shit yer pants. I can smell it. You have to take them off. Yer Momma will bop you—you come home with shitty pants. Won't she? Won't she? And she'll get Dad to beat you, too. Won't she? Won't she?

JEFF: No. No. My Mom's nice. She won't do that.

KORD: No, she won't. Because she'll never see you again, if you don't do exactly as I say. I mean exactly.

JEFF: They'll be looking for me.

KORD: People're too lazy, kid. My name's Kord, what's yours?

JEFF: You're crazy.

KORD: You're the one's crazy. You came with me. You don't know me. But I know you. I know you'll end up doing exactly what I say. (*Swipes at him with knife*) Name?

JEFF: Stop it! My name's . . . my name's Jeff.

KORD: How old are you Jeff?

JEFF: Yer not much older'n me. Why are you doing this to me?

KORD: You'll do as I say. Exactly. (*Swipes at him and nicks him.* JEFF *screams.*)

JEFF: (*Breaking*) Please, please. Please don't hurt me. (*Falls to ground and puts arms around his knees*)

KORD: You're scared shitless, aren't you? Take off your clothes or I'll cut 'em off. Jeff?

JEFF: (*Pulls off shirt*) There.

KORD: Stand up! I can't see. Get the rest off.

JEFF: (*Pulls off jeans*)

KORD: Get out of the dirt you little shit.

(JEFF *gets up on knees, falls back on ground, and takes off shoes.*)

KORD: I'm getting mad, and it's interfering with what I can see. Get up and get the rest off!

JEFF: (*Takes off socks*) There. Now can I go? I'm cold. It's cold out here.

KORD: (*Puts knife under* JEFF's *nose*) You can't stand up to us, can you Jeff? (*Swipes knife at* JEFF's *legs, draws blood*) Take 'em off.

(JEFF *screams and starts to pull off shorts as lights black out.*)

(*The woods:* KORD *confronts a half-dressed new boy. He's a bit younger than* JEFF.)

KORD: (*Brandishing knife*) You heard me. Quit stalling!

MIKEY: Why you wanna do this, man? Did Pink Kopeckney put you up to this, man? He's kinda jealous of me cuz LaVonne Hamberger's nice to me. Even tho' I'm younger than her. And he'd kind of like to get next to her but she likes me, I think she does. If it was Pink made you do this to me, man, I can straighten it all out. I'll take him over to her house, too. The both a you. Ain't that a deal? It'll be cool man. LaVonne Hamberger, she's got, you know, out to here. Triple D at least. That's what the guys say. Triple D. Can you imagine what that would feel like? Wouldn't you rather see her than me?

KORD: You're made in God's image.

MIKEY: Huh?

KORD: Didn't God say he made men in God's own image?

MIKEY: He did? When? Hey, we're all the same, man.

KORD: Are we?

MIKEY: This isn't fun anymore.

KORD: When was it fun?

MIKEY: When you said we could get high.

KORD: I'm getting high. (*Swipes knife toward boy's shorts*) Jackpot!

MIKEY: If I take off all my clothes will you put away the knife?

KORD: Take a risk.

MIKEY: I'm tired and hungry.

KORD: You should eat a big breakfast before going off to work.

MIKEY: (*Breaking down*) Didn't have no food in the house.

KORD: (*Cutting his shoulder with knife*) Don't mock me. Get the job done!

MIKEY: You made me bleed.

KORD: You made me mad.

MIKEY: You're crazy.

(KORD *cuts him again.*)

MIKEY: (*Screams*) Don't! Don't! (*He breaks all the way down and screams.*) Please don't cut me again!

KORD: There are a few things I want to know about you.

MIKEY: Why? What?

KORD: What you'll do when you have no clothes.

MIKEY: This is as far as I go.

KORD: (*Raises knife*) I'm prepared to kill you if you don't take everything off.

(MIKEY *takes off undershirt as lights black out.*)

(*The woods:* KORD *and* ROYCE, *a hyper boy of twelve, are there.* ROYCE *paces and jumps about.*)

ROYCE: Hey, this's no party! This's the dumb outdoors. Hey, I'm gone. It's too noisy.

KORD: We're just a little early.

ROYCE: You said at the 7-Eleven we were going to a party where this dude had a lot of free video games. I'm into action. I can't stand listening to birds and bees. (*He runs around kicking at dirt.*)

KORD: Don't dig up the dirt. Creatures live under the dirt.

ROYCE: (*Digging faster*) Where, where? I'm hungry. Help me, puke head, help me, grunt nose. Can't you see? (*Screams*) I'm starving!

KORD: What's your problem?

ROYCE: Don't you understand English? You wouldn't, you're from Mars. But I'm a Martian detector. I seen you, when you didn't seen me.

KORD: You talk too fast.

ROYCE: Too bad for you boo-ga-loo. Listen faster. I don't like it here and I don't like you and I hate being hungry. And I hate liars!

KORD: Don't call me a liar, you little jerk-off!

ROYCE: That's fun, isn't it? You ever jerk off in a circle? I beat everyone. Can you beat that? (*Laughs and hits himself*)

KORD: (*Cuffs* ROYCE) Shut up!

ROYCE: I won't shut up. I'm up all the time. I'm always up ain't I little pup? (*Pats his crotch*) I'm going to have you arrested. I don't dig people hitting people!

KORD: You're gonna what?

ROYCE: You got a lower IQ than worms. And speaking of worms, I could eat a plateful. Let's go back to the 7-Eleven and you can buy me a red hot chili burrito for taking up my time.

KORD: You're a pisser. Where'd you come from?

ROYCE: You said you needed some extra guys for a party. You can't remember nothing. I'm going to report you.

KORD: Shut up or I'll draw and quarter you!

ROYCE: Your head's in quarters, dick nose.

KORD: I can't stand you. Get out of here!

ROYCE: I don't know where I am so how can I get out of here?

KORD: You're totally crazy.

ROYCE: My mother thinks so, too.

KORD: Fer sure!

ROYCE: She took me to the nut inspector and they inspected my nuts and said my nuts were fine, but my mind needed to be refined. I'm gonna get locked up, Tuesday.

KORD: Get lost, ding-a-ling.

ROYCE: I'm Royce! The wrecker! I'll cut off your pecker.

KORD: You gnat, you couldn't cut my nails. You've wasted my time. I can't do anything with a crazy.

ROYCE: I'm going to report you to the thought police. You definitely need some Thorazine.

KORD: You are a total waste! I'm not getting what I want! (*Pulls knife*)

ROYCE: Little pricks like you don't know how to play with knives. Give it to Daddy Royce and I'll cut your hair for the electric chair.

KORD: I can't get worked up.

ROYCE: I want that knife!

KORD: (*Puts knife away*) I'm not gonna show you what my knife can do because you're nothing but a pinball. (*Turns away from* ROYCE) I want kids to pee their pants when they see a knife.

ROYCE: (*Pulls a blackjack out of crotch of her pants and slugs him over and over*) Kids like Jeff! Kids like Mikey!

KORD: Get out of my face! I'll kill you, you jerk-off!

ROYCE: Not if I kill you first. (*She beats and kicks him down into the dirt. Pulls out cuffs and cuffs his wrists.*)

ROYCE: (*Pushes some buttons on her wrist watch, talks to watch*) Officer Royce reporting in. Yeah . . . No . . . Better an ambulance. The scumbag tripped on his own knife. (KORD *moans and stirs. She kicks and slugs him.*) Sumbitch! You don't deserve to live on this planet! You don't lie still you'll hurt as bad as you hurt those boys! (*Speaking back into watch radio*) S'okay, I just had to give 'im another tranquilizer. You bet it worked. Shakespeare was right. (*Kisses blackjack*) A codpiece of generous weight and size will rivet gaze and addle judgment every time.

BLACKOUT

THE JANITOR

August Wilson

CHARACTERS

SETTING: A Hotel Ballroom

(SAM *enters pushing a broom near the lectern. He stops and reads the* *sign hanging across the ballroom.*)

SAM: National . . . Conference . . . on . . . Youth.

(*He nods his approval and continues sweeping. He gets an idea, stops,* *and approaches the lectern. He clears his throat and begins to speak. His* *speech is delivered with the literacy of a janitor. He chooses his ideas care-* *fully. He is a man who has approached life honestly, with both eyes* *open.*)

SAM: I want to thank you all for inviting me here to speak about
youth. See . . . I's fifty-six years old and I knows something
about youth. The first thing I knows . . . is that youth is
sweet before flight . . . its odor is rife with speculation and
its resilience . . . that's its bounce back . . . is remarkable.
But it's that sweetness that we victims of. All of us. Its sweetness . . . and its flight. One of them fellows in that Shakespeare stuff said, "I am not what I am." See. He wasn't like
Popeye. This fellow had a different understanding. "I am not
what I am." Well, neither are you. You are just what you
have been . . . whatever you are now. But what you are now
ain't what you gonna become . . . even though it is with you
now . . . it's inside you now this instant. Time . . . see, this
how you get to this . . . Time ain't changed. It's just moved.
Or maybe it ain't moved . . . maybe it just changed. It don't
matter. We are all victims of the sweetness of youth and the
time of its flight. See . . . just like you I forgot who I am. I

forgot what happened first. But I know the river I step into now . . . is not the same river I stepped into twenty years ago. See. I know that much. But I have forgotten the name of the river . . . I have forgotten the names of the gods . . . and like everybody else I have tried to fool them with my dancing . . . and guess at their faces. It's the same with everybody. We don't have to mention no names. Ain't nobody innocent. We are all victims of ourselves. We have all had our hand in the soup . . . and made the music play just so. See, now . . . this what I call wrestling with Jacob's angel. You lay down at night and that angel come to wrestle with you. When you wrestling with that angel you bargaining for you future. See. And what you need to bargain with is that sweetness of youth. So . . . to the youth of the United States I says . . . don't spend that sweetness too fast! 'Cause you gonna need it. See. I's fifty-six years old and I done found that out. But it's all the same. It all comes back on you . . . just like reaping and sowing. Down and out ain't nothing but being caught up in the balance of what you put down. If you down and out and things ain't going right for you . . . you can bet you done put a down payment on your troubles. Now you got to pay up on the balance. That's as true as I'm standing here. Sometimes you can't see it like that. The last note on Gabriel's horn always gets lost when you get to realizing you done heard the first. See, it's just like. . . .

MR. COLLINS: (*Entering*) Come on, Sam . . . let's quit wasting time and get this floor swept. There's going to be a big important meeting here this afternoon.

SAM: Yessuh, Mr. Collins. Yessuh.

(SAM *goes back to sweeping as the lights go down to—*)

BLACK

HELEN AT RISK

Dana Yeaton

HELEN AT RISK premiered at Actors Theatre of Louisville's Humana Festival of New American Plays in March 1995. It was directed by Frazier W. Marsh; the set designer was Paul Owen; the costume designer was Laura Patterson; the lighting designer was Brian Scott; the dramaturg was Michael Bigelow Dixon. The cast was as follows:

HELEN	Adale O'Brien
RONNIE GUYETTE	V Craig Heidenreich
GUARD	William McNulty

CHARACTERS

HELEN: an attractive middle-aged woman, dressed sensibly but with an artistic flair
RONNIE GUYETTE: an inmate
GUARD

TIME & PLACE: A prison rec room.

A long table center stage; downstage and to one side, a chair.

AT RISE: RONNIE *is lying on the table, a kerchief covering his hair, while* HELEN *applies the final touches to his white plaster mask.* GUARD *sits facing audience.*

HELEN (*To audience.*) Now this last piece, the little triangular, Vermont piece, or . . . (*Turns it upside down.*) New Hampshire-shaped piece, depending . . . (*She dunks it in a small Tupperware container of murky, white water. Throughout the play, she continues to shape and smooth the mask with her hands.*) This will go between the nostrils, not over the nostrils or your partner will no longer be able to breathe. Now in your kits you will find that I have precut all the pieces, which I do not like to do but I had all I could do to get plaster and paint supplies in here and they definitely were not going to let me hand out scissors. So now really, I'm just smoothing, the forehead's already hard, of course the nose will be the last to dry. *Do not hurry the mask,* it should be completely hard before you try to take it off. I will show you how to do that in a minute—(*To man whose mask she is making.*) How ya doin' there, Ronnie? Happy? No complaints, right? Yes it was an education just trying to get in here, the Arts Council had warned us about belts, so I knew to come beltless, and no gum to stick in the locks, I can understand that, but pens? Ball point pens? Apparently you boys start tattooing yourself is that right? . . . (*Responding to an inmate.*) No I don't mind tattoos, one of my friends has a lovely little tattoo . . . I'm not tellin' where! You just pay attention to what I'm doing because in a minute *you* are gonna be up here doing the same thing . . . Now doesn't Ronnie look peaceful? And look at those cheek bones . . . (*To another inmate.*) No, you are not allowed to say anything to people who are having their masks done. Especially—

(RONNIE *gives the finger.*)

HELEN: Especially . . . this is the time when the slightest little move can . . . good now the jaws are fully dry and the chin is coming. (*To* GUARD.) How we doin' for time?

GUARD: Nine-twenty.

HELEN: And we can go 'til when?

GUARD: We got room check at ten.

HELEN: Ooh. Okay. That's gonna be a little tight. (*To* GUARD.) Sure you don't wanna join in?

GUARD: I'm sure.

HELEN: Okay . . . (*Shrugs.*) Well we gotta keep uh, lemme see, why don't I tell you a little bit about what we do once the mask is *dry* . . . um . . . we may end up cutting some of the decoration time short. What I usually do in the schools is set out two or three tables of materials. Beads, feathers, ribbon, paints, glitter, knickknacks—I love yard sales—and I ask that you find some colors or objects, any combination of paints and materials that will make the mask express who *you are*. Now today, as I said, we're going to use, I was only allowed three brushes, so we're going to have to share. I'm not quite clear on what the danger of a paintbrush is but . . . What have we got here? (*Inspecting another Tupperware container, full of paints.*) Black, blue, um yellow, peach, I hope y'all won't use a lot of the peach, though I don't actually . . . I don't see my red. Pardon? . . . (*To an inmate.*) Well no you *can* use the peach, I just think, you know, I want to encourage you to experiment, use your imagination and not feel like your mask has to be the same color as you . . . though I can see that, well we, if you would LIKE to use black, some of you, or anybody, that's up to you. We're looking for something that expresses *you*, how you feel as a person, how you feel today, right now.

GUARD: (*In response to an inmate.*) Pearson!

HELEN: (*To* GUARD.) No that's okay. (*To Pearson.*) If that's how you really feel then try to imagine how that shapes your face and let that be the mask and later before you do any decorating—we're all dry through here now (*Re: chin*), we're just waiting on the nose—before you paint or do anything, make sure that you have an image in your mind, in your mind's eye, of what your mask should finally be . . . Yes I suppose you could. Sure, sort of a fantasy of what you'd *like* to be. That would be equally valid. Now we just keep—

(RONNIE *is pretending to masturbate.*)

GUARD: (*To Ronnie.*) Guyette!

HELEN: (*Placing Ronnie's hand at his side.*) We'll just put this over here . . . Ronnie doesn't seem to understand how simple it would be for us to place another piece of plaster right along here. (*Pretending to cover the nose completely.*) I should tell you that for some people having your eyes completely covered can be very . . . disorienting, very frightening. A man once, I was out in Colorado, at this convention, and this man had volunteered to be the guinea pig, he was very excited about the idea, and about ten minutes into the demonstration—

(RONNIE *bolts upright, shaking as if terrified.*)

HELEN: (*Pulling him down to flat again.*) DO NOT MOVE until the mask is off or you will—

GUARD: Guyette you're gonna be outta here.

HELEN: Ronnie will be good, won't you Ronnie? . . . There now lie back . . . Good. For some reason the nose always takes the longest to dry . . . (*To Pearson.*) Yes I am. Are you?

GUARD: Pearson! . . . Yeah, I heard what you asked.

HELEN: I don't like to wear my ring when I'm working with plaster.

GUARD: Look, these guys don't have to be in here. Anybody you want out, say so.

HELEN: We're fine. Look, I appreciate, I mean (*Laughs.*) for God's sake, I have worked in junior high schools!

GUARD: Okay.

HELEN: *Then* it would have been nice to have a guard.

GUARD: Your call.

HELEN: If I need you I can always just scream, right?

GUARD: Whatever.

HELEN: Y'all promise to be good don't you? (*In response to Pearson.*) I'll bet you are. Um . . . one thing we *may* want to do since we will be a little short on time is use *warm* water for soaking because this will speed the drying process *however* warm water *will* mean that we have to work a little faster to keep it from setting before we're . . . (*To Pearson.*) Pardon? . . . You mean today? . . . I just thought it would be fun . . . Well, *that* and I think it's important for people to learn more about who—Yes. I am . . . Well I'd rather not . . . A hundred and fifty dollars, not including the materials, which of course here don't really amount—Because that's *not* why I'm here. If I wanted to make money I'd go do that. I think people deserve a chance to, this always sounds stupid, but I *do* think there is a basic human need to create and to express yourself. See you think I'm an outsider, I don't think I'm an outsider. What happened to you *before,* what your parents did, I don't know the particulars but . . . I mean I think I know what it's like to grow up with no one caring what you think or feel. You're just some piece of furniture. And finally you blow up, of course! Thank God. You're alive! Do you ever look at other people and really think about being *them?* Which would mean everything about them, their families, their genes, every experience, but you're still *you,* you still know that you're only visiting. There was a little boy, maybe one of yours, waiting to get buzzed out while I was waiting to get buzzed in, and his mother was doing something at the front desk and through the glass, he couldn't see me I guess or didn't care but he was opening, he seemed to be practicing opening his mouth as wide as he could. And he wasn't saying anything but I could see way back in his throat.

(RONNIE *taps her arm.*)

HELEN: Oops, I think our guinea pig is telling us it's time. (*To* PEARSON.) And by the way, I *do* need the money. (*Touching the mask.*) Okay, does it feel hard all over?

(RONNIE *does a spectacular mock orgasm.*)

HELEN: That is not what I—(*Trying to restrain him.*) I can see I have to be careful what I say to *this* man. Now stay still. STOP! . . . There. (*To* GUARD.) See how well he minds? (*To all.*) Now, what I *was* going to say is that when you are having your mask made you'll notice how as the plaster hardens it cools. So you should be able to tell *from the inside* when it's ready to come off. Now I want to demonstrate how we remove the mask. You in the back, make sure you can see this. First you v-e-e-ery gently slip your fingers up under here (*Re: the cheeks.*) and you just keep working your way around, under the chin. Careful not to pinch. Nice and gentle. You should feel it coming loose. Alright, see how it starts to come away, and we . . . this is where you find out if you used enough Vaseline. Ready? . . . Voilà.

(*The mask is off.* RONNIE *sits up, bits of plaster on his face. He pulls off the kerchief.*)

HELEN: (*Handing mask to* RONNIE.) And that, my friend . . . is you.

(RONNIE *stares, unimpressed.*)

HELEN: Most people have only a two dimensional image of themselves which is what a mirror gives you or a photo. But. Here . . . (HELEN *turns the mask to show* RONNIE *its profile.*) What you're looking at right now, maybe for the first time ever, is your third dimension . . . Now before you say anything, here's your paintbrush. Kinda big but do your best— Oh first we need to get your name written on the inside so we don't get 'em confused. Don't want any arguments over whose face is whose . . . 'Course I don't have a pen.

GUARD: (*Pulling a pen from his pocket.*) I can do it.

HELEN: Great. You don't mind?

GUARD: (*To* RONNIE.) C'm'ere.

(RONNIE *crosses, hands mask to* GUARD, *who writes in it.*)

HELEN: See, I knew we'd get him participating. Now before we all get started I just want to remind you that with the Vaseline, do a good, thorough job, remember that beards and moustaches will have to be covered with *tissue* paper and make sure to go way up into the hair line. There's no such thing as—

RONNIE: (*To* GUARD.) Try it on.

GUARD: No.

RONNIE: Come on. Just try it. (*To inmates.*) Don't ya think he should try it on? (*After an enthusiastic "yeah."*) All right. Let's see.

(GUARD *holds mask to his face.*)

RONNIE *looks to the inmates, then turns and drives the large, wooden paint brush deep into the eye of the mask. He slashes side to side.* GUARD *falls to the floor, thrashes for a moment, then lies still.*

RONNIE *pulls the mask from* GUARD*'s face. He uses the paintbrush to wipe blood from the back of the mask, then flips it, and paints a trail of blood descending, like a tear, from the eye hole.*)

RONNIE: Hey, look. (*Holding the mask out to* HELEN.) It's me.

(*They stand facing each other, motionless.*)

RONNIE: Aren't ya gonna try it on?

(*Beat.*)

BLACKOUT

END

ACKNOWLEDGMENTS

We'd like to thank the following individuals for their invaluable contributions to this anthology: Linda Driekonski, Tom Ledcke, Eleanore Speert at Dramatist Play Service, Michael Bigelow Dixon at Actors Theatre of Louisville, John McCormack, David Robinson, Tom Szentgyorgi at Denver Center Theatre, Peter Franklin, Matthew Lewis, Beth Blickers and Eric Zohn at William Morris, Peter Hagen at Writers & Artists, Ron Gwiazda at Rosenstone/Wender, Seth Gordon at Primary Stages, Mary Harden at Harden/Curtis, Yaddo, and, as always, our families and friends.

Special thanks to our agents Susie Perlman and Phyllis Wenderr for their extraordinary efforts and skill. Also our editor at Vintage, LuAnn Walther, for the opportunity to publish this book. And especially, the playwrights for their wonderful plays, and the theatres that continue to develop exciting new works.

CONTRIBUTORS

JOHN AUGUSTINE is a writer, actor, and teacher. His work has been produced at HOME for Contemporary Theatre, Ensemble Studio Theatre, Naked Angels, and Manhattan Theatre Club. He received a Revson Fellowship from Playwrights Horizons. With Sherry Anderson, he is half of Dawne in the satiric nightclub act "Chris Durang & Dawne."

CATHERINE CELESIA is the author of seven full-length plays and numerous one-acts. She has been produced in Los Angeles and New York, and is the recipient of a 1993 Beverly Hills Theatre Guild Award for her play "The Essence of Being." She loves what she does.

LAURA CUNNINGHAM is a playwright as well as a novelist and journalist. Her works have been performed at Steppenwolf Theatre and on Theatre Row in New York. She is the author of the memoir *Sleeping Arrangements,* currently in its seventh printing from NAL (Plume).

CHRISTOPHER DURANG was born in Montclair, New Jersey. He is author of *A History of the American Film, Sister Mary Ignatius Explains It All for You, Beyond Therapy, Laughing Wild, The Marriage of Bette and Boo,* and *Durang Durang.* He is one third of the cabaret act "Chris Durang and Dawne."

MARY GALLAGHER's plays, including *Little Bird, Father Dreams, Chocolate Cake, Dog Eat Dog, How to Say Goodbye, Buddies,* and

¿De Dónde?, have been published by Dramatists Play Service and produced all over the United States and in many foreign countries. She also writes screenplays and novels, most recently *The Mooch.*

JOHN GUARE's award-winning plays include *Six Degrees of Separation* and *The House of Blue Leaves.* His screenplay for Louis Malle's *Atlantic City* won the New York, Los Angeles, and National Film Critics awards, as well as an Oscar nomination. In 1989, Mr. Guare was elected to the American Academy and Institute of Arts and Letters. He lives in New York City.

DAVID IVES was born in Chicago, and educated at Northwestern University and the Yale Drama School. His one-act plays were a staple at the annual comedy festival of Manhattan Punch Line for several years. Plays include *All in the Timing* and *Don Juan in Chicago.* He has also written for film, television, and opera.

JASON KATIMS's plays include *Who Made Robert DeNiro King of America?, Driving Lessons,* and *Catch!* He was the cowriter and coproducer of the motion picture *The Pallbearer.* He was executive story editor for ABC's critically acclaimed television series *My So-Called Life,* and is creator and executive producer of *Relativity.*

SHERRY KRAMER's plays include *The Law Makes Evening Fall, Napoleon's China, The Wall of Water, David's Redhaired Death, What a Man Weighs,* and *Things That Break.* Her plays have been produced in New York, regionally, and abroad. Her awards include those from the NEA, the New York Foundation for the Arts, the McKnight, the Weissberger, and the Jane Chambers. She is an alum of New Dramatists.

TONY KUSHNER's plays include *Angels in America* (1993 Pulitzer Prize; 1993 and 1994 Tony Award for Best Play); *Slavs!; A*

Bright Room Called Day; and *The Illusion,* freely adapted from Corneille. His work has been performed at theatres around the United States and in over thirty countries around the world. He lives in Manhattan.

ERIC LANE is the author of *The Gary & Rob Show, Times of War,* and *Dancing on Checkers' Grave.* He wrote, directed, and produced *Cater-Waiter,* a short film starring David Drake and Tim Deak. Honors include a Writer's Guild Award, the LaMama Playwright Development Award, an O'Neill Center Finalist, and two Yaddo Fellowships.

SHIRLEY LAURO's plays include *A Piece of My Heart, Open Admissions, The Contest, Margaret and Kit, In the Shadows, The Coal Diamond,* and *Nothing Immediate.* These have been produced on Broadway and Off-Broadway, regionally, in Europe, and in South Africa. Major awards include a Tony nomination and the Guggenheim, NEA, and NYFA grants. She serves on the Dramatists Guild Council's Steering Committee.

ROMULUS LINNEY is the award-winning author of three novels, fifteen full-length and twenty-two short plays, which have been seen over the past twenty-five years in resident theatres across the United States, as well as in New York, Los Angeles, London, and Vienna. Plays include *2, Childe Byron, The Sorrows of Frederick, Holy Ghosts, April Snow,* and *Three Poets.*

DAVID MAMET is the author of the acclaimed plays *The Cryptogram, Oleanna, Speed-the-Plow, Glengarry Glen Ross, American Buffalo,* and *Sexual Perversity in Chicago.* He has also written the screenplay for the Oscar-nominated film *The Verdict,* four collections of essays, a novel, and a book of poems. His plays have won the Pulitzer Prize and the Obie Award.

JANE MARTIN, a Kentuckian, first came to national attention for *Talking With,* a collection of monologues premiering in Actors Theatre of Louisville's 1981 Humana Festival of New American Plays. Her full-length plays include *Cementville,* the Pulitzer-nominated *Keely and Du, Criminal Hearts, Middle-aged White Guys,* and *Jack and Jill.*

MARY MILLER's *Ferris Wheel* was a Finalist at the 1993 Actors Theatre of Louisville National Ten-Minute Play Contest. It won the 1992 National Playwriting Competition in Dubuque, Iowa, and was produced at the Five Flags Theatre. Mary Miller has received over a dozen national playwriting awards and seen her work produced throughout the country.

CHIORI MIYAGAWA's *America Dreaming* premiered at Vineyard Theatre in a coproduction with Music Theatre Group in 1995. A short version of her play *Nothing Forever* was published in *Central Park.* Her new play, *Fire Dance,* was presented in the 1996 *Just Add Water* Festival at New York Theatre Workshop, where she is Artistic Associate.

JOE PINTAURO is a playwright, novelist, and poet. His plays include *Raft of the Medusa, Men's Lives, Snow Orchid,* and *Cacciatore.* He has written two novels, *Cold Hands* and *State of Grace,* and several award-winning books of poetry, among them *To Believe in God* and *The Rainbow Box.*

MARY SUE PRICE, a native of the Ozarks, writes for daytime television and teaches playwriting at the Circle Repertory Company Theatre School. Her plays have been presented Off-Broadway and throughout the United States. Her musical, *Streets of Gold,* with music by Robin and Linda Williams, is under development for a mainstage production at the Circle Repertory Company.

NICOLE B. QUINN is a playwright/screenwriter who resides in Brooklyn with her husband, two children, and a pet tortoise.

CAROLE REAL's one-act plays *Why the Beach Boys Are Like Opera, Pray to Mary* (coauthored by Maureen McDuffee), and *The Battle of Bull Run Always Makes Me Cry*, were included in Ensemble Studio Theatre's Octoberfests of 1993, 1994, and 1995. *Why the Beach Boys Are Like Opera* was subsequently produced in Los Angeles as part of the EST LA Project Summer Shorts festival of one-acts, and in the Act One Festival.

JOSÉ RIVERA is the author of *Cloud Tectonics*, which premiered at the 1995 Humana Festival at the Actors Theatre of Louisville. His play *Marisol*, winner of a 1993 Obie Award for outstanding play, premiered at the Humana Festival in 1992. Other plays include *The House of Ramon Iglesia, Each Day Dies with Sleep*, and *The Promise*.

SYBIL ROSEN's plays have been produced in New York, Los Angeles, and Boston. She is currently a ranger/educator at the Mohonk Preserve, a not-for-profit nature preserve in upstate New York.

STEVEN SATER has written for theatre, television, and film. His stage plays include *Carbondale Dreams* (Kaufman Theatre); *Perfect for You, Doll* (Rosenthal Prize; Cincinnati Playhouse); *Asylum* (Naked Angels; Greenwich Street Theatre); *Pearl's Tears* (G.M. Kernodle Prize; Shoebox Theatre); and *Umbrage* (Steppenwolf New Play Prize). Twenty of his one-act plays have been published and produced cross-country.

JOHN PATRICK SHANLEY is from the Bronx. His plays include *Savage in Limbo, the dreamer examines his pillow, Italian American Reconciliation*, and *Four Dogs and a Bone*. Films include *Five Corners, Congo*, and *Moonstruck*, which won the Writer's Guild Award and Academy Award for Best Original Screenplay.

DAVID SMILOW's theatrical career began on his first birthday the instant his father turned a home-movie camera on him and he walked—for the first time. After that, he concentrated on writing. He has written for film, television, and magazines. *Brights,* his first ten-minute play, is based on an actual fear.

DIANA SON's plays have been performed at La Jolla Playhouse, the Mark Taper Forum, and the Public Theatre. Her full-length plays include *Boy, Fishes,* and *Stop Kiss.* She lives in New York City.

FREDERICK STROPPEL has had recent New York productions of his plays at the Ensemble Studio Theatre, the John Houseman Theatre, the Theatre Row Theatre, the West Bank Cafe, and The 29th Street Repertory Theatre. In spring of 1995 his full-length comedy *Fortune's Fools* was produced Off-Broadway at the Cherry Lane Theatre. Mr. Stroppel is a member of the Dramatists Guild.

REGINA TAYLOR's writing credits include *The Ties That Bind, Watermelon Rinds,* and *Inside the Belly of the Beast* at the Goodman and Alliance theatres; *Between the Lines* at Actors Theatre of Louisville's Humana Festival; *Escape from Paradise* at Circle Rep; *Mudtracks* at Ensemble Studio Theatre; *Ghost Train* and *Sty Farm* (adaptations of one-acts by Franz Xavier Kroetz) at the Joseph Papp Public Theatre.

MEGAN TERRY is the author of more than sixty published plays. She has been changing the face of American theatre for four decades with transformation plays, the formalization of theatre games into play structures, docudramas, *"theatre verité,"* and performance art. A founding member of the famed Open Theatre, she developed this country's first rock musical, *Viet Rock.*

AUGUST WILSON, one of America's leading playwrights, has won two Pulitzer Prizes, five New York Drama Critics Circle Best Play Awards, and a Tony Award, among many other honors.

He is the author of *Ma Rainey's Black Bottom, Fences, Joe Turner's Come and Gone, The Piano Lesson, Two Trains Running,* and *Seven Guitars.*

DANA YEATON is the winner of the 1995 Heideman Award from the Actors Theatre of Louisville. His tragicomedy, *Kin Deep,* was winner of a 1994 New Play Fellowship at the Shenandoah International Playwrights Retreat. He is Playwright-in-Residence at the Vermont Stage Company in Burlington, Vermont, where he directs the Vermont Young Playwrights Project.

EDITORS

ERIC LANE and NINA SHENGOLD are editors of *Plays for Actresses* for Vintage Books. For Penguin Books, they edited *Moving Parts: Monologues from Contemporary Plays, The Actor's Book of Scenes from New Plays,* and *The Actor's Book of Gay & Lesbian Plays,* which was nominated for the Lambda Literary Award for excellence in gay and lesbian publication in the United States. In addition, Ms. Shengold edited *The Actor's Book of Contemporary Stage Monologues,* and Mr. Lane edited *Telling Tales: New One-Act Plays.*

ERIC LANE's plays have been performed at theatres in New York and around the country. Works include *The Gary & Rob Show, It Must Be Him, The Heart of a Child,* and *Dancing on Checkers' Grave.* Mr. Lane wrote, directed, and produced *Cater-Waiter,* a short film starring David Drake and Tim Deak, which is currently hitting the festival circuit. He is artistic director of Orange Thoughts, a not-for-profit theatre and film company in New York City. Honors include a Writer's Guild Award (for TV's *Ryan's Hope*), two Yaddo residencies, the first LaMama Playwright Development Award, and Finalist in the O'Neill Center National Playwrights Conference (*Times of War*).

NINA SHENGOLD won the ABC Playwright Award and the *L. A. Weekly* Award for her play *Homesteaders,* and received a Berilla Kerr Foundation grant for her work-in-progress *Grown Women.* Her one-acts have been performed all over the country. Ms. Shengold's TV scripts include Hallmark Hall of Fame's *Blind Spot,* starring Emmy nominee Joanne Woodward, and *Silent Night.* A founding member of the theatre company Actors & Writers, she lives in upstate New York with her daughter, Maya.